The Empathic Healer

An Endangered Species?

The Empathic Healer

An Endangered Species?

MICHAEL J. BENNETT, MD

Academic Press

San Diego   New York   Boston   London   Sydney   Tokyo   Toronto

Academic Press
a Harcourt Science and Technology Company
525 B Street, Suite 1900, San Diego, California 92101-4495
http://www.academicpress.com

Academic Press Limited
Harcourt Place, 32 Jamestown Road, London NW1 7BY, UK
http://www.academicpress.com

Library of Congress Catalog Card Number: 00-111402

International Standard Book Number: 0-12-088662-6

PRINTED IN UNITED STATES OF AMERICA
01 02 03 04 05 06 SB 9 8 7 6 5 4 3 2 1

To my wife and children:
You give my life meaning

and

To my mother and the memory of my father:
You gave my life direction

CONTENTS

ACKNOWLEDGMENTS

p. 1, May Sarton, *Take Anguish for Companion*, from *Collected Poems 1930–1933* by May Sarton. Copyright © 1993, 1988, 1984, 1980, 1974 by May Sarton. Used by permission of W. W. Norton & Company Inc.

p. 3, Alfredo Castañeda, *Consideration* (1986). Reprinted with permission from and through the courtesy of Mary-Anne Martin/Fine Art, New York.

p. 27, Gustav Vigeland, sculpture, Frogner Park, Oslo. Photograph by Susan Bennett (1991). The life work of Vigeland, these sculptures depict human interaction in all its rich variations. This grouping suggested attunement of the old and the young, evoked in the observer through *einfuhlung*.

p. 49, From *Revelation* from the *Poetry of Robert Frost*, edited by Edward Connery Lathern, © 1969 by Henry Holt & Co., LLC. Reprinted with permission from Henry Holt & Co., LLC.

p. 53, Rembrandt van Rijn, *Aristotle with a Bust of Homer* (1653). Oil on canvas, 143.5 × 136.5 cm. Reprinted with permission from the Metropolitan Museum of Art. All rights reserved.

pp. 54, 55, 161, 193. John Holmes, *The Eleventh Commandment*. Reprinted with permission from Doris Holmes Eyges. This poem was first read by the poet at the Phi Beta Kappa exercises at the 1956 Harvard University commencement, and was subsequently published. It is interesting to consider that college students of the 1950s were known as "the silent generation."

p. 77, René Magritte, *The Lovers* (1928). Oil on canvas, 53.5 × 72 cm. The Menil Collection, Houston. Reprinted with permission from C. Herscovici, Brussels/Artists Rights Society (ARS), New York.

p. 97, Richard Stine, *Head/Heart* (1994). Reprinted with permission from the artist. © 1994, Richard Stine. All rights reserved.

p. 99, Joshua Simons, *16 States* (1987). Reprinted with permission from the artist.

p. 133, Pablo Ruiz Picasso, *Mother and Child* (1901). Oil on canvas, 112.4 × 97.5 cm. Reprinted with permission from the Fogg Art Museum, Harvard University Art Museums. Bequest from the Collection of Maurice Wertheim, Class of 1906. Photographic Services, President and Fellows of Harvard College, printed 5 December 2000.

p. 147, René Magritte, *The Therapist* (1937). Oil on canvas, 81.3 × 65 cm. Reprinted with permission from C. Herscovici, Brussels/Artists Rights Society (ARS), New York.

p. 182, Alfredo Castañeda, *When the Mirror Dreams with Another Image* (1988). Reprinted with permission from and through the courtesy of Mary-Anne Martin/Fine Art, New York.

p. 201, Paul Klee, *Outbreak of Fear* (1939). Reprinted with permission from and through the courtesy of the Artists Rights Society (ARS), New York/VG Bild-Kunst, Bonn.

p. 218, Gustav Vigeland, *The Column*, Frogner Park, Oslo. Photograph by Susan Bennett (1991). This centerpiece suggested both interrelatedness and interdependence: a graphic portrayal of the concept of *mishpocheh*.

FOREWORD

Roger E. Meyer, MD

Clinical Professor of Psychiatry, Georgetown University
Adjunct Professor of Psychiatry, University of Pennsylvania
Senior Consultant on Clinical Research,
Association of American Medical Colleges
Chief Executive Officer, Best Practice, LLC

In terms of its scope and its timing, Dr. Michael Bennett has written a landmark book. He reaffirms the place of empathy in human experience, and its special role in the healing process. By interspersing well-chosen works of poetry and art throughout the text, he highlights the universality and timelessness of empathy in human experience, as well as the limitations of straight prose in communicating its nature to the reader. Case vignettes in specific chapters help to establish the clinical context. But this is not just another clinical "how-to" book about empathy for mental health professionals, because Dr. Bennett brings us a vision of the historical roots of empathy in the clinical encounter, and the opportunities and barriers to its expression in that encounter under managed care. He conveys an extraordinary array of knowledge, skills, and attitudes in this book—the knowledgeable and sensitive clinician who values understanding in his care of patients and the knowledgeable and experienced "maven of managed care" who has practiced and managed in these settings for thirty years. In my view, Dr. Bennett has brilliantly analyzed and decried the declining place of empathy in the practice of psychiatry. The problem did not begin with managed care, but managed care can either affirm or deny the opportunity to bring empathic understanding and collaborative resources to facilitate the healing process.

Contrary to the platforms of recent successful candidates for presidency of the American Psychiatric Association, managed behavioral health care is not "the evil empire." Indeed, the immortal words of Pogo (Kelly, 1972) are highly relevant here: "We have met the enemy and he is us." Current approaches to psychiatric training and practice de-emphasize empathy in the context of a symptom-based diagnostic system and a view of treatment that is defined by the pen and prescription pad. In its overly narrow focus, American psychiatry in its present iteration is like a caricature of the medical model—without the physical examination. Without empathic understanding, the patient's encounter with a mental health professional is at best of limited usefulness. In 1977, the late George Engel (Engel, 1977) deplored the limitations of the medical model that had not yet emerged fully in psychiatry. Indeed, Engel believed that only psychiatrists at that time possessed a biopsychosocial model of illness and treatment. He wrote as psychiatry was beginning its descent away from its biopsychosocial and empathic roots. His essay did not succeed in stopping the trend. Nearly twenty-five years later, Michael Bennett's book looks over the relatively barren paradigmatic landscape of modern psychiatry and suggests how we might restore its vitality. He proposes a clinical practice paradigm that restores empathy to a central place in the patient's encounter with the health care system. His vision of how that might work is a dramatic departure from the more limited psychoanalytic perspectives on empathy. His model is consistent with the requirements of our health care system and is compatible with an enlarging base of scientific information. Unlike the traditional psychoanalytic perspective, Bennett's vision is pragmatic and open to new information. Rather than cursing the darkness, recalling the "good old days" and condemning managed care, he suggests how we might light a candle and re-connect with our empathic roots. He also observes how we got where we are!

Over the past forty years, no area of medicine has experienced the discontinuities in paradigms and practice as psychiatry. Forty years ago, as Michael Bennett was contemplating a career in psychiatry, the favored psychoanalytic/psychodynamic paradigm emphasized the importance of the empathic understanding of patients as a central theme in psychiatric education and in clinical care. All psychopathology was presumed to have functional meaning, and treatment was aimed at bringing functional meaning into conscious awareness so that patients could free themselves from their symptomatology. Long-term psychotherapy was considered the privileged preserve of psychoanalytically trained physicians, while social workers might be engaged in supportive care of family members of the seriously mentally ill and psychologists were adjunctive diagnosticians especially prized for their ability to interpret projective tests that might reveal aspects of the unconscious. At the prestigious psychiatric teaching hospital where Dr. Bennett began his residency in 1963, assessments of medication efficacy and side effects were made by a retrained psychiatric aide who was available to residents for consultation. Unlike Dr. Bennett and his contemporaries, today's trainees in psychiatry are taught to emphasize the centrality of current symptomatology in establishing psychiatric diagnoses. Psychiatrists prize their role in making singular and co-morbid diagnoses and in managing medications and their side effects. Social workers and psychologists now compete for admission to psychoanalytic institutes, and psychotherapy practice (such as it is) is becoming the preserve of non-physician clinicians.

Because dynamic psychiatry saw psychopathology as functional, its paradigm could not easily incorporate psychopharmacological treatments aimed at treating dysfunctional cognitions, emotions, and behaviors. Psychopharmacology slowly undermined the validity and usefulness of psychodynamic explanations of the *etiology* of mental disorders, but it has never been able to sustain a consistent paradigm to explain those disorders. While advances in neurobiology may someday define the pathophysiology of the symptomatology that brings patients to psychiatrists, and while advances in human genetics may someday help to unravel the genetic/environmental conundrum of risk, neurobiologists and geneticists understand that our present syndromal approach to diagnosis represents a substantial barrier to progress. These syndromes defy validation in biological and genetic studies, even as they maintain a high degree of reliability. As we move away from linear models of etiology in the context of our appreciation of the complexity of brain function and gene expression, the importance of individual differences and of psychological and sociocultural meaningfulness are likely to regain significance. In chapter 6, Bennett describes how our expanding knowledge of brain science can relate to empathy in human experience and as a core component of the healing relationship: "empathic forms of communication are one of the hallmarks of a healthy brain; [. . .] empathy is one of the clinical variables required to correct the aberrant patterns of learning that underlie mental disorders; and, [. . .] there is a scientific basis for limited clinical interventions that are designed to *strengthen the environment in which healing may take place*" (Bennett, p. 120). Unlike his psychoanalytically oriented teachers, who could not (or would not) attempt to integrate findings from other fields within their canon, or the biological psychiatrists who were contemptuous of the psyche, Bennett believes that "bridges can be built between brain and mind that do not require abandoning the important discoveries that have been made about each." Indeed, if there is a hierarchy of science in which primacy belongs to the paradigm that can explain the totality of a phenomenon, then it is critical for neuroscientists to develop models of brain function and dysfunction that can address the healing potential of empathy.

Over the past forty years, residents have been taught about psychopharmacology and dynamic psychiatry as separate silos of learning. Their teachers never brought together an integrated vision of patient care, or of the possible causes and treatments of psychopathology. For the most part, the analysts emphasized the long-term treatment of persons who were not seriously mentally ill, while the psychopharmacologists advanced meliorative treatments for persons with psychosis and major mood disorders. Through most of the first two decades of this period, the National Institute of Mental Health subsidized the education of psychiatric residents and supported the staffing and construction of a nationwide system of community mental health centers (CMHCs). The community mental health movement embraced a population-based vision of mental health care, but its promises of prevention and treatment were seriously flawed. Like the psychoanalysts, the leaders of the community psychiatry movement never addressed the problems of the seriously mentally ill. The care system represented by the CMHCs was heavily dominated by masters-prepared social workers, nurses, and psychologists. Psychiatrists were valued for their prescription-writing authority. Whether the CMHC was the cause of this shift in practice patterns, it is not hard to discern that it legitimized the diminished role of psychiatrists in the psychosocial dimensions of mental health care. Since many academic departments were caught up in the community mental health movement as a source of funding for their programs, this shift was also transmitted in a variety of ways to trainees across the mental health disciplines.

Ultimately, the community mental health center movement paid the political price for its association with other social programs created in the 1960s, and declined in significance after the election of Ronald Reagan. The year 1980 was significant for American psychiatry in other ways as well. Commencing with the Reagan Administration, the mission of NIMH and its sister Institutes (NIDA and NIAAA) shifted to emphasize largely biological research, rather than training and service programs. The year also marked the publication of DSM-III, a symptom-based diagnostic system that explicitly rejected psychodynamic concepts and terminology. Rather than formulations about individual patients based upon an understanding of personal history and psychological defenses, residents (and medical students) were expected to learn a new diagnostic nomenclature based on a Chinese menu of presenting symptoms. In the absence of objective pathophysiology, the concepts and categories could not be validated. Yet, the goal to establish a highly reliable diagnostic system to replace the unreliable antecedent systems of diagnosis was achieved. While many of the leaders of American psychiatry have cheered in the triumph of an atheoretical, descriptive, and reliable system of diagnosis, and much of psychiatric education is now built around the successive volumes of the DSM, the field lacks a paradigm that would link its diagnostic system to brain function, heritable and non-heritable risk factors, and/or clinical decision making. With the introduction of a new class of antidepressants in the late 1980s (the selective serotonin reuptake inhibitors), even the boundaries between anxiety and mood disorders became irrelevant in terms of which class of drugs to employ. While many leading psychiatrists tout the progress of our science, in the absence of a paradigm or some candidate for a paradigm, real science is not possible (Kuhn, 1970).

By the late 1980s, the psychoanalytic hegemony over academic psychiatry had largely dissipated, and psychoanalytically based systems of inpatient and outpatient mental health care were ripe for dissection. As the public sector programs declined, there was increased advocacy for health insurance coverage for mental illness and addictive disorders. As the government's prospective payment system for Medicare decreased lengths of stay for medical and surgical patients, and as these developments were extended to other third party health systems payers, hospitals expanded their "exempt" mental health services and a growing industry of for-profit psychiatric hospitals and substance-abuse treatment facilities emerged to compete with the Ivy League of nonprofit hospitals such as McLean in Massachusetts, the Institute of Living in Connecticut, and the Menninger Clinic in Kansas. It is not surprising that the increased supply of hospital beds, when coupled with the increasing demand coming from increased mental health benefits, caused the purchasers of health care (the employers) to turn to some group to stem the rate of growth for mental health services. Enter managed behavioral health care.

Managed behavioral health care has succeeded easily in reducing the heavy reliance on inpatient care for the treatment of mentally ill and addicted patients. While not a good road map for clinical care, the DSM system gave care managers a tool to rationalize their decisions on limitations of services. The community mental health center established the possible roles of different mental health professionals, and the managed behavioral health care industry has been able to build from that base of experience to allocate service performance on the basis of cost. Masters-prepared therapists are less costly psychotherapists than psychiatrists and psychologists. Psychiatrists now fight to defend their prescribing turf from legislative lobbying on behalf of psychologists and masters-prepared nurses. General physicians (general internists, family physicians, pediatricians, and obstetrician/gynecologists) now routinely prescribe medications for their patients with anxiety or depression, and complain that the DSM-driven diagnostic input by psychiatrists is not helpful (de Gruy, 1996). They want their psychiatric consultants to tell them about their patients: the meaningfulness of their symptoms, their medical illnesses, and their current life stresses.

"In the era of descriptive psychiatry, it is often (erroneously) assumed that patients seek out therapists because they suffer from a disorder; [. . .] patients seek help because they are ill" (Bennett, p. 167). "In a population-based system of care, where all members have access to services according to need, the clinician must configure to the patient's preferred method of learning and therefore must understand the need before selecting the method. [. . .] Empathic process is central to the development and maintenance of [. . .] focus. Validation, attunement and shared meaning are central to the task" (Bennett, p. 195). Empathy involves both a caring emotional response (sympathy), and a search for understanding about another person. It is a "mode of relating in which one person comes to know the mental content of another, both affectively and cognitively, at a particular moment in time and as a product of the relationship that exists between them" (Bennett, p. 7). While psychodynamic understanding may be a component of empathic understanding, it does not define it.

At the outset, I described this book as a landmark in terms of scope and timeliness. Dr. Bennett has laid out a clinical practice paradigm to a field that is hungry for direction. He has laid out a model for collaborative practice and focal psychotherapy that is fully compatible with the best of population-based health care. Indeed, if his model were applied to judge the ways in which managed behavioral health care is practiced, it could form the framework for accreditation and defining best practice. His book describes the role of the empathic healer. The case vignettes support his concept that healing takes place in life and not in the process of long-term psychotherapy. His vision of psychiatry is honest, refreshing, traditional, and revolutionary. If embraced, it would move the field away from self-destructive complaining about the way things are, to a new and authentically idealistic vision of the psychiatrist as healer. His model incorporates the empathic forces present in self-help efforts and in interpersonal relationships. Most important, his ideas offer a new approach to psychiatric education. The educational process should be geared to the identification of the natural capacity for empathy in each trainee, and should help the trainee to strengthen that capacity over time. Trainees need to be taught the art of formulation, the art of treatment resource allocation for individuals within population-based systems of care, and the art of focal psychotherapy that enables healing to proceed beyond the therapeutic encounter. The empathic skills of trainees and teachers are undermined by our current approach to diagnosis, by the failure of mental health professionals and of managed behavioral health care organizations to understand the healing process, and by the absence of a clinical care paradigm that is consistent with the expectations of patients, the requirements of a managed health system, and the best impulses of our profession. In his poetic and encyclopedic elaboration of empathy, Dr. Bennett offers us the opportunity to heal our profession and ourselves.

REFERENCES

de Gruy, F. (1996). Mental health care in the primary care setting. In *Primary Care: America's Health in a New Era*. Washington, DC: National Academy Press.

Engel, G. L. (1977). The need for a new medical model: A challenge for biomedicine. *Science, 196*, 129–136.

Kelly, W. (1972). *Pogo: We have met the enemy and he is us*. New York: Simon & Schuster.

Kuhn, T. (1970) *The structure of scientific revolutions*. Chicago: University of Chicago Press.

PREFACE

The idea for this book came from an invited presentation given at a 1998 conference sponsored by the Institute for Behavioral Healthcare. I was asked by Dr. Michael Freeman to participate in a session that concerned the evolution of managed mental health care over the past decade, and to prepare and deliver a talk entitled, "Whatever Happened to Empathy?" George Zimmar, PhD, who was to become my editor at Academic Press, heard my presentation and suggested I turn it into a book. Since I had just left my job as a senior vice-president for a managed behavioral health-care carveout and was reflecting on the end of my 30-year romance with managed behavioral health care, the opportunity came at exactly the right time: I needed to reconcile the changes that were taking place in managed care, many of which disturbed me greatly, with my beliefs about psychiatric practice, and especially with my deep and enduring commitment to dynamic psychotherapy as a basic tool of mental health intervention. This book is the product of that attempt at reconciliation.

My career spans the transition that has taken place in psychiatry since the 1960s: the rise and subsequent decline of community psychiatry, the development of the HMO as a site for delivering mental health services, the emergence of the corporation as a dominant player in health care, privatization of resources, and the trends toward descriptive and biological paradigms. For someone who was trained in the psychoanalytic era, and whose roots lie in dynamic psychiatry, the journey has been a personal as well as a professional odyssey. All around me I see demoralization, pessimism, and confusion, even amidst the remarkable growth in knowledge and understanding about the roots and nature of mental disorder that has taken place. The historical strengths of my profession remain at variance with the economic forces that drive it to reconfigure, and its art and science have never been more sharply divided from each other. It is those schisms, and the dualistic thinking that results from them, that this book aims to address.

Why another book on empathy? Surely, as I found in my research on the topic, the literature is vast. Over the past 100 years or so, it would be difficult to find a major theorist who has not tackled this subject. Theories about the nature of empathy and its relevance to health care abound. Because of the forces that drive mental health practice at the dawn of the twenty-first century, however, empathy as a clinical variable has become suspect. Where is its legitimate place in the practice of biological psychiatry? How can this feature of the clinician–patient relationship, which historically derives from the psychoanalytic and experiential traditions, both of which involve the types of enduring dyadic relationships that have become the exception rather than the rule, be reconciled with time-limited interventions and biologically based therapies?

It is the central premise of this book that, not only is empathy consistent with contemporary beliefs about the brain as the target organ of the mental health practitioner, but empathic attunement to the patient's perspective is also an essential feature of focused and time-efficient interventions. Although this is not a book about managed care, the realities of current and imminent practice make it essential that mental health practitioners adapt their practice patterns to the care of populations. To do so effectively, it is necessary to allocate our services rationally and to exploit the opportunities for recovery and healing outside the formal health-care setting: opportunities that are ubiquitous if recognized, mobilized and harnessed. As treaters, our consummate role is to pave the way for the healing that will take place within the patient's own life context. If we are to subordinate our function in this manner, then we must carefully attune to the patient's perspective as a prerequisite for formulating treatment needs and planning interventions. Such attunement, I will argue, is achieved largely through the use of empathically derived understanding. Empathy, then, is the indispensable bridge that links the subjective world of the patient with the objective parameters by which we identify the presence of a disorder of the brain. Only such a balance of subjective and objective data can lead us to think holistically about the work that we do.

No book is written in isolation, and there are many people to thank for this one. First, my loving and most patient partner, my wife, Susan; her tolerance of my long absences at the library or at my computer, her willingness to indulge my immersion in this topic (best characterized as marination), and her faith that eventually I would bring the project to a close, are deeply appreciated. If I have forgotten to be empathic at times while writing a book on empathy, I wince at the irony and apologize. My children, Kate, Lauren, and Natana, who were curious and interested, and who made their own contributions in our many discussions of the topic, inspired and propelled me as they always do. It was Kate who helped me understand the relationship between empathy and musical performance and led me to the writing of Robert Levin; Lauren, on the threshold of her own PhD in psychology, helped me think in pragmatic terms about the clinical implications of my theories; Natana, who gave birth to our granddaughter, Talia, in January of 2000, reminded me in the beauty of her mothering how natural empathic linkages truly are. My own mother, Helen Bennett Ross, whose love and approval have always been there for me, gave her unstinting support. Portions of the text were reviewed by my good friend and colleague, Roger Meyer, MD, who helped me place my reading about brain science in perspective and who was my scientific gyroscope; by Bruce Roberts, MD, Rich Fitzpatrick, PhD, and Arthur Bohart, PhD, who contributed suggestions for improving the manuscript and helped me find my way. Thanks are due to my friends, Pia and Per Stampe, who introduced me to the work of Tor Norretranders; to Rita Addison, whose own work on the topic and whose interest in the health-care potential of virtual reality led me to reconsider my doubts about the compatibility of empathy and technology; to Frances Chuning, who led me to Stanislavski and to considering the relationship between acting and empathy; to Michael Leuci for facilitating the logistics during the writing phase; and to my students, who allowed me to try out my ideas during our supervisory sessions. A special thanks is due to my crusty production editor, Tim Oliver, who first suggested enhancing the text with reproductions of works of art and who labored mightily to meet the book's deadline. Finally, I owe a continuing debt to my patients, present and past, who are ultimately the source of what I believe and know about treatment and healing.

This book is dedicated to the memory of H. Richard Nesson, MD. Dick was my mentor and friend during my early and formative years at the Harvard Community Health Plan. He, more than anyone else, encouraged and facilitated my development as a manager and planner of mental health services: roles that shaped my career for 30 years. A giant figure on the Boston and national scenes, who went on to become president of the Brigham and Women's Hospital and the first chief executive officer of Partners HealthCare System, Dick was a believer in integrated systems and primary care long before these were popular. His unique vision, and his warm and personal style of leadership, led him to become a beloved mentor to countless others as well. I had the privilege to know and work with him as a clinician, and to share patients with him during those early years; it would be difficult to find a better example of a practitioner who combined practical thinking with empathy. When Dick left HCHP, I wrote a poem for him that concluded with the following sentence, repeated here in tribute: *"And well we'll remember the lessons of Nesson he taught us while fressin' on delicatessen."* Thank you, Dick.

Michael J. Bennett, MD
Boston, December 2000

CHAPTER 1

The Health Care System Has Lost its Heart

If the one certainty is suffering,
And if the only absolute is doubt,
From these alone belief must be wrung
Or else the bitter poverty found out:
Take anguish for companion and set out.

May Sarton

INTRODUCTION

The health care system appears to have lost its heart. We are regaled daily in the media with anecdotes that graphically portray a system gone awry, one that fails to provide for the needs of a substantial portion of our population while underserving many of the rest. Claims of wrongdoing, such as denial of nec-

1

essary services and disregard for patient safety, inflame a public that demands less restrictive practices while politicians debate the scope of protections against the perceived abuses of managed care. Some clamor for the government to take a hand, while others are terrorized at the prospect that the folks who brought you the IRS and the Postal Service might be your recourse when you are ill from other causes.

The concept of *patients' rights* has been advanced as a remedy for health system wrongs (Patients' Rights, 2000; Stone, 1999; Sorian & Feder, 1999). Organizations that represent the interests of health care professionals, themselves perceived victims of the upheaval in our medical care system, lobby for a return to practitioner autonomy and seek redress for their members, whose lives and practices have been assaulted by the furious pace of change. Many are in flight from patient care, while others seek new careers entirely (Barnard & Tong, 2000). The seemingly universal perception is that things are spinning out of control. Surveys of physicians and nurses document their frustration and conviction that patients are being denied necessary care and, by implication, they are unable to succeed as advocates (Collins *et al.*, 1997; Gold, 1999). Ironically, clinicians, ordinarily staunchly opposed to such measures, encourage the burgeoning body of regulations that now impact on both the practice and management of medicine. This being a litigious society, lawsuits and threatened lawsuits abound. In such a climate, sensitivity to the emotional needs of individual patients can hardly be expected; for many, personalized care appears to have been temporarily, or perhaps permanently, lost.

But is this new? Consider the following discussion between the idealistic physician, Lucas Marsh, and his colleague and mentor, Avery, in Morton Thompson's novel, *Not as a Stranger*:

> "Sixty patients an afternoon! That's what we handle! Sixty! Two or three operations every morning. Calls at night. And sixty patients an afternoon."
>
> "Sixty! But you can't—"
>
> "No, you can't possibly do them justice. That's right. All you can do is treat their symptoms. The ones you don't miss. A pill here, a prod there, adhesive tape, tonic, soothing lotions, keep 'em going. Just dab a little on and keep 'em going. That's not Medicine, Ave. That's not Medicine. And every patient I handle I know it's wrong, it's dead wrong, and I'm doing it, and my guts turn over." (1954)

Another victim of managed care? Hardly. These words were written in 1954.

In *The House of God*, Samuel Shem's pseudonymous account of his internship at a hospital considered by many to be a model for humane care, the author described the personal impact of his training experience:

> All of us had become deaf to the murmur of love.

and,

> What had happened in the House of God had been fierce, and I had been hurt, bad. For before the House of God, I had loved old people. Now they were no longer old people, they were gomers, and I did not, I could not, love them, anymore. (1978)

The impact of managed care? In 1978, when *The House of God* was published, managed care was still a blip on the practice landscape.

The breakdown of caring in our health care system is symbolized for many in the term "managed care," but its roots lie far deeper. In order to understand these roots, it is necessary to examine how we got into the plight we are in. As might be expected, through good intentions.

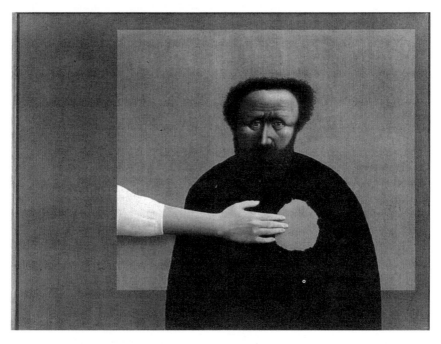

Alfredo Castañeda, *Consideration* (1986).

MANAGED HEALTH CARE

> The best-laid schemes o' mice an' men
> Gang aft agley,
> An' lea'e us nought but grief an' pain
> For promised joy!
>
> *Robert Burns*

Prepaid group practices were the early prototype of health maintenance organizations (HMOs), the antecedents of managed systems of care. These systems, which were designed to bring affordable health care to populations at need, united two developmental lines: group practices and prepaid financing. The first of these dates back to the late 1800s, originating with the Mayo brothers, while the latter can be traced to the practice of contracting physicians during the days of the American Revolution. These two lines of development converged in the late 1920s in two sites: rural Oklahoma, in farm cooperatives, and Los Angeles, in a consumer-controlled program for the Department of Light and Power (Bennett, 1988). Over the next 50 years, the development of prepaid group practice was spurred by industry, through what became known as "corporate paternalism" (Starr, 1982), by consumers, by government, and by unions. The ideals associated with HMOs were democratic in nature, even socialistic in the minds of many, in that health care was regarded as a social right. This vision was underscored in the 1960s by the two great initiatives, Medicare and Medicaid. To this point, HMOs appeared to represent a vehicle for coordinating the care of populations without compromising the core ideals of medical practice.

Beginning in the 1970s, the situation began to change. Concerns about spiraling costs led to initiatives designed to contain them. The HMO movement was permanently altered, as both government and then other payers envisioned the management of care as practiced in the closed systems known as HMOs as a strategy to contain costs (Bennett, 1992). Advocates called for an expansion of such programs so that larger segments of the general population might be cared for in such configurations. Theorists such as Alain Enthoven advocated cost containment through free market forces, in which multiple health care enterprises would compete for members and costs would be contained through choices made by informed and prudent purchasers (Starr, 1982; Enthoven, 1989).

The so-called "pro-competitive scenario" (Starr, 1982), in which health care costs would be reined in through open market forces alone, while the quality of care was maintained, has clearly failed. Though costs were contained for a time, they have begun again to escalate (Savage *et al.*, 2000; Greenberg 1998).

More importantly, the implicit assumption that the quality of care might be maintained through the exercise of free market forces alone has proven illusory. Quality of care must be at least partially characterized by satisfaction: of patients, clinicians, the public at large. This has long since ceased to be the case. The public has gradually become disenchanted with the limitations imposed by managed systems of care, and there is growing doubt about the quality of care provided. There is also a growing perception in the public mind, rightly or wrongly, that practitioners who work in managed systems cease caring. The public has demanded less restriction on access and broader choice. Such demands are magnified by the response of the community of health care providers, whose professional and personal lives have been drastically altered by the economics of managed care. Gradually, the inspectors of care have themselves become the target of inspection, which has led to a host of new regulations designed to provide oversight of the overseers. The result is that everyone appears to be inspecting everyone else's work, and few appear to be satisfied with the resulting climate.

FROM PHYSICIAN-HEALER TO PHYSICIAN-SCIENTIST

Managed care is a product (some would claim it is a breakdown product) of our times, and largely a consequence of our failure to establish a floor for the cost of health care; as a result, we have become obsessed with the ceiling. Increases in cost, in the absence of a national policy that regards health care as a right of citizenship, as it is in most developed nations, are regarded as untenable. This is so despite the fact that such increases are associated with remarkable changes in the nature and quality of the treatments available to some. These advances in treatment methodologies have impacted not only on cost, but have had a profound effect as well on the core of the health care system: the relationship between patients and treaters. The humanistic tradition has become progressively reshaped by scientific advances and rapidly expanding knowledge about diseases and their causes and remedies. The physician-healer has become a physician-scientist.

These trends in medicine have also reshaped mental health care, where advances in understanding brain anatomy and physiology, genetics, and the biological basis of the most severe mental disorders have transformed the service sector. With the advent of the DSM system of descriptive psychiatry, with newer emphases on evidence-based care, disease management, best practice guidelines, and manualized forms of treatment, the mental health professional has become, like his/her medical colleagues, a treater rather than a healer. Emphasis on the uniqueness of the individual patient, which is the foundation of the humanistic tradition, has given way to standardization, which involves a focus on commonalities; often it appears that the disorder rather than the patient who suffers from it is regarded as the target of treatment and the measure of its success. Descriptive psychiatry, largely dormant during the psychoanalytic era, holds sway again, while psychodynamic theories are regarded by many as anachronistic or simply inefficient as a basis for treating the mentally ill. Practitioners have become providers of services, and the term *healer* is rarely used. Driven from the medical setting, the fugitive healer has increasingly sought a home outside mainstream medical care, in the various alternatives to traditional care that have become known as "complementary medicine." (Eisenberg *et al.*, 1998; Goldbeck-Wood *et al.*, 1996)

The relationship with individual patients (or, for some practitioners, "clients") is at the core of the healing arts, and empathy has long been associated with those arts. Although this association prevails throughout medical practice, it has been seen as particularly important for the mental health professional. From its origins in aesthetics, empathy as a mode of knowing, communicating, and behaving has become the hallmark of the humanistic therapist. Most schools of psychotherapy have something to say on the topic, though empathy as a curative element in psychotherapy has been primarily associated with two pioneers, Carl Rogers and Heinz Kohut, and those who have followed in the traditions of client-centered therapy and self-psychology, derived respectively from their work. In considering the evolution of the concept and its contemporary application, one factor stands out: empathy as a vehicle for promoting healing is associated with extended forms of psychotherapy. Where the briefer forms of psychotherapy are concerned, or in discontinuous forms of treatment, empathy has either been seen only as a means of obtaining information or as a factor that promotes or sustains treatment alliance, but not as a source of healing itself. But what is the source of this dichotomy and is it unavoidable?

This book will explore the matter of empathy primarily as it relates to the provision of mental health treatment services, where the relationship between a treater and a patient has received greater attention than in any other field of medicine. An emphasis on the treatment milieu has been particularly important with regard to the practice of psychotherapy, which is still perceived by many as the central and defining activity that characterizes the mental health professional. But this is beginning to change. For example, psychiatrists are increasingly called upon to configure their practices around somatic therapies and consultation and liaison with the medical setting, and are less likely to define themselves as psychotherapists than were their predecessors. Alan Tasman, a recent president of the American Psychiatric Association, referred to the decline in teaching empathic listening skills to psychiatrists as "a tragic phase in the history of psychiatric education" ("Drug focus shortchanges psychodynamics,"

2000). Most of the literature on empathy concerns its nature and value in two-person treatment relationships, which have been the core of the mental health system for many years. Since reliance on dyadic relationships as the basis of mental health treatment has given way to patterns of collaborative practice and subspecialization with a disease focus, the role of empathy has become less clear.

Because of the financing mechanisms involved, managed systems of care tend to prioritize the needs of populations rather than individual patients (Bennett, 1996, 1997). Patient advocacy, once seen as the primary obligation of practitioners, now must be reconciled with responsibility for a larger family: the members of a given population who are eligible to receive services, whether or not they have yet demanded such services. What happens to empathy under such circumstances? It is a thesis of this book that not only is empathy consistent with population-based models of health care, but that the provision of effective and efficient treatment may depend upon it. This position is in sharp contrast to the popular point of view, which holds that treatment of mental disorder in a managed system is by its nature impersonal. We will question this assumption.

A Working Definition of Clinical Empathy

Empathy as it occurs in the clinical setting has been varyingly defined. For purposes of simplicity, we will consider empathy in this book as it appears in a two-person therapeutic relationship, putting aside for the most part the broader social ramifications of the concept. We will use the following working definition, to be built upon as we progress through the chapters:

> Empathy refers to a mode of relating in which one person comes to know the mental content of another, both affectively and cognitively, at a particular moment in time and as a product of the relationship that exists between them.

The belief that empathy involves reciprocity is not universally accepted. For example, some would say that empathy resides in the observer and is a measure of certain attitudes, capacities, or skills, independent of the cooperation or even the knowledge of the person so observed. In this book, we will regard empathic knowing as the end result of an interactive process that may begin in various ways, but that has as its defining moment the experience of engagement in another's frame of reference, as reflected in his/her subjective mental state at a given moment. This knowing is both personal and immediate, though the result of a process that may go on over a period of seconds to minutes or longer.

By this definition, affective resonance alone, though it may be a route to achieve empathic knowing, falls short of it. I believe that all forms of psychotherapy rely, to some degree, on the exercise of empathy; that the capacity for empathy is universal, and that this capacity can be both blunted and enhanced; therefore, in its potential for enhancement, it is teachable. We will consider later in the book how such teaching might take place, and why it is important for it to take place.

If the capacity for empathy is universal, then questions follow about its utility and value, its appropriate use in psychotherapy, its compatibility or lack of compatibility with the mental health care system likely to be in place in this country in the foreseeable future, and its relationship to the healing arts. Furthermore, if empathy can be blunted, it behooves health care planners as well as educators to understand the reasons for such blunting and, if it can be enhanced, to understand how to enhance it as we train tomorrow's practitioners. These are the topics we will address in this book.

EMPATHY FROM 10,000 FEET

Empathy is a much discussed, misunderstood, and abused concept. Historically, it is related to the attitude of sympathy (More, 1994), which implies both a personal connection and a feeling of concern, that is, the sympathizer is both in harmony with the feelings or experience of another person and is affected by them. Olinick (1984) has distinguished empathy from sympathy largely by the call to action and subjective nature of the former and the more neutral nature of the latter. Most theorists agree that sympathy involves a commitment to the other, while empathy is a more neutral attitude, though responses to empathic awareness may involve caring actions. But responses may also involve the opposite of caring: exploitation, manipulation, or inaction are also possible (Shlien, 1997).

Inherently related to the act of listening, empathic knowing has been linked with healing, and with the "listening healer" (Jackson, 1992). Among the various schools of psychotherapy, the followers of Carl Rogers and Heinz Kohut in particular regard such knowing as central to the therapeutic process, though in vastly different ways. The importance assigned to reciprocal empathic engagement serves as a measure of the degree to which a practitioner or theorist considers psychotherapy to be an interpersonal activity. For Kohut, empathy was a treatment tool dependent on the therapist's observational skill, while for Rogers it represented a mode of relating interpersonally in the collaborative enterprise of healing. Within the psychoanalytic tradition, empathy is primarily a mode of understanding, while for the client-centered and experiential therapist it is a mode of relating. These distinctions will prove relevant to the central question of this book: what is the fate of empathy in the evolving health care environment?

In order to answer this question, it is necessary to embrace a broad view of empathy and its relationship to human development and interaction. In the words of the philosopher Martin Buber, empathy has to do with an individual's state of "being" as experienced by another in dialogue (Buber, 1957). The origin of the term is in the field of aesthetics, where a comparable challenge to that of psychotherapy is present: the appreciation of a work of art requires that barriers that separate the observer from the work be crossed. So it is with human interaction. If the generally accepted view that one person can not truly know the inner state of another is true, then the empathic function represents an attempt to transcend the barriers that separate us and approximate such knowing in the course of trying to be helpful. How is this possible? Buie has stated that empathy is primarily a method of careful and systematic observation followed by inference, and pointed to its fallibility (Buie, 1981). While other theorists have argued that empathy involves some form of merging with the patient, Rogers and others have insisted on its "as-if" quality; that is, that the therapist becomes aware of the patient's feeling state while maintaining his or her own identity (Rogers, 1959). Robert Lindner's *Jet-Propelled Couch* is an evocative account of the relationship between a psychoanalyst and his psychotic patient, in which the therapist decided to immerse himself in the world of the patient. Lindner pointed to the dangers of identification and the possible loss of boundaries when the therapist abandons his observational perspective and embraces the patient's inner state (1982). Still, some theorists hold that empathy requires subordinating one's separate self to the task of assuming the patient's inner state as one's own (Mahrer, 1997).

In attempting to understand the essential features of an empathic transaction, some distinction must be made between empathy and other psychological phenomena having to do with traversing interpersonal boundaries. How does one person traverse the boundaries between self and other and make the type of connection with the patient's state of being that empathy presumes? It appears that a leap of some kind is required. But what kind of leap? Is empathy an intuitive act, or a reasoned one that is based on the therapist's having had similar or related personal experiences to those being described by the patient? What precisely do we mean when we speak of "mental content"? Most theorists have focused on what is in the patient's conscious awareness, but others have expanded the concept to include what is preconscious and unarticulated by the patient or what is outside of the conscious mind entirely. This position raises the even more complicated question of what type of mental activity takes place outside of consciousness. By broadening the scope of an empathic trans-action to embrace mental activity outside of conscious awareness we place a burden on the therapist to use this faculty with greater care lest she or he lead the patient or, worse, mislead. Bolognini (1997) has raised the problem of what he calls empathism: "a dogmatic, hyperconcordant attitude" by which the therapist presumes to know the patient's inner state and uses such presumptions to control the treatment.

In this book, the assumption will be made that empathy involves primarily what is conscious in the other though unexpressed, that is, the empathic therapist may give voice at times to ideas or feelings that the patient has failed to see as relevant or even as present. In such situations, some type of confirmation by the patient is important in order to ascertain the accuracy or, even more important than accuracy, the utility of the therapist's impression. Additionally, we will consider empathy as consistent with but distinct from compassion, sympathetic action, or benign intent: a tool to be used with discretion in the care of the patient. Finally, we will consider empathy to be a faculty that is ubiquitous, available to facilitate healing and change, both for the individual and for the group of which the individual is a part, both within and outside the formal health care system.

EMPATHY AND THE ARTS

Returning to the origins of the term, empathy, to be explored further in chapter two, aestheticians of the middle and late nineteenth century used the German *Einfuhlung* to describe the capacity on the part of the observer to feel his way into a work of art and know it from within. Buber has characterized this as "to glide with one's own feeling into the dynamic structure of an object" (Buber, 1947). In contemporary psychological parlance, this would be a good definition of projection; some theorists hold that all empathic transactions involve projective identification (Tansey & Burke, 1989), a position that I consider extreme and untenable.

Two forms of artistry address the matter of crossing interpersonal boundaries and help us to understand how this might take place. First, there is the musician, whose job it is to bring to a listener the spirit and intent of the composer as preserved in the score and as retrievable through playing the music. In a review in the *Boston Globe* of October 2, 1999, critic Richard Dyer, in describing the previous night's performance of Mahler's *Second Symphony* by the Boston Symphony Orchestra, had the following to say about conductor Seiji Ozawa:

> Last night's performance spoke and sang of desperate experience, compassion, hope, and faith, just as Mahler intended it to. (Ozawa Conducts Transcendent Mahler Second, 1999)

How is it possible for Ozawa to know what Mahler intended? According to the musicologist and fortepianist Robert Levin, the performer must be in part a composer him/herself. Levin believes that a creative act is involved, requiring that the performer understand the context and language of the composer. Language encompasses both the specific means by which the composer transmits his or her ideas and the affect associated with them, and requires an understanding of the context within which the work was created (Levin, 1997). The question arises as to whether the performer creates based on his or her own vision, or is the performer's personality to be subordinated to the task of becoming a vehicle for communication between composer and audience? Three sets of boundaries must be overcome: that between the composer and the performer, between the performer and his or her instrument (except for singers), and between the performer and the audience. This sequence is not unlike the therapist's striving to overcome barriers of culture, history, and personal psychology in order to enter the world of the patient and appreciate his/her dilemma as a prelude to assisting in resolving it. Havens has spoken of the importance of language in transcending interpersonal barriers (Havens, 1978, 1979), and suggested that there is a particular language of empathy.

Music may help us understand the nature and value of empathy in another way as well. A chamber musician must overcome not only the barriers indicated above, but also those between self and others in the collaborative musical act. The essential point here is that the collaboration is not hierarchical; participants are on the same plane, facing the same barriers, and all are equally responsible for achieving the result. The objective is to sense the composer's state of mind through the music, using the notes on the page as one might break a code to discern underlying meaning. So it is with the therapist, who is presented with the patient's narrative and must discern the meaning, for the patient, behind it. We all speak in code.

A second form of art can further inform us about the phenomenon of empathy: acting. Constantin Stanislavski, actor and director in the Moscow State Theater, developed a systematic method for training actors in the early part of the twentieth century. Known in this country as *The Method*, Stanislavski's ideas have been adapted and used to guide and train actors both within Russian and American theater. This great teacher conceived of the actor's task as imbuing the author's character with life by drawing on his or her own internal reservoir of experience (Stanislavski, 1936). In other words, the performance is built from within the actor, and the character comes alive. Exercises in affective recall, emotional and sensory memory, relaxation, and other tech-

niques are essential elements in training and provide the actor with the necessary skills to accomplish this task (Easty, 1981). Psychotherapists generally
lack such honing of personal capacities, but may find other routes to gain
access to the internal world of memory and experience: for example, for those
who enter psychoanalytic training, through a required personal analysis, or
through learning various meditative techniques.

The actor's challenge is to be real, rather than to simulate, drawing on the
author's words and an inner reservoir of experience that is relevant. This
challenge bears similarity to the therapist's efforts to experience first hand what
the patient's narrative suggests. If the successful actor thus can approximate
the intent of the author, and the successful musician can sense the composer,
then the therapist who wishes to fully appreciate the patient's inner state must
learn similar skills: to draw on his or her common humanity, whether or not
there is a history of specific shared experiences with the patient.

By understanding the ubiquity of empathy, we may benefit from the wisdom
of allied arts and preserve the art associated with psychotherapy. It is my
conviction that the advent of scientific medicine and its gradual assumption of
dominance among psychotherapists as well as medical practitioners makes it
more vital than ever that we know how to do this. Furthermore, if we are to
avoid the loss of humanism in our profession, and retain the balance between
the objective and subjective aspects of our patient's disease, it is essential that
we not lose the empathic attitude. In the chapters that follow, I will suggest
how this is feasible.

THE EVOLVING HEALTH CARE SYSTEM

Although this is not a book about managed care, some attention to the nature
of changes taking place within the health care system is relevant to its central
question. The current atmosphere is one of turbulence, instability, and apprehension on the part of many. The relationship between patients and treaters
has altered greatly within the mental health care system, affected by mechanisms of financing, scientific advances, the development of the internet and
other information processing technology, and the challenge of extending services to the full range of persons who require them. Parity, as a goal and as a
likely reality, forces us to define our work with a broader population in mind
and with limitations in the budget available to serve it. If the message can be
separated from the messenger, managed care is here to stay, but the ownership
of the health care system is in transition and the relative roles of government,
regulators, the public, and the business community are less certain. That some
form of prospective payment system will be involved is very likely; that we

must learn to live within a limited budget and do our work efficiently, a certainty.

The patient in tomorrow's health care system will be viewed as a member of a population who has emerged from the status of "insuree" for a time, and who is in need of a treatment intervention to address an illness. That illness will be reflected by a diagnosis, with particular emphasis on impairment of function, premorbid or baseline state, treatability, and need for services beyond acute care: for example, to promote or support habilitation or rehabilitation. Outcome will become the gauge of a successful intervention, and both the patient's satisfaction and objective evidence of recovery will be expected. Appraisal of the patient's life context, both as it undermines health and as it supports recovery, will be viewed as an important feature of the treatment planning process, and the patient and his or her family will be looked to as active participants in the process of recovery and healing. The use of self-help and community resources will increase, as a more knowledgeable public regards mental disorder with less prejudice and a clearer appreciation of the state of the art of treatment. The boundaries between traditional medical practice and complementary medicine will become blurred, as the reality of a global community exerts its impact and the concept of "Western medicine" is replaced by a more eclectic and evolving retinue of treatment options.

The patient in such a system will be treated in increasingly standardized fashion, based on evidence of what works and what does not. Because of the specialized techniques and services involved in diagnosis, treatment, and outcome assessment, the practice of a single therapist providing continuous psychotherapy to a single patient over an extended period of time will become the exception rather than the rule, and most patients will be cared for collaboratively, with multiple treaters operating either concurrently or in sequence. The transcendent aim of treatment will be to promote recovery in the shortest time possible. The relationship with primary care and other medical services will become more functional, as the longstanding quest for integration of the somatic and psychological realms of illness and treatment continues. Biological psychiatry will continue to be dominant, but psychotherapy will remain an essential activity, financed in part through third-party payment and in part through self-payment. Psychosocial need will remain a consideration in the care of the mentally ill, with increasing attention to the needs of a growing elderly population and preventive activities directed toward the young.

This admittedly optimistic perspective is based on the conviction that major social change is often preceded by chaos and change is both overdue and desirable. The chapters that follow will address the role of empathy in psychotherapy in a health care system that I believe will be characterized by the following:

1. Prospective payment, which prioritizes the needs of populations rather than individual patients.

2. Patients who are treated for documentable states of illness that may be characterized in terms of impairments relative to baseline states.

3. Interventions that are evidence-based, focused, and directed toward recovery of function.

4. Collaborative patterns of care that involve multiple treaters and significant others.

5. Blurred boundaries between the formal health care system and alternative or complementary medicine.

6. Increasing use of technology in diagnostic appraisal, treatment, and assessment of outcome.

7. Selective use of psychosocial treatment methods, including psychotherapy, alone or in combination with biologically based interventions.

8. Psychotherapies that are configured to the specific goals of therapy and based on evidence of efficacy and effectiveness.

9. Improved integration of mental health and medical practice.

10. An atmosphere characterized by scrutiny of treatment, resulting in continued erosion of the insular environment in which psychotherapy has historically taken place.

The question that this book poses is as follows: what is empathy and what is its fate as an element of treatment in the health care system to come; specifically, how may it be reconciled with the ten predictions above? Our primary concern will be with empathy as it operates in the clinical setting: ergo, "clinical empathy." As the title suggests, the empathic healer is an endangered species. The reasons for this are more complicated than might at first be thought. Not only do certain features of the current and emerging context of health care practice militate against such a role, but there are other reasons for jeopardy as well. We will explore these reasons and suggest how the role of empathic healer may be adapted in order to overcome them. The operative term is "adapted," that is, preservation of the role of empathic healer will require changes in the way mental health professionals conduct practice and structure their relationships with patients.

The book is divided roughly into three sections, which may be understood as a thesis, an antithesis, and a synthesis. The first three chapters will explore the concept of empathy as it relates to healing and establish the basis of its value, and the following two will examine the various extrinsic and intrinsic factors that shape clinical practice with particular attention to their impact on clinical empathy. Chapters six and seven will suggest new ways of thinking about clinical empathy, first by reconciling empathy with contemporary understanding of its biological locus and importance, and then by suggesting how our ideas about healing might be modified to take into account the realities of contemporary health care. The final three chapters will offer a model for eclectic psychotherapeutic practice within the type of environment I have predicted above, and offer a set of predictions for the continuing evolution of the role of empathic healer as the art and science of health care practice continue to change.

OUTLINE OF THE BOOK

The utility and value of empathy can be understood by first tracing its origins and its several lines of evolution, with particular emphasis on the emergence and description of the empathic healer, and an understanding of how such a role contributes to health care in general and the role of the psychotherapist in particular. Chapter two traces the history of the concept and its application to psychology and the practice of psychotherapy.

In chapter three, we will consider the relationship between empathy and healing in psychotherapy, with particular attention to the psychoanalytic and experiential traditions. The work of Carl Rogers and Heinz Kohut will be considered, as well as several of the representative theorists associated with contemporary psychodynamic, client-centered, experiential, existential, and self-psychological treatment paradigms. Specific attention will be paid to the idea that listening is an essential feature of healing. Miller's five stage process for empathic communication will be explored (Miller, 1989), as well as the work of Havens, with its emphasis on language and the role of language in clinical engagement (Havens, 1978). Through case examples, we will consider how empathy might lead to ripple effects that begin a process of healing that extends beyond formal treatment. This aspect of healing will be important to our later consideration of healing environments outside the health care system.

Empathic transactions do not occur in a vacuum: a reciprocal relationship exists between the context of practice and the attitude brought to the clinical interface by its participants, patients and their treaters. In chapter four, we will review those factors that promote the use of empathic communication in psychotherapy and those that tend to undermine or interfere with it. As a feature of human interaction, empathy makes demands on both (or all) participants:

risk is involved. In order to venture beyond the presumptive boundaries that separate us from each other, we must offer something of ourselves. Our willingness to do so depends not only on our personal makeup, including the degree to which we have developed our empathic capacities, but on various aspects of the relationship established between the participants as well: their objectives, expectations of each other, commitment to the process, degree of stability and comfort with the intimacy involved, and their states of mind as they approach the encounter. All of these factors are influenced by the context within which the exchange takes place. In this chapter, I will raise the question "Whatever happened to empathy?" What are the historical factors that have altered the context of practice, such as the advent of scientific and, later, corporate medicine, the changes in financing and organization as well as ownership of health care resources, and the increasing emphasis on parsimony of interventions and evidence-based treatment methods? Changing methods of training in the mental health disciplines as well as general medical practice may favor a less empathic practitioner; why is this the case and what can be done about it?

If context shapes practice and inclines toward or away from the willingness of participants in the health care transaction to offer their subjective selves to each other, ideological considerations on the part of practitioners are of equal or even greater importance. In chapter five, we will consider the impact of the overall frame of reference from a historical perspective, with two features in mind: the oscillations of the health care system between materialism and idealism over the past two thousand years, and the manner in which practice patterns configure to the template that is in vogue. We will explore the themes of dualism, reductionism, and determinism as they have shaped attitudes toward mental health care during the twentieth century and as they continue to do so.

With the advent of scientific medicine and the increasing "medicalization" of psychiatry during the latter half of the twentieth century, psychoanalysis and the dynamic psychotherapies have fallen into disfavor. The subjective elements of practice, which include empathically attained knowledge of the patient's state of mind, have been diminished in importance with the dominance of descriptive psychiatry, the advent of powerful new biological techniques of treatment, and growing understanding of the brain as the target organ of mental disorder. Third-party payment, considered in the previous chapter as one of the factors that lead therapists to seek expeditious treatment strategies, also exerts a powerful reinforcing influence by endorsing patterns of care that reduce the ambiguities associated with growth therapies and favor a disease model of mental health care. But the presumed polarization of the science and art of treatment is illusory. At the gross, microscopic, cellular, and molecular levels, our new understanding of how the brain works in health and in illness, and how mind and brain are related, is reshaping our thinking and leading us away from rigid choices between a mindless or a brainless psychiatry and toward a holistic duality. In chapter six, we will consider how empathy may be understood as a core feature of our biological makeup, essential to our continuing adaptation as a species, as well as to our ability as individuals to function effectively within the social environment. We will examine the role of empathic communication from both an ontogenetic and phylogenetic perspective, and consider its role in contributing to the constant reshaping of neuronal activity that occurs throughout the life cycle. Such reshaping has great relevance to mental disorder and its treatment.

As new information about how the brain works revises our ideas about mind, consciousness, learning, and adaptation to the environment, there is mounting evidence that empathy has a biological locus and biological, genetic, and evolutionary roles to play. We are learning that the healthy brain is characterized by well-developed empathic capacities. These changes in thinking are reinforced by changing ideas about science itself: gradual replacement of the mechanistic models in place since the time of Newton with a dynamic vision of the universe as less predictable, knowable, and manageable than classic science had assumed it to be. Quantum, relativity, and chaos theory have all come on the scene and provided us with an emerging picture of the world and of ourselves that is sharply different from materialistic and deterministic models of the past. With a recognition of the importance of subjectivity in science, empathy has returned to respectability; its place in the context of contemporary practice now must be redefined.

We are left with the challenge of how it is possible to practice with one eye turned toward the emerging science of brain and the other turned to the realities of the emerging practice climate: a threat to binocular vision, to say the least. The context, current and likely for the future, requires models of treatment that are practical, limited in scope, and effective. Empathy may be central to *healing*, but how does the concept apply to the role of *the treater*? In chapter seven, we will turn our attention to the overlapping phases of healing, with treatment referring to the mitigation of illness and healing referring largely to the social reintegration and realization of life potential that takes place following treatment, and occurs largely outside and beyond the bounds of the formal health care system. How does this reality impact on the practice of psychotherapy? We will consider the distinction between treatment and healing and use case examples to demonstrate how effective treatment frees up healing elements within the patient as well as within his or her environment.

Chapters eight and nine will involve a closer look at the type of psychotherapy that may be practiced within an organized health services environment where the mission is to provide useful service to the large numbers of people who require it. In chapter eight, we will introduce practice patterns that seek to maximize a psychotherapist's impact through specificity of focus. By examining how a psychotherapist might optimally function in a population-based system of care, using case examples to illustrate the use of empathically derived understanding to facilitate focused treatment, we will consider how it is possible to mitigate barriers to recovery from illness and set the stage for healing aftercare within a limited service framework. The role of subjective data in developing and sustaining an appropriate focus will be discussed, with case examples used to illustrate how a managed system of care might optimally assume the responsibility for caring for a population without abandoning generally accepted principles of effective treatment. We will consider the achievement of patient alliance, as opposed to the more common concept of compliance: how an alliance may be best established and maintained through careful attention to the subjective elements of the patient's presentation and his or her own treatment agenda(s). The idea of *formulation*, the term used to characterize the integration of data about *disease* with data about *a particular patient's illness*, will be explored in detail, and the importance of empathy in developing a working formulation illustrated through case discussion.

In chapter nine, we will further refine the ideas introduced in chapter eight about the practice of targeted or "focal psychotherapy" by suggesting a sequence of evaluation that is designed to identify core themes and targets for formal treatment, while setting the stage for the healing process. This process begins with a clear understanding of the context in which the patient's presenting problems have developed and the agendas that s/he brings to the treatment encounter. In order to set the stage for healing, the *empathic treater* must develop a working model of the patient's areas of necessary change and conduct an inventory of those personal strengths and resources that may be drawn on so as to further and facilitate the task, as well as those that will interfere. The treatment, then, aims to reinforce the first while mitigating the second: the barriers to change. Through case examples, we will examine how the empathic treater wends through the data each patient presents to accomplish this aim.

Some, but not all, healers carry black bags: many healers are not health care professionals. In chapter ten, we will leave the office of the practitioner and consider the means by which healing proceeds beyond or outside the formal health care setting. Relationships, especially love relationships, and supportive social contexts in general can foster healing through reinforcement of adaptive behavior and may also contribute to changes in the function and structure of neural networks. Through repetition and the promotion of new learning, with its biological, psychological, and social dimensions, the impact of old wounds may be mitigated and sometimes reversed. A burgeoning literature links empathic interactions with healing, for example, through enhancement of the integrity of the immune system, contributing to both emotional and physical health. The ubiquity of empathic interactions suggests that the locus of healing activities is diffuse, offering support for the distinction made between treatment and healing, and creating a rational basis for the limited use of formal health care resources.

In the concluding section of the book, we will note the explosion of technology in mental health diagnosis and treatment, ranging from the development of diagnostic aides, computer-based interventions, and the potential in virtual reality and other emerging treatment adjuncts. We will consider how the old hierarchical doctor–patient relationship is being reshaped by information technology, leading to the possibility of partnership with an informed patient population who, through the internet and other sources of information, bring a different set of demands and expectations to the health care encounter.

How does the march of science and technology shape psychotherapeutic transactions themselves, and what happens to empathy when psychotherapists turn toward technology to exploit the treatment potential it offers? I will suggest that technology offers unprecedented opportunity to enter the patient's world therapeutically while respecting the necessary boundaries between treatment and healing. The role of empathy remains the bridge that links the subjective with the objective aspects of care and bridges the treatment with what comes after it.

In concluding, I will review the argument that has been made and suggest that empathy is alive and well and continues to play an indispensable role in the healing process, both within and outside the formal health care system, in the myriad sites where healing takes place. Returning to the ten predictions about the coming health care system that were offered earlier in this chapter, I will suggest what the implications are for training practitioners to function within such a system without blunting their empathic capacities. We will consider initiatives that are already taking place in general medicine, both within the practice community and in medical school, and suggest how the mental health disciplines may follow suit.

CLINICAL EMPATHY: REFORM OR RELIC?

Is empathy old hat? There is ample evidence that the caregiving climate, including the relationship with treaters, is important to patients and to the process of recovery and healing, and this will continue to be the case. Clinicians who work in the mental health field often presume they have a grasp of empathic transactions, or, in some instances, a unique skill. With the pressures of managed care, training programs have come to de-emphasize the more humanistic aspects of mental health care in the mistaken belief that this will increase efficiency and ready their trainees for the real world. Nothing could be farther from the truth. Depersonalized medical practice is evoking a backlash. While there is an upsurge of interest in integrated systems, there is also public pressure for a return to more personalized care, for restoration of the human dimension of the doctor–patient relationship and for more humane treatment in general. As competing systems of care vie for patients, satisfaction with services becomes another important factor in reshaping health care. An informed public creates pressure for reform, while the media, as a glance at any newspaper will reveal, has made such issues headline news.

Other changes in the world around us are also germane to the topic of empathy. Our world is becoming smaller, and the boundaries that separate nations, diverse cultures, and ethnic groups are becoming blurred. Most of the writing on empathy comes from the Western Hemisphere, where primary importance is placed on the sense of a unique, bounded personal self. O'Hara has characterized this as "egocentric" and suggested an alternative: a sociocentric perspective, in which the group becomes primary (O'Hara, 1997). This position raises important questions about psychotherapy in general and about the empathic function in particular. Given the increasing focus on populations that is an essential feature of managed systems, this perspective is especially timely. How does empathy relate to the well-being of the group? How do emerging ideas about the global community shape our ways of thinking about the work that we do? Of what importance are the differences in experience, worldview, and perspectives between therapist and patient as one seeks to understand the frame of reference of the other? And how should individual goals in treatment reflect the family, the community, and society in general? The increasing popularity of complementary medicine suggests that our patients place value on what such alternatives have to offer. We must do a better job of understanding and integrating those that can be demonstrated to be effective in promoting recovery from illness as well as healing. If empathy originates in similarity of experience, how is it possible with an increasingly diverse patient population and in an environment that calls for less hierarchical and therapist-centered approaches to care? These factors must be considered as part of the backdrop against which this book is written, and against which an increasingly scientific medicine continues to evolve.

The chapters that follow will present an argument for the compatibility of empathic transactions with the limits imposed by organized and managed systems of care. Though its focus is mental health care, many of the points to be made have applicability to the general health care system as well. In considering the relevance of empathy to healing, we will examine how conceptions of health and illness are being modified by discoveries in pathophysiology, neurochemistry, and the various somatotherapies, as well as by economically driven reconfigurations of the context in which care takes place. How will empathic communication take place in a formal health care system that is increasingly based on technology, artificial intelligence, and biological forms of intervention? What use may be made of empathic exchanges in treatment that is increasingly biological in nature, and in systems of care that are based less on two-person relationships and extended forms of psychotherapy and more on collaborative patterns of practice and brief or intermittent contacts between patient and treater? The relationship between treatment and healing raises questions about how broad the boundaries of formal health care should be, who should pay for which types of intervention, and how we will determine outcome. Concluding chapters will seek to reconcile the reality of managed care with healing, suggesting where and how healing might take place and what the health care professional's role might be in promoting it, drawing on both the science and the art of medicine. We will consider how scientific medicine has altered the role of the mental health provider but not diminished its importance, how the concept of cure has largely given way to those of recovery and rehabilitation and how these may be reconciled with the idea of healing.

The questions that have been raised in this introduction will occupy us in the chapters that follow. Exciting possibilities exist, but they demand change. The heart of the health care system remains the relationships that are established between treaters and their patients, and empathic communication is vital to the preservation of those relationships. It is the thesis of this book that with appropriate change the prospect of a humane and effective health care system, which lies beyond our grasp, is not beyond our reach.

REFERENCES

Barnard, A., & Tong, K. (2000, July 9). The doctor is out: more and more physicians, frustrated with managed care, are trying new professions and finding life less stressful. *The Boston Globe*, p. 17.

Bennett, M. J. (1988). The greening of the HMO: Implications for prepaid psychiatry. *American Journal of Psychiatry*, 145(12), 1544–1549.

Bennett, M. J. (1992). Managed mental health in health maintenance organizations. In S. Feldman (Ed.), *Managed mental health services* (pp. 61–82). Springfield, IL: Charles C. Thomas.

Bennett, M. J. (1996). Is psychotherapy ever medically necessary? *Psychiatric Services*, 47(9), 971–974.

Bennett, M. J. (1997). Focal psychotherapy. In L. I. Sederer & A. J. Rothschild (Eds.), *Acute care psychiatry: Diagnosis and treatment* (pp. 355–373). Baltimore: Williams & Wilkins.

Bolognini, S. (1997). Empathy and "empathism." *International Journal of Psycho-Analysis*, 78(Pt. 2), 279–293.

Buber, M. (1947). *Between man and man*. London: Routledge & Kegan Paul.

Buber, M. (1957). Elements of the interhuman. *Psychiatry*, 20, 105–113.

Buie, D. H. (1981). Empathy: its nature and limitations. *Journal of the American Psychoanalytic Association*, 29, 281–307.

Collins, K. S., Schoen, C., & Sandman, D. R. (1997). *The Commonwealth Fund survey of physician experiences with managed care*. http://www.cmwf.org/programs/health_care/physrvg.asp.

Drug focus shortchanges psychodynamics, Tasman says. (2000, July 7). *Psychiatric News*, p. 18.

Dyer, R. (1999, October 2). Ozawa conducts transcendent Mahler Second. *The Boston Globe*, p. F4.

Easty, D. (1981). *On method acting*. New York: Ivy Books.

Eisenberg, D. M., Davis, R. B. Ettner, S. L., Appel, S., Wilkey, S., Van Rompay, M., & Kessler, R. C. (1998). Trends in alternative medicine use in the United States, 1990–1997. *Journal of the American Medical Association*, 280(18), 1569–1575.

Enthoven, A. C. (1989). Effective management of competition in the FEBHP (Federal Employees Health Benefits Program). *Health Affairs*, 8(3), 33–50.

Gold, M. R. (1999). ISO quick fix, free lunch, and share of pie. *Journal of Health Politics, Policy and Law*, 24(5), 973–983.

Goldbeck-Wood, S., Dorozynski, A., Lie, L. G., Yamauchi, M., Zinn, C., Josefson, D., & Ingram, M. (1996). Complementary medicine is booming worldwide. *British Medical Journal*, 313, 131–133.

Greenberg, D. S. (1998). Rapid rise for U.S. health-care costs, yet again. *Lancet*, 351(9116), 1639.

Havens, L. (1978). Explorations in the uses of language in psychotherapy: simple empathic statements. *Psychiatry*, 41, 336–345.

Havens, L. (1979). Explorations in the uses of language in psychotherapy: complex empathic statements. *Psychiatry*, 42, 40–48.

Jackson, S. W. (1992). The listening healer in the history of psychological healing. *American Journal of Psychiatry*, 149(12), 1623–1632.

Levin, R. (1997). Speaking Mozart's lingo. In B. D. Sherman (Ed.), *Inside early music* (pp. 315–338). New York: Oxford Press.

Lindner, R. (1982). The Jet Propelled Couch. In *The fifty minute hour* (pp. 163–216). New York: The Dell Publishing Company.

Mahrer, A. R. (1997). Empathy as therapist–client alignment. In A. C. Bohart & L. S. Greenberg (Eds.), *Empathy reconsidered: New directions in psychotherapy* (pp. 187–213). Washington, DC: American Psychological Association.

Miller, I. J. (1989). The therapeutic empathic communication (TEC) process. *American Journal of Psychotherapy*, 43(4), 531–545.

More, E. S. (1994). Empathy enters the profession of medicine. In E. S. More & M. A. Milligan (Eds.), *The empathic practitioner: Empathy, gender and medicine* (pp. 19–39). New Brunswick, NJ: Rutgers University Press.

O'Hara, M. (1997). Relational empathy: Beyond modernist egocentrism to postmodern holistic contextualism. In A. C. Bohart & L. S. Greenberg (Eds.), *Empathy reconsidered: New directions in psychotherapy* (pp. 295–321). Washington, DC: American Psychological Association.

Olinick, S. (1984). A critique of empathy and sympathy. In J. Lichtenberg, M. Bornstein, & D. Silver (Eds.), *Empathy I* (pp. 137–167). Hillsdale, NJ: The Analytic Press.

Patients' rights, M.D. unions inch forward in Congress. (2000, July 21). *Psychiatric News*, pp. 1 & 26.

Rogers, C. R. (1959). A theory of therapy, personality, and interpersonal relationships as developed in the client-centered framework. In S. Koch (Ed.), *Psychology: A study of a science. Foundations of the person and the social context*, Vol. 3 (pp. 210–211). New York: McGraw-Hill.

Savage, G. T., Campbell, K. S., Patman, T., & Nunnelley. L.L. (2000). Beyond managed costs. *Health Care Management Review, 25*(1), 93–108.

Shem, S. (1978). *The House of God* (pp. 12, 13). New York: Michael Marek.

Shlien, J. (1997). Empathy in psychotherapy: A vital mechanism? Yes. Therapist's conceit? All too often. By itself enough? No. In A. C. Bohart & L. S. Greenberg (Eds.). *Empathy reconsidered: New directions in psychotherapy* (pp. 63–80). Washington, DC: American Psychological Association.

Sorian, R., & Feder, J. (1999). Why we need a patients' bill of rights. *Journal of Health Politics, Policy and Law, 24*(5), 1137–1144.

Stanislavski, C. (1936). *An actor prepares*. New York: Theatre Arts Books.

Starr, P. (1982). *The social transformation of american medicine*. New York: Basic Books.

Stone, D. (1999). Managed care and the second great transformation. *Journal of Health Politics, Policy and Law, 24*(5), 1213–1218.

Tansey, M. J., & Burke, W. F. (1989). *Understanding countertransference: From projective identification to empathy*. Hillsdale, NJ: Analytic Press.

Thompson, M. (1954). *Not as a stranger* (p. 391). New York: Charles Scribner & Sons.

CHAPTER 2

The History of Empathy in Mental Health Care

Canst thou not minister to a mind diseas'd
Pluck from the memory a rooted sorrow,
Raze out the written troubles of the brain,
And with some sweet oblivious antidote
Cleanse the stuff'd bosom of that perilous stuff
Which weighs upon the heart?

William Shakespeare

*E*mpathy is a relatively new concept, which has its roots in aesthetic theories developed in the middle to late nineteenth century. With its application to psychology, and later to psychotherapy, this concept has been expanded and applied with great enthusiasm and even greater variability. In considering the history of its origins and its application to psychotherapy, I will focus attention on two overlapping lines of development: *strategic empathy*, as represented primarily in the psychoanalytic tradition, and *experiential empathy*, as represented in the work of and followers of Carl Rogers. Briefly defined, the first of these refers to the belief that empathy is a mode of enquiry used by a therapist to acquire information that will facilitate treatment, while the second regards empathy as an attitude or interpersonal posture on the part of a therapist that contributes directly to healing. This distinction, though perhaps overstated, is germane to the central question of this book: what is the appropriate place of empathy in contemporary mental health care?

ORIGINS: FEELING INTO A WORK OF ART

No idea or concept has a single traceable origin. Most theorists agree, however, that the concept of empathy originated in aesthetic theories of the nineteenth century, first articulated by Robert Vischer and based on ideas advanced by his father, Friedrich (Wind, 1963). The Vischers elaborated a theory of art appreciation based on muscular and emotional responses in the viewer to properties of the work of art. Consistent with much of German thought in the late nineteenth century, these ideas sprang from the philosophy of Immanual Kant, which held that the beauty of an object was grounded in the observer, rather than in the object itself (Gauss, 1973–74). Calling the activity involved, *Einfuhlung*, literally, "feeling into," Vischer proposed that the viewer unconsciously imbues the object of contemplation with his own vitality. These ideas were taken up independently by two other individuals, Theodor Lipps and Violet Paget, the first a psychologist and the second a novelist and literary critic who wrote under the name Vernon Lee. Lipps and Paget both advanced the idea that we "lend our life" (Wellek, 1970) to the form that we perceive; *Einfuhlung*, therefore, was an act of projection. What we project, Paget theorized, is both our feelings and body sensations as they are evoked through the act of observation (Gauss, 1973–74). For Lipps, this projection involved more than muscular actions and feelings, encompassing as well the fund of experiences and the basic drives of the viewer, and resulting in a merger of self and other. Lipps held that this type of merger involved a loss of self-awareness on the part of the observer during the act of observation.

The two core themes—that *Einfuhlung* involves an active process of feeling one's way into an external object, experiencing it, as it were, from within, and that one's identity is either suspended or otherwise affected by the activity— emerged as important considerations over the next half century as the idea of empathic knowing was applied to the interpersonal realm. Lipps is credited with introducing the concept of "feeling into" to the field of psychology, suggesting that the inner process associated with appreciating a work of art is also involved when we seek to know the mind of another person (Sharma, 1993; Wispe, 1987).

Language shapes ideas and ideas shape behavior. So it is with the transformation of *Einfuhlung* into *empathy*, a translation suggested by the English

Gustav Vigeland, sculpture, Frogner Park, Oslo.

psychologist Edward B. Titchener in a lecture delivered in 1909 at the University of Illinois (1926). Titchener expanded on the idea that we learn about something outside of ourselves through muscular mimicry, including both imitation of the various physical features observed and visual imagery evoked by the object, that is, we engage in mental activity and experience movement images as well as actual sensations of movement in response to our observations. This internal activity in the mind, occurring in response to something external, he called "empathy." Titchener's model of the mind placed emphasis on visual imagery drawn from experience, which served as the basis for empathic knowing. Shlien has noted that this translation involved a shift from an essentially pleasant activity (experiencing something beautiful) to one associated with *patheos*, illness or suffering (Shlien, 1997), an association that may account for its subsequent application to the process of treating illness.

The idea of empathy as a method of knowing another person presents certain problems, and these have preoccupied psychological theorists. First, unlike inert objects, human beings have a mental as well as a physical life. Is it possible to transcend the boundaries that separate us from each other and to know another's mind? The most extreme answer to this question is known as *solipsism*, the belief that the only reality is one's own mind, and even the idea of the existence of other minds is a matter of doubt. Although no philosopher has seriously proposed this extreme view, Descartes raised it as a possibility (Russell, 1945) while the philosophy of Leibniz, and particularly his metaphysics, proposed that all entities are forever separate and perceptually cut off from each other, though caught up in the greater scheme of God's design (Pfleiderer, 1886). Derived from the Greek word for *passion*, empathy requires that the "feelings, thoughts and motives of one are readily comprehended by another" (*American Heritage Dictionary*, 1969, p. 428). How is such a thing possible?

A second question, if we assume that other minds do exist and that it is possible to know them in some fashion, involves the manner in which we may transcend the boundaries that separate us one from the other. Is it a matter of intuition? Imagination based on similarities of experience? Careful observation? Imitation? Identification? Projection? Is it a matter of extrapolating from objective data about another person and his or her nature and life experiences? Is empathy a process or an event, and, if a process, is it an active or passive one? Can we bring it about or only create circumstances in which it may occur? All of these points of view have been advocated at one time or another by the various theorists concerned with this topic. How can they be reconciled with each other?

A third question pertains to the relationship between the object of observation and the observer. If it is indeed possible to know another's mind, what happens to the observer in the process? Does his or her self become merged with the other? Is his or her identity temporarily absorbed, suspended in some fashion, or given over in the process, or does s/he maintain a state of separateness and objectivity?

A fourth question concerns the utility or value of empathy, and especially its contribution to psychotherapy. Is empathy primarily a method of obtaining information? Is its value limited to the process of forming or sustaining a relationship and thus laying the groundwork for the *real work* of therapy, or is it in itself therapeutic? If it is therapeutic, in what way is it so?

Finally, is empathy a concept that applies only to the activities that take place between individuals or does it have broader implications for groups, communities, and the culture in which we live? If these broader implications are believed to exist, what is their relevance to our major concern in this book, the role and value of empathy in contemporary health care and especially mental health care.

As a topic of interest to philosophers, social and developmental psychologists, sociologists, and a variety of others, empathy has been widely studied. Since our concern is with its relevance to mental health care, and to psychotherapy in particular, we will not pursue it into all realms; neither will we consider research on empathy or the various methods that have been proposed to measure it. What follows is a brief review of the evolution of the concept of empathy, focusing on the questions I have raised about its nature and value to the psychotherapist. For a fuller exposition on the history of empathy in psychotherapy the reader is referred to other accounts (Eisenberg & Strayer, 1987; Sharma, 1993; Basch, 1983; More & Strayer, 1994).

EMPATHY AS A THERAPEUTIC STRATEGY

Although most practitioners of psychotherapy would probably agree that a good therapist is empathic, they would have varying opinions about its nature and use. Basch summarized the ambiguity about its nature when he asked, "Is empathy an end result, a tool, a skill, a kind of communication, a listening stance, a type of introspection, a capacity, a power, a form of perception or observation, a disposition, an activity or a feeling. Is empathy to be equated with love, understanding, sympathy?" (Basch, 1983). This volley of questions underscores the lack of agreement about empathy but, as we shall see, over-states the differences among theorists.

The development of the concept of empathy as a factor in psychological healing took place over the first half of the twentieth century, primarily within the psychoanalytic movement; therefore, any discussion must begin with Freud. Though it is sometimes assumed that he had little interest in the concept, it is mentioned a number of times in his writing. Freud (1921/1959a) appeared to consider empathy as essential to the task of knowing anything at all about another person's mind, and therefore as indispensable in psychoanaly-sis. In considering the phenomenon of identification as it relates to the ties developed among members of a group, Freud stated that "we are far from having exhausted the problem of identification and that we are faced by the process which psychology calls 'empathy (*Einfuhlung*)' and which plays the largest part in our understanding of what is inherently foreign to our ego in other people" (p. 40). Empathy is, therefore, a process rather than an event, one that we use in order to visit a foreign place. Considering how this process might unfold, he went on to state, "A path leads from identification by way of imitation to empathy, that is, to the comprehension of the mechanism by means of which we are enabled to take up any attitude at all toward another mental life" (p. 42).

As Basch has clarified (1983), Freud was saying that our ability to form any impression of another person's mental life depends on the process of empathy, which includes imitation and identification as precursors to awareness. This position is reminiscent of Lipps. Freud was familiar with Lipps and quoted him

widely in his work on humor (Freud, 1905/1960), a subject written about by
Lipps as well. In considering the relationship between the receiver and pro-
ducer of a joke, Freud stated that, "we take the producing person's psychical
state into consideration, put ourselves into it and try to understand it and
compare it with our own. It is these processes of empathy and comparison that
result in the economy in expenditure which we discharge by laughing" (p.
186). Empathy was for Freud a matter of identification as well as understanding. The use of the words "try" and "compare" suggest he regarded this
as an active rather than a passive process.

Freud (1907/1959b) also made reference to empathy in *Delusions and
Dreams in Jensen's Gravida*, when he distinguished between understanding a
person's illness (in this case, a psychosis) and understanding the personal
mental makeup of the person with the illness. It is through empathy that we
understand the personal dimension that might "give rise to such a state" (p.
45). We will come back to this important point later in the book, when we
consider the importance of the distinction between the subjective and objective
aspects of mental disorder and the role of empathy in appreciating the former.

Development of the concept of empathy within the psychoanalytic tradition
for the most part presumed that it took place within a dyadic and hierarchical
relationship in which a therapist worked on a continuous (and usually lengthy)
basis with a patient. This therapist (psychoanalyst) sought to use the knowledge obtained about the patient's mental state to foster insight through facilitating the emergence of unconscious determinants of the patient's disorder into
consciousness. The curative mechanism for accomplishing this was believed
to be interpretation, especially directed at the patient's development of transference phenomena that were the derivatives of developmental impasses. In
this paradigm, empathy was generally considered a tool used to gain the
necessary understanding that formed the basis for interpretations. For Freud
and his followers, the core matter was the conflict between drives and external
and internal constraints.

Following Freud, but distancing himself from Lipps, Theodore Schroeder
wrote a paper in 1925 in which he cautioned against the idea that empathy
involved simple projection, which is an unconscious process. He regarded it
instead as a conscious activity that he characterized as *reading out* rather than
reading in, that is, the analyst investigates the psychological experience that
the patient relates through drawing on his own recollection of similar experience, which informs him about the patient's state of mind. Schroeder (1925)
placed great emphasis on the fact that the analyst had been analyzed, and was
therefore in a position to correct projections, thereby making it possible to
"read another's mind" and experience the patient's feelings and thoughts "as if
from within" (p. 162). This sequence, which might be termed *projection fol-*

lowed by correction, was possible only because of the analyst's self-knowledge and ability to process his impressions. The analyst thus placed his "own consciousness at the disposal of the unconscious determinants" of the patient's personality. Many years later, Schafer would also propose that empathy involved projection followed by correction (Schafer, 1959). Schroeder's transformation of *Einfuhlung* from *feeling into* to *reading in* and thence to *reading out* suggested that empathy involved mental activity by the therapist with the patient a passive participant.

Patients, however, are not works of art but human beings who, like the therapist, live in a context; therefore, the mental state that is targeted is multidimensional, reflecting various aspects of the patient's unique identity. The question of how the analyst, who has his/her own identity, might be able to experience the patient's mental state was addressed by Helene Deutch (1926/1963). Deutch hypothesized that an *identification with the patient* took place, based on the similarity between the developmental process experienced by both the analyst and the patient and the fact that the analyst's unconscious had been made accessible through his or her own analysis and could thus be drawn on and used in the treatment process. The assumption is that beneath their differences in life experience lies a reservoir composed of common developmental themes that patient and analyst have in common. The therapist, therefore, is in a position to know what goes on beneath consciousness in the patient.

Using identification as the core mechanism in empathy presented problems because of the orthodox definition of identification as a process leading to lasting or even permanent change. A series of suggestions was made to create a special category for the type of identification that purportedly took place. Fliess (1942) spoke of it as a "trial" or "transient" phenomenon; Greenson (1960) referred to it as "tentative"; Schafer (1959) as "segregated" (distinct from more permanent aspects of the identity of the analyst), and Beres and Arlow (1974) called it "momentary." Despite these qualifications, the idea that empathy requires identification of the therapist with the patient continued to trouble clinical theorists. "Identification" usually refers to the assumption of features, traits, attitudes, or behaviors of one person by another, with lasting impact on the identity of the identifying party. Identification, therefore, implies a *taking in* of some feature of the other and making it one's own. In that sense, it is the opposite of projection, though both raise the matter of crossing boundaries. By these permutations, psychoanalytic theorists had now reversed the polarity of *Einfuhlung*.

In *Listening with the Third Ear* (1948/1983), Theodore Reik proposed an alternative to identification. He proposed that empathic listening is a process that involves an affective response induced in the analyst, presumably directly by the evocative power of the patient's presentation, rather than an identification with the patient. This affective response is then processed by the analyst, who draws on his own mental content to develop an idea of the patient's state of mind. There are two important aspects to Reik's theory: first, that empathy is a process and, second, that it is initiated by an affective communication (in Reik's terms, an "induced impulse") (p. 465). The analyst's mental activity relies on his ability to process the communicated affect, which is a product of his mastery of his own unconscious as a result of having been analyzed. Reik was clear in distinguishing the analyst's consciously recalled life experiences from those stirred by the patient's affect, which are unconscious: "it is not the other person's impulse as such, but its unconscious echo in the ego that is the determining factor in psychological conjecture" and "the analyst seizes unconsciously upon the expression of his patient's emotion before becoming conscious of it himself" (p. 466). He distinguished this from both projection and identification, emphasizing the need of the therapist to use the conscious part of his mind to avoid entangling himself in the patient's affective state. Although his thinking remained true to the psychoanalytic tradition, Reik's idea of an induced impulse anticipated later work on affective resonance.

A consistent feature of empathy within the orthodox psychoanalytic tradition is that knowing applies not only to the patient's conscious (and communicated) experience, but also to ideas and feelings that are out of consciousness or defended against. This suggests a unidirectional flow of empathy, a basically hierarchical relationship between patient and therapist, and special powers in the therapist to know more about the patient than s/he does about him/herself. For example, Olden (1953) suggested that the therapist may "trespass the [. . .] screen of defenses" of the patient through empathy. What is proposed is that the therapist may bypass the patient's defenses and gain direct access to unconscious mental content, a position that requires belief in the enhanced capacity of the trained psychoanalyst to be master of his or her own inner world. In drawing on inner resources, the analyst oscillates between an introspective and a cognitive mode, as a number of theorists have suggested: the first in order to attune to the patient's affective state and the second to understand it. This sequence amounts to a controlled regression in the observer, which is balanced by disciplined attempts to confirm, disconfirm, or clarify hypotheses generated through immediate unconscious resonance.

Belief that the analyzed therapist is in a position to correct for empathically derived hypotheses about the patient's mental state has been a core feature of the psychoanalytic use of this concept. Sandor Ferenczi (1955), who advocated a central role for empathy in therapy, cautioned about the need to be sensitive to the patient's readiness to receive interpretations. He associated empathy with the form of protection that he termed "tact." Ferenczi believed that the analyst, based on "the dissection of many minds, but above all from the dissection of our own," was in a position to conjecture on the patient's unexpressed thoughts and their unconscious determinants but was bound to use this information with great caution lest he unwittingly increase the patient's resistance to treatment. For Ferenczi, empathy referred to the analyst's appreciation of the patient's mental state, including resistances, and was a guide to the clinical process. Ferenczi's contribution was to present the feelings and activities of the analyst as central to the healing process, departing from the notion that the analyst was strictly a neutral figure, and recognizing the need to create a therapeutic ambience conducive to healing. It is ironic that Ferenczi rationalized his ideas about not harming the patient by stating that his major concern was that the insufficiently tactful (empathic) therapist might unwittingly reinforce the patient's resistance, leading to a (premature) disruption of treatment. For Ferenczi, this explanation was most likely a response to criticism that his methods were too much based on subjective factors.

If the reliability of empathy is contingent on successful self-mastery, its use involves risk. The boundary between empathic resonance and countertransference may not always be clear. Empathy, both as experienced by the therapist and also as experienced by the patient, may be misleading or inaccurate. Constant checking may not be a sufficient safeguard. These considerations may have served to constrain theorists from a broader exploration of this aspect of treatment and its value and applicability. Shapiro (1974), in discussing the distortions in the patient's own empathic capacities, failed to consider similar problems emanating from the therapist; Buie (1981) addressed the matter of fallibility, but attributed it to the patient's resistance to being understood. The fear of subjective responses to the patient continued to plague therapists concerned about neutrality. Reik's (1948/1983) opinion, which deviated sharply from orthodoxy, was that "The assertion of the unfeeling attitude, of the impassibility of the analyst, is a fairy tale" (p. 468).

In an attempt to return empathy to the realm of the objective and the scientific, Basch (1983) sought to explain the unsettling question about the transmission of affect by drawing on the work of Sylvan Tomkins, who postulated nine basic affects universally present from birth and evoked through various stimuli. Basch proposed that knowledge of the patient's emotional state was accomplished in three overlapping steps. First, the therapist unconsciously resonates to the patient's affect via his own somatic (autonomic) structures. This is accomplished, as suggested earlier by Freud and his predecessors, through unconscious imitation. The experience of affective arousal then leads to conscious processing in the therapist, based on familiarity with and similarity to the patient, and presumably accomplished through inference. The perception of affects leads to assumptions about associated feelings (subjectively experienced affects) and emotions (complex mental states encompassing feelings and their meaning to the individual) as these might be present in the patient. Beres and Arlow (1974) spoke of the initiating cue as a "signal affect," an experience that impels the therapist to consider what the significance of the signal, in the patient's mind, might be.

These considerations, which are based on the idea that members of a species have the capacity for attunement to each other, are reminiscent of the concept of *entrainment*, an idea traceable to the physicist Christian Huygens, who noted three hundred years ago that two clocks mounted on a common support will tick in unison. Restak (1984) pointed out that there are many examples of similar phenomena in biology, including human biology, suggesting that our ability to resonate may be part of our physiological makeup. The study of kinesics also suggests that human communication takes place through body movements, voice quality, and other nonverbal means. Though the mechanisms are more sophisticated, the similarity to the aesthetic theories of Paget and Lipps are interesting. Recent findings about infant development suggest that such attunement plays a significant role in the mother–child relationship.

The notion of affective resonance followed by inferential thinking has been advanced as a basic element in empathy by other theorists as well, with growing emphasis on the patient's role in empathic communication. Schafer (1959) related empathy to the Eriksonian concept of generativity, and considered it to be growth promoting, *in the patient*, *the therapist*, and *in their relationship*, a point of view that departed from the conventional psychoanalytic view that empathy was only a tool for gaining knowledge. In considering empathy to be bidirectional, Schafer appears to have anticipated the experiential therapists to be considered later in this chapter. Similar to the psychoanalytic theorists noted above, however, he understood the ability to experience the feelings and thoughts of another person as a projection of the analyst's remembered feelings and thoughts (i.e., conscious) in similar circumstances, tested then by further observations. Significantly, Schafer also regarded empathy as a corrective device in therapy, drawn on when a break occurred in the relationship between therapist and patient, an idea that would be developed more fully by Heinz Kohut. For Schafer, empathy required an incomplete form of identification that developed over time in treatment, based on the creation in the therapist's mind of a working model of the patient's world. The idea that therapy might involve a "corrective emotional experience" had been proposed earlier by Alexander and French (1946), who were not referring to empathy per se, but to the idea that the therapist's ability to understand the patient's vulnerability as it unfolded in the transferential relationship and correct for it might be, in itself, therapeutic. Kohut (1959) was to expand this idea considerably by relating the processing of faulty empathy in the therapeutic relationship to the healing process in the patient.

Greenson (1960) also viewed empathy as part of the relationship between therapist and patient, but focused his attention not on the interaction but on the therapist's internal version of the patient. For Greenson, the therapist's ability to empathize was based on the development of a working mental model of the patient, one that was comprehensive, embracing "appearance, affects, life experiences, [. . .] modes of behavior, [. . .] attitudes, defences, values, fantasies, etc." (p. 421). This model is not a replication of the patient, but a modified version shaped by the therapist's expectations for the patient. Greenson saw empathy as reciprocal in that it depended both on the therapist's ability to empathize and also on the patient's willingness for empathic resonance to take place. Buie (1981) and Shapiro (1974) have both argued that empathy has its limits and may be faulty in the absence of this type of alliance. Greenson viewed empathy as most useful as a corrective device in therapy, invoked when contact with the patient fails to take place or is lost.

For Buie (1981), the empathic process was an inferential one that did not involve identification. He also emphasized its fallibility and its dependence on an alliance between a therapist seeking to empathize and a patient who allows him or herself to be understood. An empathic sequence begins with the observation of behavioral cues provided by the patient, which then leads the therapist to draw on certain inner referents in the course of understanding the meaning of these cues. He postulated four types of referents: conceptual, experiential, imaginative, and resonant. The first of these relates to a model of the patient that the therapist constructs in his mind; the second, the therapist's own reservoir of experiences; the third, the creative imagination of the therapist; and the fourth, a generic ability we seem to have to experience strongly communicated affect. Resonance appears similar in this sense to the notion of contagion. The use of imagination was also emphasized by Schafer (1959), who pointed out its fallibility. Margulies (1989), who emphasized the creative nature of clinical empathy, suggested that a two-step process is involved: the therapist initially frees himself from bias about the patient and then opens his mind to perceptions, allowing him to feel his way into the inner world of the patient, which he termed, "the inscape." For Margulies, not only is this a process of discovering what is unique and unexpected, but it is inherently creative, and should occasion both surprise and wonder. The key point for both Buie and Margulies is that the therapist uses his own creative energies in the process of discovery. Margulies and others have pointed to the similarity between empathy in the therapist and the creative process employed by the artist, as described by Kris (1952).

The concept of empathy reached its fullest psychoanalytic expression in the work of Heinz Kohut, who departed radically from orthodox psychoanalytic thinking and established empathy as a central factor in therapy. His work eventuated in the theories and practice of self-psychology, an offshoot of dynamic psychotherapy that regards empathy as an essential tool of treatment with all patients. Although empathy remained largely a strategic tool, Kohut's major contribution was to place it squarely at the hub of the therapeutic process and suggest that it represented a sustained activity on the part of the therapist, whose introspection was directly linked to the grasp of complex psychological constellations within the patient. Though not credited to them by Kohut, this holistic concept is similar to ideas expressed earlier by the gestalt psychologists. Kohut termed this capacity for grasping the patient's state of mind "vicarious introspection" (1959).

Kohut's revisions were initially a response to the difficulties encountered in treating patients with certain types of personality disorders, those associated with pathological narcissism, who were seen as refractory to the usual psychoanalytic methodology. In understanding his profound impact on psychoanalysis, psychiatry, and psychology, and the fundamental change in thinking that his work provoked, the fact that these disciplines were already in transition must be taken into account. With the development of the first *Diagnostic and Statistical Manual* by the American Psychiatric Association (DSM-I) and the advent of psychopharmacology, descriptive and biological psychiatry was on the rise. The old psychodynamic models, derived from orthodox Freudian precepts, had proven inadequate to treat major mental disorders; behaviorism and cognitive theory offered other alternatives but implied a mechanistic vision of man that failed to account for uniqueness and individual variation. A new spirit of optimism and humanism opened the way to treatment innovations. Against this backdrop, Kohut's work amounted to nothing less than a revolution in psychoanalytic thinking, presenting an alternative to drive theory that was based on the concept of narcissistic fulfillment as an appropriate, lifelong need. Bitter opposition within the orthodox psychoanalytic community predictably occurred, further distancing this subgroup from the mainstream. The psychology of the self had a Copernican impact, renewing interest in dynamic therapies while establishing the place of the self as central.

According to Kohut (1971), narcissism represents a line of development rather than an infantile antecedent to adult love. Health in adult life depends on empathic relationships during upbringing. The failure of early relationships to provide narcissistic nurturance leads to personality disturbances refractory to ordinary psychoanalysis but curable through the provision of treatment designed to correct the flawed sense of self. Such treatment depends on the therapist's empathic resonance with his patient, and especially on the inevitable small failures of empathy that naturally occur in treatment and prompt the development of new and reliable structures within the patient to sustain healthy self esteem. For Kohut, empathy was both a method of gathering information and a vehicle for healing; it could be understood as an extension of the introspective mode to the mind of the analysand:

> The best definition of empathy—the analogue to my terse scientific definition of empathy as "vicarious introspection" [. . .] —is that it is the capacity to think and feel oneself into the inner life of another person. It is our lifelong ability to experience what another person experiences, though usually, and appropriately, to an attenuated degree. (p. 82)

Though he never explained how such vicarious introspection might take place, Kohut's later work indicated that he saw the capacity for empathy as a basic human endowment allowing for a unified grasp of complex states of mind. He distinguished empathic knowing from intuition and did not regard it as an identification with the patient. His work is consistent with a number of theorists associated with the experiential therapies as well as with the work of Edith Stein (1964), an assistant to the phenomenological philosopher Edmund Husserl. Stein considered empathy to be a "kind of act of perceiving [. . .] how man grasps the psychic life of his fellow man" (p. 11). Margulies (1989) has made the same point; drawing on the work of Havens and others, he has linked empathy to phenomenology: the belief that we learn about the world solely through our perceptions and, for these to be authentic, we must first rid ourselves of the ideas that distort them. This perspective is antithetical to the current emphasis in psychiatry on diagnostic entities, a point to be developed in greater detail by the experiential therapists.

Kohut's progress from orthodox analysis through the development of his ideas on the centrality of the concept of the self led him eventually to consider empathy even more broadly as a vehicle for continuing personal growth through deeper connections to others: a fundamental mode of human relatedness that is essential for individual and collective survival (Teich, 1992). Within the therapeutic context, however, he appears to have restricted his use of empathy to a strategic tool of intervention, used in a dyadic relationship to gather information, understand the patient's state of mind and vulnerability, and explain the source of his/her self pathology. Thus, while Kohut had a great deal in common with Carl Rogers and the client-centered and experiential therapists who followed, he appears to have remained committed to a hierarchical rather than an interpersonal model of treatment.

Following the work of Kohut, other psychoanalysts took up the new pathways he opened. Schwaber (1979), who understood empathy to be a particular type of listening that is characterized by attention to the patient's attempts to use the therapist as though an extension of the self (a *self-object*), argued that such listening requires that the therapist be sensitive to the patient's experience, especially the experience taking place with the therapist. Data gathered empathically should take into account the manner in which the presence of the therapist shapes the experience of the patient. Empathy, then, seen from a self-psychological perspective, allows the therapist to learn both about the patient's attempt to use the therapist as a self-object (in order to meet unfulfilled need) and also his/her adaptive responses when the therapist (inevitably) fails as a self-object. This strategic use of empathy is an extension of Kohut's thinking, and is also consistent with Winnicott's ideas about therapy, to be described later. As with many thinkers who experimented with the concept of empathy actively in their work over an extended period of time, Schwaber seems to have moved closer to those who regard empathy itself as healing.

As Freud must be distinguished from the Freudians, so Kohut should be seen as distinct from the Kohutians: those who have taken his ideas in new directions based on the notion of the self as the core element in identity. Self-psychology now permeates not only the dynamic psychotherapies that are the successors to orthodox psychoanalysis, but contemporary psychoanalysis as well. Spawned by Kohut and his various predecessors, self-psychologists have reshaped the dynamic landscape. Their contributions, which have been summarized elegantly by Barbara Seruya (1997), are the various treatment models that use empathic interaction to treat a range of disorders that are presumed to stem from a faulty development of the self. Based on the Kohutian idea of internalization of self-object functions from the therapist, the versions of brief psychotherapy that are associated with self-psychology seek to stabilize the patient's sense of self and mobilize resources within his/her life context that will lead to more lasting repair. We will return later in the book to considering how a patient may be prepared to draw on such resources through relatively brief psychotherapy.

EMPATHY AND EXPERIENTIAL HEALING

The work of Carl Rogers, the core of which is his model of client-centered therapy (CCT), represents the fullest development of empathy as a healing element in treatment. The roots of his system of treatment lie in his background as a social scientist and in his approach to counseling. For Rogers, empathy was a sustained attitude on the part of the therapist toward the patient that was, in itself, healing.

As with any theorist who works with a core concept over a period of many years, Rogers's views on empathy evolved. Their wellspring was his belief in the universal and inherent tendency toward growth and well-being (self-actualization) that, if supported during development, led to health. The conflict for Rogers was not between drives and constraints (as orthodox psychoanalysts believed) but between tendencies toward self-fulfillment and an environment that thwarted such tendencies, replacing healthy self-regard with a self-concept that is shaped according to the conditional acceptance experienced earlier with significant others. The role of the therapist was not to *treat* in the ordinary sense, but to promote recovery of health through creating an ambience that might reawaken the innate capacity for growth. Under such circumstances, healing would come from within. This ambience is characterized by an attitude that includes three features: *congruence* (genuineness on the part of the therapist), *unconditional positive regard for the patient* (acceptance of the patient's communicated experience without judgment or criticism), and *empathy*. Empathy was defined initially as follows:

> The state of empathy, or being empathic, is to perceive the internal frame of reference of another with accuracy and with the emotional components and meanings which pertain thereto as if one were that person, but without ever losing the "as if" condition. (Rogers, 1980, p. 140)

This initial understanding of empathy contained four important ideas. First, empathy is a manifestation of the therapist's attitude; second, it is not necessarily connected with activities or clinical strategies; third, it consists in an identification with the patient that is limited by certain boundaries beyond which the therapist ought not go; and fourth, it does not depend on unconscious communication. In response to criticism that the nondirective approach to treatment advocated was passive, Rogers said the following:

> This misconception of the approach has led to considerable failure in counseling—and for good reasons. In the first place, the passivity and seeming lack of interest or involvement is experienced by the client as a rejection, since indifference is in no real way the same as acceptance. In the second place, a laissez faire attitude does not in any way indicate to the client that he is regarded as a person of worth. (1951, p. 27)

In his later work, Rogers revised his thinking about empathy as a state of mind to considering it a process. The "as-if" condition, so important early, was laid aside in favor of "entering the private perceptual world of the other and becoming thoroughly at home in it" (1980, p. 143). The therapist not only perceives the patient's frame of reference, but senses the patient's world, communicates that sense to the patient, and constantly checks to determine its accuracy. The therapist may investigate ideas about which the patient is "scarcely aware," but is cautioned not to "uncover totally unconscious feelings, since this would be too threatening" (p. 142). The emphasis is on *meaning* and on the patient's unfolding experience of the world. For Rogers, empathy had become *a way of being* with the patient, rather than only a way of listening. Unlike Schroeder's earlier guidance that the therapist place his consciousness at the patient's disposal, Rogers was proposing that it was *the person of the therapist* that was offered for the client's use.

The goal of treatment in CCT is personality change, which is brought about as a result of attitude; this is in sharp contrast to the central curative element in psychoanalysis, its *hermeneutic* or interpretive function. The patient is believed to benefit because of a diminished sense of alienation, a greater sense of being valued, improved self-acceptance, and a changed self-concept based on new discoveries facilitated by the validating environment. In other words, s/he is presumed to become more of what s/he is capable of being. Diagnosis, formulation, and conceptual models of the patient are inconsistent with this approach to psychotherapy. In considering the characteristics of a helping relationship, Rogers saw the demands that his method placed on therapists: to be strong enough to remain separate from the client and permit the client separateness as well, to lose all desire to judge, to attune sensitively to both explicit and implicit meanings and to sustain such attitudes through the work (Rogers, 1961).

The idea that empathy promotes healing directly is related to an emphasis on the subjective element in treatment: the world of the patient as perceived by the patient, the meaning of his/her personal experience. For Rogers, empathy focuses our attention on the person with the problem. This position also presupposes the importance of interpersonal learning. Among the antecedents to later Rogerian thinking is the work of the philosopher Martin Buber, whose influence on Carl Rogers appears to have come after Rogers's initial formulations occurred, shaping later modifications (Shlien, 1997). Buber contrasted the version of empathy that was based on *Einfuhlung* with what he called, "experiencing the other side" In *Between Man and Man*, he stated:

> It would be wrong to identify what is meant here with the familiar but not very significant term "empathy." Empathy means, if anything, to glide with one's own feeling into the dynamic structure of an object, a pillar or a crystal or the branch of a tree, or even of an animal or a man, and as it were to trace it from within, understanding the formation and motoriality of the object with the perceptions from one's own muscles; it means to "transpose" oneself

over there and in there. Thus it means the exclusion of one's own concreteness, the extinguishing of the actual situation of life, the absorption in pure aestheticism of the reality in which one participates. Inclusion is the opposite of this. (1947, p. 96)

Buber went on to define "inclusion" in a manner that sounds very much like the later Rogerian definition of empathy:

> It is the extension of one's own concreteness, the fulfillment of the actual situation of life, the complete presence of the reality in which one participates. Its elements are, first, a relation, of no matter what kind, between two persons, second an event experienced by them in common, in which at least one of them actively participates, and, third, the fact that this one person, without forfeiting anything of the felt reality of his activity, at the same time lives through the common event from the standpoint of the other. (p. 97)

The idea of a dialogue of this kind was further explained in *Elements of the Interhuman* (1957), where Buber presented his dynamic version of what we currently call the capacity for empathy, "a gift which lives in man's inwardness as a Cinderella":

> Some call it intuition, but that is not a wholly unambiguous concept. I prefer the name, "imagining the real," for in its essential being this gift is not a looking at the other, but a bold swinging, demanding the most intensive stirring of one's being, into the life of the other. This is the nature of all genuine imagining, only that here the realm of my action is not the all-possible, but the particular real person who confronts me, whom I can attempt to make present to myself just in this way, and not otherwise, in his wholeness, unity, and uniqueness, and with his dynamic center which realizes all these things ever anew. (p. 110)

What Buber envisioned was an active use of our capacity to engage with each other empathically. Transposed into the clinical realm, "imagining the real" might serve as a prelude to healing activities or might be seen as healing in itself. The interpersonal ("interhuman") field is highlighted, in contrast to the emphasis on self that was the central preoccupation of the Freudians and the later self-psychologists as well as the early Rogers. Not only does this position support the use of the self therapeutically, but it implies something else as well: the healing potential of relationship and of social context in general. We will return to this idea frequently in this book.

At the core of interpersonal healing is the notion that our most basic needs are for human contact and fulfilling relationships. The great psychiatrist and teacher Harry Stack Sullivan saw the self in a negative valence when our social nature was considered. Although Sullivan saw empathy as central to the mother–child relationship and the development of a self, he considered the self to be a part of the personality that was concerned primarily with managing anxiety. For Sullivan (1940), empathy was a term used to describe the emotional linkage of the infant with significant people; in particular, empathy refers to "a certain direct contagion of disagreeable experience from significant adults to very young children" (p. 215), which in turn leads to the development of anxiety and then to the development of a self. Anxiety springs from the experience of disapproval from significant others. In our efforts to avoid anxiety, we limit and constrain ourselves and tend to develop the idea that we are "unique, isolated individuals in the human world" (p. 219). Mental illness, for Sullivan, consists in

> disordered living of subject-persons in and within their personal complexes. It is not an impossible study of an individual suffering mental disorder; it is a study of disordered interpersonal relations nucleating more or less clearly in a particular person. (1931, p. 978)

The essence of psychiatry for Sullivan was its art, and at the heart of its art, intuition followed by thinking (formulating). Treatment must therefore take place in an interpersonal context that is capable of reversing disordered interpersonal relations; it is, by its nature, sensitive to the patient's affective state, and especially anxiety, as experienced in the context of the therapist–patient relationship, where distortions in relating can be observed and addressed. For Sullivan, interpretation was not the primary healing vehicle, but it was useful insofar as it allowed the development and use of an empathic relationship to promote healing (Marcia, 1987).

The object relations theorists/therapists, although they did not always use the same terminology, also saw relationship as healing. Like Kohut and Sullivan, they placed great emphasis on the early mother–child relationship as a shaper of interpersonal behavior and the seed of self development. For Winnicott, the self was a core element of identity that might be adversely affected by failures in the mother–child relationship. As Kohut would emphasize later, Winnicott saw the inevitable failures in mothering as sources of health and strength in the child if they occurred gradually and in a manner that the child could tolerate, and regarded the therapist's function as maternal and corrective. His concept of the "holding environment" applied both to the mother's attunement to the infant and willingness to meet his/her needs, which he termed "good-enough mothering" (Winnicott, 1965), and to the therapist's willingness to provide an optimal ambience for healing. The reciprocity of the therapist–patient relationship is expressed best in his statement:

> Psychotherapy takes place in the overlap of two areas of playing, that of the patient and that of the therapist. Psychotherapy has to do with two people playing together. (1968, p. 591)

And, from Harry Guntrip's account (1975) of his treatment by Winnicott, this evidence of reciprocity:

> I'm good for you, but you're good for me. Doing your analysis is almost the most reassuring thing that happens to me. The chap before you makes me feel I'm no good at all. You don't have to be good for me. I don't need it and can cope without it, but in fact you are good for me. (p. 153)

An example of Winnicott's empathic resonance comes from the same paper. Describing his inability to tolerate silence or inactivity, Guntrip quotes:

> I began to be able to allow for some silences, and once, feeling a bit anxious, I was relieved to hear Winnicott move. I said nothing, but with uncanny intuition he said: "You began to feel afraid I'd abandoned you. You feel silence is abandonment." (p. 152)

The object relations theorists exerted considerable influence on psychoanalysis, leading to modifications of Freudian theory and the development of methods of treating children as well as adults. Though not all used the term, empathy was clearly an important element in their treatment methodology. Some, though not all, advocated the use of the real relationship as opposed to the transferential one, in gaining access to the patient and undoing the presumed damage done by empathic failures during development.

The use of the real relationship between therapist and patient as a vehicle for healing poses certain problems. First, there is the need to assure that the therapist does not exploit the relationship in order to meet personal needs. It is interesting in this regard to note the comment attributed to Winnicott by his patient Guntrip. Winnicott was able to present himself as a three-dimensional person who had his own feelings about the treatment and who could be disappointed, while reassuring his patient that he would not be damaged as a result. This highly empathic form of self-revelation took into account the need of this particular patient to be a helper while freeing him from a sense of obligation to Winnicott. The comment was paradoxical at the same time that s to have been genuine (an example of what Rogers might have termed *ice*). In this example, Winnicott's empathy is reminiscent of Ferenczi's *tact*.

Another problem with using the real relationship as a healing vehicle was addressed by Havens in his comments about the therapist's attempt in existential psychiatry to reduce or dissolve the boundary between therapist and patient. How is it possible to eliminate preconceptions about the patient, in order to "arrive where the other is"? Havens (1974) proposed that the therapist maintain a disciplined attitude and resist the temptation to draw conclusions. One way to understand this discipline is to compare inductive with deductive reasoning, the former involving data gathering that might lead to the generation of hypotheses, and the latter efforts to test an existing hypothesis by determining whether phenomena predicted by it actually occur or not. The ability to sustain an inductive posture is similar to the reduction suggested by phenomenologists in order to arrive at a purity of perception. This attitude runs counter to the search for generalities that is a core feature of descriptive psychiatry, and the imperative to draw conclusions about the patient's disorder rapidly so that it may be rapidly treated.

In sharp contrast to the prevailing attitudes in the era of descriptive psychiatry, Havens (1974) characterized the attitude of the existential method of psychotherapy as a search for the unique, an attitude he termed "radical subjectivity" (p. 4) in which the therapist must take at face value all that the patient says: the existential method commits the therapist to "accepting the patient's point of view, and to living as fully as possible in that point of view." This use of empathy is consistent with Buber and with the later Rogers, though Havens considered CCT to be a more passive version of the approach.

Elsewhere, Havens (1978) has suggested that empathic engagement is accomplished by a process of selective response, and involves a language that facilitates it. In a style that might be characterized as "hunt and peck," the therapist attempts to match his affect to that of the patient through various utterances, translations, and nonverbal responses that validate the patient's state of mind as understandable under the circumstances. This detailed model of empathic listening involves the therapist's willingness to "exist less as a person" (p. 341) in order to experience the patient's state of mind. It may be either active or passive, that is, the therapist may attempt to put into words what the patient has not yet expressed (an objective that was described by Rogers) through "imagining the real" (Buber) or s/he may proceed more slowly in an effort to deepen the connection.

Margulies and Havens, in a separate paper (1981), have stated that the empathic encounter seeks the unique essence of the other and is therefore the major therapeutic instrument. These two authors also raise the interesting notion that such an approach is by its nature a search for the patient's health and disease is found only to the extent that the search is unsuccessful. We will return in later chapters to the idea that the psychotherapist should be concerned with the patient's *overall state of health* rather than with disease, per se, since disease may be best understood in relative rather than absolute terms.

CONCLUSIONS

This review of the evolution of the concept of empathy concludes without following our topic into the other realms it now inhabits. By necessity, we have focused on only a small number of the clinical theorists who have been concerned about the nature and use of empathy in the therapeutic process. As we proceed to examine how listening in an empathic manner may be therapeutic, it is necessary to decide on a characterization of empathy in psychotherapy.

In this book, I will use the term to indicate a mode of knowing another person's state of mind through utilizing an ability that is universal, though variably possessed, developed, and drawn on. Additionally, I believe that the capacity for empathy may be interfered with or enhanced, and that it depends on the senses and cognitive capacities of the empathizer as these are employed with a willing subject. In other words, empathy requires some degree of reciprocity, though not necessarily an alliance (though alliance is one of the goals of the empathizer). I do not believe empathy involves an identification with the patient, but it does require venturing beyond the boundaries that separate us one from the other in order to place oneself in the patient's *life space* and see his/her agendas, priorities, and concerns from his/her own perspective. Projection, insofar as it occurs, depends on the imaginative capacity of the empathizer to know the other, which I understand to be a creative act based on perceived similarities, shared experience, or the ability to modify one's fund of experience and knowledge to encompass the unknown: imaginative extrapolation.

The empathizer must have tolerance for ambiguity, the discipline of avoiding premature closure, and the willingness to listen and learn. I do not believe empathy depends on engagement with unconscious mental content, but that it proceeds as a nonlinear process involving both affect and cognition as these occur in both participating parties. The beginning of an empathic exchange may be either affective or cognitive, one eventually leading to the other in the complete cycle. The attitude associated with empathy is not, as Rogers suggests, empathy itself: sustained states of empathy do not appear to me to be either possible or desirable, though sustained attitudes toward the patient that are consistent with empathy are possible. Of these, I would place caring first, curiosity second, and the ability to sustain an inductive posture and regard clinical hypotheses as presumptive as the third. All of these depend on a disciplined attitude on the part of the therapist who seeks to be fully present at the same time, a demanding feat; hence, the value of training and experience. Finally, empathy is relevant to the process of healing as it takes place both within the formal health care setting and, even more importantly, outside that setting. In the following chapters, I will amplify these beliefs and suggest how they apply to the emerging culture of health care.

The history of empathy in mental health care suggests two overlapping lines of theoretical development, which I have termed *strategic* and *experiential*. Both of these depend to a great extent on the same sets of skills and attitudes in the practitioner: receptivity to the ideas of the other and the willingness to listen attentively. The tradition of what Jackson has referred to as *the listening healer* (1992) is an old one, predating modern medicine by thousands of years. In the following chapter, we will consider its roots, nature, and evolution and attempt to discern at a higher power of magnification what we have considered only in general terms to this point: what is it that happens during an empathic exchange and in what way does the event contribute to the process we know as healing?

REFERENCES

Alexander, F., & French, T. M. (1946). *Psychoanalytic therapy: Principles and applications*. Lincoln: University of Nebraska Press.

American heritage dictionary of the English language (1969). Boston: Houghton Mifflin.

Basch, M. F. (1983). Empathic understanding: A review of the concept and some theoretical considerations. *Journal of the American Psychoanalytic Association, 31*, 101–126.

Beres, D., & Arlow, J. A. (1974). Fantasy and identification in empathy. *Psychoanalytic Quarterly, 43*, 26–50.

Buber, M. (1947). *Between man and man*, London: Routledge & Kegan Paul Ltd.

Buber, M. (1957). Elements of the interhuman. *Psychiatry, 20*, 105–113.

Buie, D. (1981). Empathy: Its nature and limitations. *Journal of the American Psychoanalytic Association, 29*, 281–307.

Deutch, H. (1963). Occult processes occurring during psychoanalysis. In G. Devereux (Ed.) *Psychoanalysis and the occult* (pp. 131–146). New York: International Universities Press. (Original work published in 1926.)

Eisenberg, N., & Strayer, J. (Eds.) (1987). *Empathy and development*. Cambridge: Cambridge University Press.

Ferenczi, S. (1955). *Final contributions to the problems and methods of psychoanalysis*. New York: Bruner/Mazel.

Fliess, R. (1942). Metapsychology of the analyst. *Psychoanalytic Quarterly, 11*, 211–227.

Freud, S. (1959a). Group psychology and the analysis of the ego. New York: W. W. Norton. (Original work published 1921.)

Freud, S. (1959b). *Delusions and dreams in Jensen's Gravida*. In J. Strachey (Ed. and Trans.), *The standard edition of the complete psychological works of Sigmund Freud* (Vol. 9, p. 45). London: Hogarth Press. (Original work published 1907.)

Freud, S. (1960). Jokes and their relation to the unconscious. In J. Strachey (Ed. and Trans.), *The standard edition of the complete psychological works of Sigmund Freud* (Vol. 8, p. 186). London: Hogarth Press. (Original work published 1905.)

Gauss, C. E. (1973–74). Empathy. In P. P. Wiener (Ed.) *Dictionary of the history of ideas: Studies of selected pivotal ideas* (Vol. 2, pp. 85–89). New York: Scribner.

Greenson, R. R. (1960). Empathy and its vicissitudes. *International Journal of Psycho-Analysis, 41*, 418–424.

Guntrip, H. (1975). My experience of analysis with Fairbairn and Winnicott. *International Review of Psychoanalysis, 2*, 145–156.

Havens, L. (1974). The existential use of the self. *American Journal of Psychiatry, 131*, 1–10.

Havens, L. (1978). Explorations in the uses of language in psychotherapy: Simple empathic statements. *Psychiatry, 41*, 336–345.

Jackson, S. W. (1992). The listening healer in the history of psychological healing. *American Journal of Psychiatry, 149*(12), 1623–1632.

Kohut, H. (1959). Introspection, empathy and psychoanalysis: An examination of the relationship between mode of observation and theory. In P. H. Ornstein (Ed.) *The search for the self* (Vol. 1, pp. 205–231). New York: International Universities Press.

Kohut, H. (1971). *The analysis of the self*. New York: International Universities Press.

Kris, E. (1952). *Psychoanalytic explorations in art*. New York: Shocken Books.

Marcia, J. (1987). Empathy and psychotherapy within a developmental context. In N. Eisenberg & J. Strayer (Eds.), *Empathy and its development* (pp. 81–102). Cambridge: Cambridge University Press.

Margulies, A. (1989). *The empathic imagination*. New York: W. W. Norton & Company.

Margulies, A., & Havens, L. (1981). The initial encounter: What to do first. *American Journal of Psychiatry, 138*(4), 421–428.

More, E. S., & Strayer, J. (Eds.) (1994). *The empathic practitioner: Empathy, gender and medicine*. New Brunswick, NJ: Rutgers University Press.

Olden, C. (1953). On adult empathy with children. In B. Charles (Ed.), *The psychoanalytic study of the child* (Vol. 8, p. 115). New York: International Universities Press.

Pfleiderer, O. (1886). *The philosophy of religion on the basis of its history* (Vol. 1, p. 68). London: Williams and Norgate.

Reik, T. (1983). *Listening with the third ear: The inner experience of a psychoanalyst*. New York: Farrar, Straus & Giroux. (Original work published 1948.)

Restak, R. M. (1984). Possible neurophysiological correlates of empathy. In J. Lichtenberg, M. Bornstein, & D. Silver (Eds.) *Empathy I* (p. 13). Hillsdale, NJ: Analytic Press.

Rogers, C. R. (1951). *Client-centered therapy: Its current practice implications and theory*. Boston: Houghton Mifflin.

Rogers, C. R. (1961). *On becoming a person*. Boston: Houghton Mifflin.

Rogers, C. R. (1980). *A way of being*. Boston: Houghton Mifflin.

Russell, B. (1945). *A history of western philosophy*. New York: Simon and Schuster.

Schafer, R. (1959). Generative empathy in the treatment situation. *Psychoanalytic Quarterly, 28,* 342–373.

Schroeder, T. (1925). The psycho-analytic method of observation. *International Journal of Psycho-Analysis, 6,* 155–170.

Schwaber, E. (1979). On the "self" within the matrix of analytic theory: Some clinical reflections and reconsiderations. *International Journal of Psycho-Analysis, 60,* 467–479.

Seruya, B. B. (1997). *Empathic brief psychotherapy.* Northvale, NJ: Jason Aronson.

Shapiro, T. (1974). The development and distortion of empathy. *Psychoanalytic Quarterly, 43,* 4–25.

Sharma, R. M. (1993). *Understanding the concept of empathy and its foundations in psychoanalysis.* Lewiston/Queenston/Lampeter: The Edwin Mellen Press.

Shlien, J. (1997). Empathy in psychotherapy: A vital mechanism? Yes. Therapist's conceit? All too often. By itself enough? No. In A. C. Bohart & L. S. Greenberg (Eds.) *Empathy reconsidered: New directions in psychotherapy* (pp. 63–80). Washington, DC: American Psychological Association.

Stein, E. (1964). *On the problem of empathy.* The Hague: Martinus Nijhof.

Sullivan, H.S. (1931). Socio-psychiatric research: Its implications for the schizophrenia problem and for mental hygiene. *American Journal of Psychiatry, 10,* 977–992.

Sullivan, H. S. (1940). *Conceptions of modern psychiatry.* New York: W. W. Norton & Company.

Sullivan, H. S. (1964). *The fusion of psychiatry and social science.* New York: W. W. Norton & Company.

Teich, N. (1992). *Rogerian perspectives: Collaborative rhetoric for oral and written communication.* Norwood, NJ: Ablex Publishing.

Titchener, E. B. (1926). *Experimental psychology of the thought processes.* New York: Macmillan.

Wellek, R. (1970). *Discriminations.* New Haven: Yale University Press.

Wind, E. (1963). *Art and anarchy.* London: Faber & Faber.

Winnicott, D. W. (1965). *The maturational process and the facilitating environment: Studies in the theory of emotional development.* New York: International Universities Press.

Winnicott, D. W. (1968). Playing: Its theoretical status in the clinical situation. *International Journal of Psycho-Analysis, 49,* 591–599.

Wispe, L. (1987). History of the concept of empathy. In N. Eisenberg & J. Strayer (Eds.), *Empathy and development* (pp. 17–36). Cambridge: Cambridge University Press.

CHAPTER 3

Empathy and the Listening Healer

We make ourselves a place apart
Behind light words that tease and flout,
But oh, the agitated heart
Till someone really finds us out.

'Tis pity if the case require
(Or so we say) that in the end
We speak the literal to inspire
The understanding of a friend.

But so with all, from babes that play
At hide-and-seek to God afar,
So all who hide too well away
Must speak and tell us where they are

Robert Frost

I thought: what sort of doctor, what sort of person, is this?
He didn't even listen to me. He showed no concern.
He doesn't listen to his patients— he doesn't give a damn.

Oliver Sacks

*J*n his remarkable personal account of recovery from a serious leg injury complicated by a profound and frightening disturbance of body image, the neurologist Oliver Sacks (1984) described his attempt to convey his concerns to the orthopedic surgeon:

> "The leg doesn't feel right."
> "This is very vague and subjective. Not the sort of thing we can be concerned with. We orthopods are really carpenters, in a way. We are called in to do a job. We do it. And that's that."

Persisting, Sacks is informed that his complaints are unique, to which he responds,

> "I can't be unique," I said, with anger, and rising panic. "I must be constituted the same way as everyone else! Perhaps (my anger was getting the better of me now), perhaps you don't listen to what patients say, perhaps you're not interested in the experiences they have." "No, indeed, I can't waste time with 'experiences' like this. I'm a practical man, I have work to do." (pp. 106–107)

The idea that listening is central to the care of patients is an old one. Sacks, the patient, was in need of reassurance that he was not freakishly unique: normalization, as well as validation of his *feeling* about his illness. Certainly he was seeking information, but something else as well: he wanted to be heard by a listener. A listener is someone who does more than hear; a listener also understands the other person. Listening is therefore a channel for empathic communication.

The association between listening and healing is a complex matter, in which empathy plays an important, perhaps the central, part. If psychological healing may be distinguished from physical healing (not as simple a matter as it may seem on the surface), then the role of the listener in the healing process must somehow be linked to our understanding of the target of treatment: the patient's altered state of health. For the most part, scientific medicine (including psychiatry), makes the patient's *disease* (for the mental health professional, *disorder*) the target. Kleinman (1980) has pointed out that Western medicine has been concerned with *disease* rather than *illness*, two linked but different aspects of impaired health. Disease refers to the malfunctioning of biological or psychological processes while illness refers to the psychosocial experience and meaning of disease as perceived by the sufferer (p. 72). If we accept this distinction, then it follows that healing may be defined in a narrow or a broader sense. With the increasing emphasis on biological mechanisms, in mental health care as well as in general medical care, the importance of the patient's perspective has been progressively deemphasized and, with it, the importance of listening. *Looking at* the patient, which includes the visual aspects of diagnosis as well as the full array of evaluative technologies that complement it, has become the dominant mode of acquiring the understanding required for treatment of disease. Illness, however, in which subjective elements are predominant, may not be successfully addressed in this manner.

If we return to Sacks' frustration with his caregivers, the failure to listen reflected a narrow perspective in which his disease but not his illness was being addressed. Healing, as it later took place in his account, was catalyzed by what Kleinman referred to as the *popular sector* of the health care system: "a matrix containing several levels: individual, family, social network, and community beliefs and attitudes" (p. 50). In Sacks' account of personal healing it was music that proved to be the spark igniting his recovery.

If illness is a complex mix of attitude, belief, and behavior, then appreciation of these personal elements *as understood from the patient's perspective* will be important in addressing it. We achieve such understanding by placing ourselves empathically in the patient's world, as described in the previous chapter. Listening, in the broadest sense, encompasses both what we hear and what we infer from observations of the patient's behavior as well as his/her words. Listening, in contrast to hearing, involves more than our auditory sense: it involves us more fully. The process begins with attention to the patient's narrative, his/her story of illness (Kleinman, 1988), which conveys the patient's beliefs about the source, meaning, and impact of the disease: his/her state of impaired health. The oft-quoted statement "listen to the patient; he will tell you the diagnosis," attributed to William Osler (Jackson, 1992), might be expanded to "Listen actively to the patient, s/he will tell you what you need to know about restoring his/her health."

Is listening, itself, curative? Marsha Linehan (1997), commenting on her work with patients who are repeatedly self-destructive, suggested that there must be a dialectic between acceptance of the patient as he/she is and the commitment to work toward necessary change. That acceptance is expressed through *validation*. Her definition and use of this term is consistent with the Rogerian notion of unconditional positive regard, but Linehan views this type of acceptance as only the first step in treatment; as such, it constitutes a strategy for balancing the imperative toward change. For Rogers, empathy, positive regard, and genuineness are sustained attitudes on the part of the therapist that establish an ambience conducive to patient growth and change, but there is no imperative. Linehan posited six levels of validation that are necessary in order to place the therapist in a position to facilitate change. The first of these, which is achieved through listening and observing, allows the therapist to understand the patient's current state relative to her/his goals, while subsequent levels of validation involve an iterative process aimed at clarifying with the patient where the adaptive process has failed and must be modified if those goals are to be achieved.

Listening and healing have been associated in philosophical and religious traditions. Jackson traced the importance of hearing to Aristotle's theories of the senses. Although he regarded vision as superior, Aristotle considered hearing to be most important in receiving communication and, therefore, in gaining knowledge of other minds (Jackson, 1992). Listening has occupied a central place in religion, where the belief in a God that listens to our prayers, and knows our innermost thoughts, has been a core feature of many religions. The Confessional and the prayers of contrition associated with the Day of Atonement for Jews are other examples of efforts to communicate with an attentive God who sees us as we are and forgives us our faults. The need to feel a sense of order in the world and personal relevance is expressed in the idea of a caring and attentive God. Not only do these ideas render the world a more familiar and homelike place, but they have spawned a host of associated counseling and caregiving activities that exploit the sense of belonging to something greater than oneself.

In his classic essay *Caring for the Patient* (Blumgart, 1964), the eminent physician and teacher Herman Blumgart noted that Hippocrates encouraged separation of medicine from religion, with the idea of a purer version of science in mind. The spiritual aspect of healing, however, has never been far from the essence of successful medical practice. Modern psychiatry, in its effort to be "scientific," treats mind as something concrete and structural, analogous to, rather than the expression of, brain. But mind is something more. In housing our past, experiencing our present, and imagining our future, mind is also our spiritual core: the essence of who we are and who we seek to become. Mind is also the channel through which we experience both health and illness. Though multiple routes of access to brain exist, there is only one to mind: listening.

Returning to the idea of a God who listens, Fleischman (1989) commented on human yearnings to be recognized and valued as the wish for "witnessed significance." There is, however, something else as well: though it begins with listening, there is a wish for healing through active intervention. In The Bible, the Book of Psalms, for example, there are repeated entreaties to be heard, recognized and guided:

> In my distress I called upon the Lord,
> And cried unto my God;
> Out of His temple He heard my voice,
> And my cry came before Him into His ears. (Psalm 18)

Rembrandt, *Aristotle with a Bust of Homer* (1653).

> O Lord, Hear my prayer,
> And let my cry come unto Thee.
> Hide not Thy face from me in the day of my distress;
> Incline Thine ear unto me;
> In the day when I call answer me speedily. (Psalm 102)

The listening God does more than hear words, however. He also answers and intervenes:

> Lord, Thou has heard the desire of the humble:
> Thou wilt direct their heart,
> Thou wilt cause thine ear to attend;
> To right the fatherless and the oppressed. (Psalm 10)

> I waited patiently for the Lord;
> And he inclined unto me, and heard my cry.
> He brought me up also out of the tumultuous pit,
> Out of the miry clay.
> And he set my feet upon a rock,
> He established my goings. (Psalm 40)

Pain and suffering are recognized and healed:

> Give ear, O God, to my prayer;
> And hide not Thyself from my supplication.
> Attend unto me, and answer me;
> I am distraught in my complaint,
> And will moan. (Psalm 52)

> O Lord my God,
> I cried unto Thee, and Thou didst heal me;
> O Lord, Thou broughtest up my
> Soul from the nether-world. (Psalm 30)

The Listening God hears not only the words of the supplicant, but also their meaning and internal significance:

> O Lord, thou has searched me, and known me.
> Thou knowest my downsitting and mine uprising,
> Thou understandest my thought afar off,
> Thou measurest my going about and my lying down,
> And art acquainted with all my ways.
> For there is not a word in my tongue,
> But, O Lord, Thou knowest it altogether. (Psalm 139)

If God is expected to listen, should anything less be demanded of His people? The American poet, John Holmes, has put the moral imperative in verse, positing an eleventh commandment:

> It is not enough that one's own inner voice
> Make of one's life a lifelong monotone.
> I, Me, Mine, to-for-because-of me, rejoice
> A man but little, then less, less and none.
> What does he hear for news who has only heard
> From his own island? It is a treasure of dust
> On the wind when he unlocks his word-hoard.

Moses' commandment opens the world's mouth
To utter the memory of life. One listener
Is man multiplied, man taking in time's breath
To be in one body ancestor and heir,
He owes one duty thus: attention. Man
If he means to live shall hold his whole mind
At ready awake. With this the law began.

So Moses brought the eleventh commandment down,
Knowing his will stir, his blood hasten
That the one word be said aloud, the word be known,
That on it all men might take hold and fasten
On it, and hear it in all tongues: Listen.
He lifted the tablets up before them saying
The word that gave them all words: Listen. (Holmes, 1956)

This enduring wish for understanding as a prelude to healing is, by its nature, spiritual. Disease, and its subjective sequel, the experience of illness, represents one type of suffering, the type that brings a person to a provider of health care. Listening skills must encompass more than a receptive ear; they must include, as well, evidence that the listener is personally engaged and cares about the sufferer. Listening, then, cannot be separated from such responsiveness. But what is responsive listening, that engages the hearer in a personal and caring way and leads to corrective intervention? It is empathy.

Within the helping professions, a great deal of attention has been paid to the development and refinement of specific types of listening skills as a prelude to intervention. Breuer's patient, Anna O, referred to the technique used in her treatment as "the talking cure" (Breuer & Freud, 1895/1955). Freud went on to characterize the optimal approach to impartial listening as establishing and maintaining a state of "evenly suspended attention" (Freud, 1912/1958), the cornerstone of psychoanalysis for more than a hundred years. Although there has been and still is contentious disagreement about what, exactly, Freud meant by this, it implies a neutral, uncritical receptivity, in which the biases of the analyst were to be held in abeyance while the patient, following the primary rule of psychoanalysis, said whatever came into his or her mind. The idea of listening in order to gather information, and the need to hone listening skills, was emphasized by Reik (1948/1983). As described in the previous chapter, his emphasis was on a particular mode of communication between the unconscious of the therapist and that of the patient, in which the analyst develops a "faculty for fine hearing that enables him to find the secret meaning here as there" (p. 104). "The analyst," he goes on to say, "hears not only what is in the words; he hears also what the words do not say. He listens with the 'third ear,' hearing not only what the patient speaks but also his own inner voices, what emerges from his own unconscious depths" (p. 105).

How is it, however, that listening in such a concentrated, unbiased manner, in which one person attempts to come to understand what is being said from the perspective of the speaker, contributes to healing? As noted in the previous chapter, empathic listening may be healing in its own right. For Rogers, with his optimistic vision of human potential, empathic listening permits the patient to emerge as a fuller, more actualized human being. He pointed to four consequences of the empathic milieu established: reduction in the sense of alienation or isolation, increase in self-esteem as a result of feeling valued by another person, reduction in harsh self-judgment through sharing the worst and not being judged, and an increase in self-awareness that may then lead to experimentation with new behaviors, as the self-concept changes in the facilitating environment (Rogers, 1980).

For Kohut, listening involved an active process of attunement to the patient's yearnings for perfect understanding. He theorized that the patient was able to benefit most from the inevitable limitations in such attunement: failures in empathy. He believed that such failures eventually contributed to the development of a stronger self through internalization of functions expected from the analyst but not fully forthcoming. The successfully treated patient did not outgrow the need for empathic listening, but was in a position to seek the necessary resources that might provide it independently in his/her own life context (Kohut, 1971, 1977; Goldberg, 1978). Schwaber (1979), who considered empathy to be a particular type of listening, echoed this when she called attention to the patient's adaptive responses to self-object failures occurring in the transference and the emergence of a stronger sense of self as a result.

The existential psychiatrists have brought a different approach to establishing a nonjudgmental bond with the patient, similar to Rogers' CCT but, in Havens' opinion, more active (Havens, 1974). Using language that enhances the empathic bond, the therapist seeks to project himself/herself into the life of the patient: to make the patient's perspective his/her own. The process depends on careful listening and attunement to the patient's verbal and nonverbal communications. The ability of the therapist in this manner to reduce the gap between him/herself and the patient is linked with Havens' ideas about healing.

Teich (1992) has commented on the pluralistic nature of empathy, in that it refers to both active immersion and passive resonance, which require fundamentally different listening attitudes on the part of the empathizer. This seeming contradiction can be resolved by considering alternative postures as considered responses to the variables encountered—for example, the nature of the therapist–patient relationship and the optimal channel of access to a specific patient at a given moment in time. This view suggests that empathy is not a sustained but an intermittent mode of engagement, useful at specific times and not at others. Each attitude makes different demands on the therapist, but both contribute to establishing the type of interpersonal connection that will permit the goals of treatment to be accomplished. This view of empathy as pluralistic fits best with an attitude of clinical flexibility.

LISTENING AND RECIPROCITY

For the most part, the theories referred to above suffer from several persistent problems. First, they treat empathy as though it were an experience in the therapist who, by either active or passive means, and either episodically or in a sustained manner, establishes a place within the patient's world through drawing on certain capacities, which may be characterized broadly as listening skills. While s/he must check impressions with the patient, and utilize personal discipline and self-restraint in order not to confuse his/her own mental state with the patient's, empathy is characterized for the most part as *intra*-rather than *inter*-personal. A second problem is that the phenomenon of empathy appears to be unidirectional: while some have noted that the patient must cooperate and his/her own empathic capacities may be involved in some way, there has been little consideration of empathy as a reciprocal feature of the relationship. Third, empathic transactions appear to be understood as linear in nature, proceeding from the patient's state of mind to the therapist's, and then to some form of response on the part of the therapist. All three of these suppositions fail to adequately address the process by which an empathic transaction takes place and the reciprocity involved. In addition, they fail to take into account the transient, constantly altered states of mind involved or the degree to which the empathizer influences these states of mind in the patient.

Barrett-Lennard (1993), drawing primarily on the work of Rogers, has proposed a model for empathy as a process that involves three steps: reception or resonance by the empathizer, communication of this awareness, and reception of the communication. Proceeding from a state of active attention (listening), the empathizer recognizes and resonates to what is being communicated; s/he then *expresses* to the patient what has been experienced (by which Barrett-Lennard appears to mean shows, and perhaps verbalizes, what has been personally experienced, rather than simply reflecting back what has been said); the third step involves the patient's reception of the empathic communication.

It is the third step in Barrett-Lennard's model, the patient's reception of an empathic communication, that carries the potential for an immediate healing impact: the patient may feel validated or experience his/her state of mind as normalized through being understood in such a manner. A fourth step (actually a return to step one) may then take place, in which the patient may offer feedback to the therapist about whether s/he feels understood and what the impact of received empathy is. This model allows for correction and also takes into account the dynamic and interactive nature of empathic transactions, in which success depends on the emotional expressiveness of both parties and their willingness to engage with each other in this fashion. By implication, listening skill is required of both. In considering this sequence, it is important to distinguish affective arousal alone, which might take place for a variety of reasons, from empathy, in which the therapist's affective arousal corresponds to the patient's communicated state of mind. Each step in this process may be characterized in terms of factors that facilitate and those that interfere with it. In succeeding chapters, we will examine the implications of this type of analysis.

This model is helpful in that it presents a cyclic rather than a linear view of the empathic process, underscores the interactivity involved, and attempts to distinguish between reflective feedback alone and empathically derived reflective feedback: a situation that creates a *"channel for the flow of empathy"* (Barrett-Lennard, 1993, p. 8). The fourth phase of this sequence, restatement, allows the imaginative and communicative capacities of the two parties to emerge, which points to the creative dimension of empathy in the clinical situation. The patient is in a position not only to benefit from the specific communication, but also to learn about the empathic potential involved in a relationship—in other words, to learn not only about him/herself, but about the other person in the treatment relationship and thereby about relationships in general. Since we live in a context of relationships, the reciprocity of an empathic transaction offers the possibility of strengthening the patient's own capacity for empathy as well as directing attention to relationships in general. This has implications for the process of continued healing, which we will consider at some length in later chapters.

Ivan Miller (1989) has described the empathic transaction as taking place in a five step process. Drawing on both the work of Kohut and Rogers, he pointed to the importance of the patient's role both in sending signals and in receiving empathic communication. Miller's sequence is as follows: the patient first sends cues about his/her inner experience; the therapist receives the cues, becomes immersed in the patient's experience, and then processes the associated cognitions. This immersion is largely affective in nature, while the processing is largely cognitive. Processing draws on the therapist's knowledge of the patient (by an internal model such as that suggested by Greenson (1960)), and requires that multiple perspectives be taken into account, that is, the therapist is both a participant and an external observer as well as a transference object and an ally of the patient. The therapist then sends a response to the patient, using verbal and nonverbal means, and the patient receives the communication. Once again, active listening on both parts are central to the sequence.

Miller distinguished among empathy, empathic responsiveness, and empathic communication, and considered the types of factors that either facilitate or interfere at each stage of the process. Though his model is more linear than that proposed by Barrett-Lennard, it does allow for correction by the patient and therefore for refinement of the empathic experience. Like Barrett-Lennard, Miller recognized that empathy is likely to be only partially accurate, but may be beneficial nonetheless. The therapist's ability to immerse in the patient's world requires the ability to suspend cognitive processing temporarily, while listening. Like Margulies (1989), who referred to the "negative capability" of the therapist, Miller appears to be saying that premature judgment and closure is to be avoided through self-discipline. This is reminiscent of Freud's (1912/1958) idea of "evenly suspended attention" and Schwaber's (1979) characterization of a particular kind of receptive listening. The healing potential of empathy in Miller's model is vested primarily in the fifth stage, in which the patient receives the communication and its implicit validation, which gives "recognition, credence, definition to the intrapsychic experiences" (p. 537). This is similar to Barrett-Lennard's third step. An important feature of Miller's model is its attention to the difficulties that may be encountered in the various phases of the therapeutic empathic process; like Kohut and the self-psychologists who followed him, Miller saw the failure to navigate this sequence as an opportunity to address those aspects of the patient's pathology that interfere. Thus, failure of the process is regarded as important, perhaps even more so than its success. Like Kohut, Miller perceived the strategic value of empathic understanding.

Kleinman's (1988) idea of the personal narrative is also relevant to the healing potential of the listening as it takes place in an empathic process. Our narratives are subject to disruption, distortion, and inner contradiction. Warner (1997) has theorized that the experience of empathy in therapy allows the patient to sustain a focus on present experience without defensive avoidance; not only does this carry the potential for a more profound and immediate sense of personal authenticity, but it may also lead to reexamination of long-held theories of both self and other; in that sense, the narrative may become more internally coherent. This position is similar to Winnicott's (1965) idea of the facilitating environment and, in particular, the idea of "holding" the patient. With such holding, the patient is more able to tolerate and experience an uncomfortable inner state.

A sequence that might be termed *empathic contagion* may expand the benefit of empathic transactions in psychotherapy. A number of observers have spoken of the patient's benefiting from an empathic milieu by learning to be more validating and accepting toward the self, both present and past, which then may lead him/her to be more empathic toward others, present and past, including the therapist. Jordan has written extensively on the importance of connection with others. In a relational model of treatment, the focus is less on self-definition and more on developing what Jordan calls "relational competence" (1997, p. 345). The achievement of such competence involves enhanced empathic capacities, which follow from the experience of being listened to empathically by others, including the therapist. Depending on the goals of treatment, these attainments may contribute substantially to healing. The following case descriptions involve such a sequence.

Vera J was 39 when she entered therapy because of a major depression occasioned by the departure of her only child for college. Since her divorce many years earlier, she had devoted her life to being a good mother, a role she now felt had come to a successful end, leaving her no reason to continue living. She refused medication for her depression, which appeared to be both acute and chronic. A psychologically sophisticated woman, Ms. J had sought help as a last resort, in the hope that her pain might be relieved enough for her to change her mind about committing suicide. She made it clear, however, that the therapist had to accept the reality of her lethality as a condition of working with her.

When he attempted to focus on the issue of grieving the loss of her child, the therapist soon learned that Ms. J was resistant to any therapeutic strategy that involved categorizing her. She had a strong need to control the therapy in order to protect herself against the type of narcissistic injuries she had repeatedly sustained during her life and, in particular, her early life with a chronically ill mother, who had thrust her prematurely into the role of an adult child. She had a profound and lifelong conviction that others would bend her to their needs and fail to recognize and understand her. Any attempt at formulation was regarded as a denial of her unique identity and, in that sense, abusive. Thus, clarifications were frequently dismissed as unhelpful. What was most important to Ms. J was that the therapist be fully present as a person seeking to understand her. She wanted him to be a full and equal participant, wanted not only his mind but his whole self to be engaged in the work. This required constant attentiveness, open sharing of responses to her, and a nonjudgmental attitude toward her accounts of the hurts and injustices she had experienced.

The course of treatment involved repeated ruptures and repair of the empathic bond, with gradual strengthening of the relationship. The therapist, once trained by his patient, was able to suspend belief in his original dynamic formulation and entertain other ideas based on his experience with Ms. J. Eventually, he came to see that the matter was not loss of a child, but loss of her own childhood. She had adapted by becoming the mother she had never had and now faced the need to lose what she had retrieved vicariously in the years of single parenthood: a loving partnership. The loss of this adaptation had catapulted her back into her original depressed state, in which she had walled off her own vital self in an effort to prevent further exploitation.

With growing trust, Ms. J was able to reestablish contact with the child she had been. This took place in the office, as this long buried younger self emerged and experienced safety with the therapist; taking on the role of an observer, Ms. J began to form an empathic linkage with that child's plight, much in the way she felt the therapist had been able to do with her adult self. Though she remained intermittently suicidal, her depression began to lift and she was able to recognize that her feelings about her stolen childhood were at the core of her inability to accept the loss of her maternal role with her son and move on to rebuild her life. The insights gained were of little use to her, however, in moving beyond fixed ideas about her early life and her place in the world. She continued to feel exploited and abused despite understanding the source of such responses, though she learned to manage them better both within and outside therapy.

In a pivotal session, after referring to the importance of the relationship with the therapist and her sense that his full and attentive presence had allowed her to recover a sense of an authentic and vital self, ideas expressed with intensity and warmth, Ms. J suddenly had a sense of what it must have been like for her mother to have been so severely ill and out of control of her life, and never to have had access to the type of help Ms. J had received. Although she had spoken with compassion about her mother's plight before, this awareness was different; her awareness was, in Kohut's terms, "experience near" (1977, p. 303). This powerful experience, in which she established an empathic understanding of her mother's pain, proved to be a healing one in that it allowed her to begin, for the first time, to forgive her.

Empathic transactions with Ms. J rarely involved active probing by the therapist; most commonly, they required restraint from the tendency to comment prematurely, avoidance of interpretation, and intense concentration on remaining receptive: the "negative capability" referred to by Margulies. He did not experience this, however, as passive, since he was often called on to share his experience of the patient with her, an opportunity for collaborative processing. Over time, her early concerns about being too intense to be tolerated evolved into an empathic concern for the therapist's limits of tolerance as she imagined them. Though there was projection involved, her assumptions were often accurate. Her empathic communications were helpful to the therapist and may have increased his ability to stay fully present and resist premature closure, an example of the power of reciprocal empathic transactions.

If empathy with Ms. J was keyed largely through affect (in Schafer's terms, "signal affect"), the empathic process was quite different with the following patient, Ms. P, where entry into the cycle of empathy was usually by other means, though empathic contagion occurred for her as well:

Hilda P was a 52-year-old teacher who presented because of inability to write creatively. She had been known to the therapist for some years, during which time she had been seen in several courses of brief individual and couples treatment for problems related to marital and life-stage issues. She had suffered from a profound lifelong impairment in her sense of self that had been compensated for through a good (second) marriage to a charismatic man with whom she shared a deep and mutually affirming love. With his decline in health, she had begun to assume more control of their joint affairs in preparation for losing him. This required of her that she stabilize her sense of self and rely less on him to do so. An independent woman who prided herself on not asking much from others, she preferred to use the therapist as a mentor and guide and saw him only intermittently. One strategy for helping her involved her longstanding ambition to write creatively. She found a professional writer to help her to do so, and began to process difficult issues from her early life through writing about them autobiographically, using the therapist to assist her when she bogged down.

The present treatment episode was occasioned by her attempt to write about a phase of her childhood in which a particular woman, whom we will call R, was important. R had been her grandfather's lover over many years. She was a warm and attentive woman who had provided Ms. P with the validation she was unable to obtain from her mother, a self-absorbed and chronically dissatisfied woman whose relationship with her own mother had been deeply flawed. Ms. P's father was an aloof man whose neglect of his family drove Ms. P's mother to turn to the patient for her needs, abusing her when she failed to meet them. Ms. P felt scapegoated and turned to R, but, because of R's dubious place in the family, Ms. P had felt guilty about her attachment to her. Over the years, and especially while enjoying the validation of her marriage, Ms. P had managed her feelings about her childhood by largely suppressing them. The effort to write about R had led to a resurgence of strong feelings of shame: that her needs were illegitimate and should be suppressed.

Ms. P treated the therapist essentially as a teacher or mentor as well as a friend. She would present her understanding in the form of a hypothesis to be reviewed and commented on. She did not ask for his understanding, but his ideas. In sessions, some of which took place by telephone (since Ms. P lived at a distance), she would present the impasse that occasioned her request for consultation in a controlled fashion, only giving way to emotion in response to the therapist's probing attempts to understand the affect that underlay the matter at hand.

With regard to R, Ms. P was asked about her recollections of herself at that point in her life. In a series of meetings, she spoke poignantly of her self as a "skinny, buck-toothed girl with glasses." The therapist found himself imagining the plight of this girl in a loveless home where so much was expected of her and commented on his impression. In tears, Ms. P found herself feeling for this child who was caught up in a household of tension and neglect and who was scapegoated by her mother when she turned to R. Her empathic connection with her former self led her to reconsider her mother's opposition to her relationship with R, since mother, herself, had turned to R earlier in her own life. Was her mother jealous of her? Did her mother, herself, have feelings of guilt associated with R? The therapist commented on the patient's dilemma: trying to be loyal and get her needs met at the same time. She suddenly had a picture of her mother as a person who had found herself in the same plight as Ms. P: not knowing how to find a place in her home and in her heart for the woman who had replaced her own mother. This empathic connection with her mother helped her to understand her mother's attitude toward the patient's love for R and freed her up to resume her writing.

For this patient, who considered him one of her array of healing resources, the therapist's major contribution was his ability to process the information she provided and help her to understand its meaning to her. She needed his mind, shared as an act of caring; she also needed him to bear witness to her attempts to heal herself from early hurts and cumulative losses. Like Ms. J, her presentation for help was prompted by the threatened loss of a compensatory relationship: an important figure in her current life structure that stabilized a fragile sense of self and kept negative cognitions at bay. Unlike Ms. J, however, who saw the therapist as a once-in-a-lifetime healer, an antidote to her early depri-vations and injuries, Ms. P had already had such a healing figure in her life. Her need of the therapist was for reactivation of the function that her husband had played, though without the need for him to share himself in a fuller and more personal way. Empathic listening and empathic communication were important in both cases, and for each woman the ability to draw on her own empathic capacities was pivotal. The nature of the empathic transactions with the therapist was quite different, but central for each.

These vignettes underscore the importance of the empathic process in therapy as a vehicle for healing. The role of the listener is an active one that invites the patient to listen to himself/herself as well. Much of what we seek to accomplish in psychotherapy is best done through example; our own flexi-bility may serve as a model for the patient seeking to make personal change. If we wish the patient to be able to achieve necessary change, then we must facilitate it through identifying and mitigating whatever the barriers are to such change. We cannot understand those barriers purely from an external, obser-vational position, since resistance to change is likely to include forces within the patient that perpetuate the illness; we are left puzzled by our success in treating the disorder while the person with the disorder feels no better. The missing element is the subjective reality of our patient, which we have sought to objectify by placing him/her in a diagnostic category and then seeking to treat the diagnosis. The type of listening that this requires of us may vary from person to person, but in all cases we must, in Schroeder's (1925) words, be prepared to put ourselves at "the disposal of" our patient (p. 162).

CONCLUSIONS

If we are to treat illness rather than only disease, we must be able to address the subjective as well as the objective aspects of our patients' pain. This requires consideration of the healthy self as it existed before and continues to exist in modified form, and then seeking to understand how it has been altered. As with Ms. J, the wellspring of healing exists within each of us, but we and our patient first must identify and then mitigate the barriers to its emergence. The patient will ordinarily find it difficult to recognize health in the midst of disease, and so it is our job to find it. We do this best when we obey the eleventh commandment: we listen to the narrative, but we listen for health as well as for illness. The empathic process represents a particular form of attunement to the patient's world for a specific purpose: to diminish barriers to healing. As we have seen, the empathic process is not a linear one; it is suffused with ambiguity, and it places demands on both participants to take interpersonal risks. It requires openness, restraint, a sustained attitude of curiosity, willingness to adapt language to the patient's preferred method of learning, and communicative skills that are both verbal and nonverbal.

Attunement to the patient may be achieved in different ways. In the analytic tradition, the important communication is between the patient's and the therapist's unconscious; the target is understanding, the basis of interpretive actions. Psychiatrist Morton Reiser (1999), drawing on the earlier theories of Otto Isakower, has raised the question of whether empathic listening involves a lower level of consciousness on the part of patient and therapist, achieved through following the cardinal rules of the psychoanalytic situation: for the patient, freely associating and for the analyst, resonating to the patient's material while scanning his or her own spontaneous responses. Reiser has proposed that such an altered state, with its minimization of external stimuli, might facilitate the activation of a reservoir of unconscious memory. Reiser is not limiting his theory to the unconscious of Freud, however, with its defensive armor serving to contain and manage warring impulses. As we will see in a future chapter, contemporary theories of memory distinguish between explicit and implicit memory, and suggest a neurological substrate for unrecalled experience. While explicit memory concerns factual data that can be recalled, implicit or procedural memory concerns habitual forms of behavior that are not subject to conscious recall. Reiser has suggested that the analytic situation may predispose to evocation of memory that is not, and may have never been, conscious, but that may be profoundly important to interpersonal patterns of behavior. Reiser does not suggest, however, that the retrieval of unconscious mental content is, in itself, healing.

Within the experiential psychotherapy tradition, access to such founts of memory carries different implications. The idea that the ambience of the psychotherapeutic milieu may predispose to the emergence of memories involving meaningful life experience, and that these memories may be implicit rather than explicit, is central to experiential therapies, where evocation is the healing strategy rather than interpreting. In such an approach, it is the moment-to-moment experience of the patient that is the focus of an intervention, and the therapist attempts to discern both the emotion that is present and emotion that may underlie what is being expressed but is not manifest. Greenberg and Paivio (1997), for example, point to the powerful shaping effects of experience encoded in the emotional memory system, at times outside the purview of cortical influence. These authors argue for the healing potential of psychotherapy that arouses painful emotion in a safe environment and thereby promotes adaptive processing. The evocation of such emotional states may be accomplished through a combination of careful listening and empathic attunement. The attunement process, itself, as Barrett-Lennard and Miller suggest, is iterative; Bohart and Rosenbaum (1995), have compared empathy to a dance.

Bohart and Tallman (1997), in characterizing the different ways empathy may promote healing, have suggested that empathic attunement for the experiential therapist may not always involve placing him or herself imaginatively into the patient's subjective reality, but may also come about through focusing on the communications being offered by the patient: a shared focus of attention. Unlike the psychoanalytic perspective, emphasis is placed less on knowing the person and more on knowing what it is that concerns the person.

The experiential therapist Alvin Mahrer (1997) has offered suggestions for establishing what he terms "therapist–client alignment," an extreme version of focusing on the communication rather than the person and a form of empathic listening. By directing attention "out there," on the topic of importance, patient and therapist come to share in the emotional experience. The therapist, according to Mahrer, achieves sustained immersion in the patient's world and experiences his or her feelings and thoughts as though coming from within. Once again, listening is central, but the person of the patient is not its object.

We have examined empathy and its relationship to healing thus far in this chapter through assuming a certain paradigm. That paradigm involves a dyadic relationship between a person who suffers and a person who seeks to heal through the means of active listening. The two players are at liberty to follow where the work leads them. The therapist, resisting attempts at premature closure, seeks to attune to the patient in a manner that will create the conditions for healing. The implicit assumption is that healing activities should and do take place within the therapeutic setting, leaving open the matter of what should happen in the office and what should happen outside it. As Kleinman (1980) has suggested, however, most healing takes place outside the professional sector of health care (p. 382).

The position I will take in the following chapters is that healing and treatment are overlapping but different matters, and that the helpers who reside within the formal health care system should be primarily concerned with mitigating the barriers to healing rather than with healing, itself. Although this somewhat overstates the case, since the healing process may begin in the office of a treater, the distinction is of vital importance if we are to preserve the species I regard as endangered. This is so because of the various contextual factors that shape the activities of treaters and healers in the current health care environment: factors that will be reviewed in some detail in the following two chapters.

The practice environment is changing rapidly. In the following two chapters we will consider how these changes affect empathic transactions: which ones favor such transactions, which undermine them or make them less likely to occur. We will consider two types of environmental factors: those that are extrinsic to practice, and those that are intrinsic. The first of these refers to general matters of context as the health care system undergoes tumultuous change; the second pertains to the core values and ideologies that determine who will become a caregiver and determine which clinical strategies are in vogue and will be considered optimal. The type of dyadic relationship considered as the prototype for empathic transactions is becoming less the norm as patterns of subspecialization and collaborative care become more common. For that reason, I have characterized it as *endangered*. Our opportunity to work with patients in insular privacy is a thing of the past: information technology, the interests of third-party payers, regulators, and a host of others now create a crowd in the consulting room.

What happens to empathy when our relationships with patients are less insular, and what is the impact on the listening healer when s/he is expected to work expeditiously? Is there such a thing as empathic psychopharmacology? Empathic transcranial magnetic stimulation? Empathic eye movement desensitization and reprogramming? What would they look like? We, no less than our patients, live in the real world: subjectivity has its limits. It is these questions, how to bring the power of empathic transactions to the work that we do in the real world, that will concern us in the chapters that follow, and it is our success as a society in addressing such questions that will determine the ultimate fate of the empathically listening healer.

References

Barrett-Lennard, G. (1993). The phases and focus of empathy. *British Journal of Medical Psychology*, 66, 3–14.

Blumgart, H. L. (1964). Caring for the patient. *New England Journal of Medicine, 270*(9), 449–456.

Bohart, A., & Rosenbaum, R. (1995). The dance of empathy: empathy, diversity, and technical eclecticism. *The Person-Centered Journal, 2*, 5–29.

Bohart, A. C., & Tallman, K. (1997). Empathy and the active client: An integrative, cognitive-experiential approach. In A. C. Bohart & L. S. Greenberg (Eds.), *Empathy reconsidered: new directions in psychotherapy* (pp. 393–415). Washington, DC: American Psychological Association.

Breuer, J., & Freud, S. (1955). Studies on hysteria. In J. Strachey (Ed. and Trans.), *The standard edition of the complete psychological works of Sigmund Freud* (Vol. 2, pp. 30, 33–37). London: Hogarth Press. (Original work published 1895.)

Fleischman, P. R. (1989). *The healing spirit: Explorations in religion and psychotherapy* (pp. 5–20). New York: Paragon House.

Freud, S. (1958). Recommendations to physicians practicing psychoanalysis. In J. Strachey (Ed. and Trans.), *The standard edition of the complete psychological works of Sigmund Freud* (Vol. 12, pp. 111–112). London: Hogarth Press. (Original work published 1912.)

Goldberg, A. (Ed.) (1978). *The psychology of the self: A casebook*. New York: International Universities Press.

Greenberg, L. S., & Paivio, S. C. (1997). *Working with emotions in psychotherapy*. New York: Guilford.

Greenson, R. R. (1960). Empathy and its vicissitudes. *International Journal of Psycho-Analysis, 41*, 418–424.

Havens, L. (1974). The existential use of the self. *American Journal of Psychiatry, 131*, 1–10.

Holmes, J. (1956). The eleventh commandment. *Harper's, 213*, 53–54. (As quoted in K. Menninger (1963), *The vital balance* (p. 350), New York: Viking Press.)

Jackson, S. W. (1992). The listening healer in the history of psychological healing. *American Journal of Psychiatry, 149*(12), 1623–1632.

Jordan, J. V. (1997). Relational development through mutual empathy. In A. C. Bohart & L. S. Greenberg (Eds.), *Empathy reconsidered: New directions in psychotherapy* (pp. 343–351). Washington, DC: American Psychological Association.

Kleinman, A. (1980). *Patients and healers in the context of culture*. Berkeley: University of California Press.

Kleinman, A. (1988). *The illness narratives*. New York: Basic Books

Kohut, H. (1971). *The analysis of the self*. New York: International Universities Press.

Kohut, H. (1977). *The restoration of the self*. New York: International Universities Press.

Linehan, M. (1997). Validation and psychotherapy. In A. C. Bohart & L. S. Greenberg (Eds.), *Empathy reconsidered: New directions in psychotherapy* (pp. 353–392). Washington, DC: American Psychological Association.

Mahrer, A. (1997). Empathy as therapist–client alignment. In A. C. Bohart & L. S. Greenberg (Eds.), *Empathy reconsidered: New directions in psychotherapy* (pp. 187–213). Washington, DC: American Psychological Association.

Margulies, A. (1989). *The empathic imagination*. New York: W. W. Norton & Company.

Miller, I. J. (1989). The therapeutic empathic connection (TEC) process. *American Journal of Psychotherapy, 43*(4), 531–544.

Reik, T. (1983). *Listening with the third ear: The inner experience of a psycho-analyst*. New York: Farrar, Straus & Giroux. (Original work published 1948.)

Reiser, M. F. (1999). Memory, empathy, and interactive dimensions of psychoanalytic process. *Journal of the American Psychoanalytic Association, 47*(2), 485–501.

Rogers, C. R. (1980). Empathy: an unappreciated way of being. In *A way of being* (pp. 150–161). Boston: Houghton Mifflin.

Sacks, O. (1984). *A leg to stand on*. New York: Summit Books.

Schroeder, T. (1925). The psycho-analytic method of observation. *International Journal of Psycho-Analysis, 6*, 155–170.

Schwaber, E. (1979). On the "self" within the matrix of analytic theory: Some clinical reflections and reconsiderations. *International Journal of Psycho-Analysis, 60*, 467–479.

Teich, N. (1992). *Rogerian perspectives: Collaborative rhetoric for oral and written communication*. Norwood, NJ: Ablex Publishing.

Warner, M. S. (1997). Does empathy cure? A theoretical consideration of empathy, processing and personal narrative. In A. C. Bohart & L. S. Greenberg (Eds.), *Empathy reconsidered: new directions in psychotherapy* (pp. 125–140). Washington, DC: American Psychological Association.

Winnicott, D. W. (1965). *The maturational process and the facilitating environment: Studies in the theory of emotional development*. New York: International Universities Press.

CHAPTER 4

Empathy: Facilitators and Barriers

Poor naked wretches, wheresoe'er you are,
That bide the pelting of this pitiless storm,
How shall your houseless heads and unfed sides,
Your loopt and windowed raggedness, defend you
From seasons such as these? O, I have ta'en
Too little care of this! Take psychic, pomp;
Expose thyself to feel what wretches feel,
That thou mayst shake the superflux to them,
And show the heavens more just.

William Shakespeare

*J*n the earlier chapters of this book, we have reviewed the matter of
empathy, its application to psychotherapy and healing in general, and the
manner in which empathic modes of listening may contribute to healing.
We have focused on the activity rather than the players in the empathic
transaction. What motivates them? What limits their ability to use this mode
of relating? Aside from brief consideration of the importance of a personal

psychoanalysis to a psychoanalyst, we have not given much attention to the circumstances that determine whether or not a professional helper is likely to be able and willing to employ an empathic mode of listening in doing the work of psychotherapy. We will now turn our attention to this question, beginning with a brief consideration of the human variables that are involved.

The empathic psychotherapist seeks exposure to what his/her patients feel as a means of engagement, a method to sustain and deepen a helping relationship, and a vehicle for understanding the dilemma that leads to the request for help. The rewards of empathic transactions, as we have explored them in the previous chapters, may be even greater, as validation creates a ripple effect that may lead the patient toward greater acceptance of self and others and a renewed sense of belonging: a person in a human context, and therefore less alone. Mental illness is often associated with profound isolation, and for some, a sense of being less than human. There is also reason to believe that those who seek psychotherapy, though they may suffer from a wide variety of conditions, are motivated to do so for similar personal reasons. Jerome Frank (1974), in his comparative study of the various psychotherapies, made the following statement:

> [W]e must ask: is there a state common to all persons seeking psychotherapy that this treatment alleviates, just as aspirin relieves aches and pains? I believe that there is such a state, which may be termed, "demoralization." (p. 314)

Frank characterized demoralization as the sense of powerlessness that a candidate for psychotherapy has experienced as the result of inability to cope with some pressing problem or meet his/her own or others' expectations; he went on to state that

> the demoralized person feels isolated, hopeless and helpless, and is preoccupied with merely trying to survive. (p. 314)

In making the argument that the curative or healing elements in the various psychotherapies are the same, Frank identified one of these elements as a particular kind of helping relationship, in which the therapist understands the patient empathically and accepts him/her "if not for what he is, then for what he can become." Such validation reduces the sense of alienation and improves morale.

Empathic transactions make demands on both participants and involve risk for both as well: for the patient, risk of disappointment, pain, and possibly exploitation; for the therapist, risk of overinvolvement or loss of the protection of professional boundaries, with possible activation of the therapist's own sources of pain. If the idea of a locus of action may be employed to characterize empathy, then it can be found at the boundary between therapist and patient, and each party must be willing to approach that boundary and venture to its other side in search of the other. This venturing requires assurance of safety. Havens (1989) characterized the optimal therapeutic setting as "a safe place," while Winnicott spoke of the therapist's willingness to provide a secure inter-personal ambience as "holding" (Winnicott, 1965). Although a great deal has been written about the patient's willingness to engage in psychotherapy in a forthright and nondefensive manner, it is less clear what the requirements may be for the therapist to come to the encounter similarly open and receptive. What factors support empathy in psychotherapy and what factors serve to undermine it or reduce the likelihood that such transactions will occur? In this chapter, we will consider the variables and how they may be affected by the profound changes taking place in the context of practice.

SYMPATHY AND EMPATHY

In his 1927 lecture to the students of the Harvard Medical School, Francis Peabody (1927/1984) concluded with the following sentence: "One of the essential qualities of the clinician is interest in humanity, for the secret of the care of the patient is in caring for the patient" (p. 818). Although Peabody placed the greatest emphasis on patients whose complaints stemmed from "nervous influences emanating from the emotional or intellectual life" (p. 815), he encouraged the development of an intimate personal relationship with all patients and urged that "time, sympathy and understanding must be lavishly dispensed." Hermann Blumgart (1964), in an attempt to reconcile Peabody's advocacy of sympathy with the need to be objective, pointed to the loss of perspective that sympathy may entail and recommended what he termed "neu-tral empathy," by which he meant "emotional appreciation of the patients' feelings without becoming engulfed by them." It was a matter, said Blumgart, of "compassionate detachment," an appreciation of the patient's feelings with-out joining in them (p. 451). Sympathy, according to Blumgart, was a riskier attitude.

The distinction between sympathy and empathy is not always clear. *Webster's New Universal Unabridged Dictionary* (1979), for example, provides the follow-ing definition for empathy:

the projection of one's own personality into the personality of another in order to understand him better. (p. 594)

While sympathy is defined as:

1. sameness of feeling; affinity between persons or of one person for another
2. an action or response arising from this.
3. agreement in qualities; harmony; accord.
4. A mutual liking or understanding arising from sameness of feeling
5. The entering into or ability to enter into another person's mental state, feelings, emotions, etc., especially pity or compassion for another's troubles, suffering, etc. (p. 1848)

While the definition of empathy is concise, it tends to neglect the emotional aspect of the type of transaction involved, and it rests on the idea of projection, a problematic notion for reasons already noted. The definitions offered for sympathy, which rest on a connection that might be termed *fellow feeling*, emphasize the affective at the expense of the cognitive; the exception is the first part of the fifth, which sounds very much like definitions of empathy we have considered. A notable distinction between sympathy and empathy appears to be concern on the part of the sympathizer and actions that may arise from such concern. Since both empathy and sympathy derive from the evocative power of one person's mental state on the mental state of a second person, the distinction appears to rely primarily on the nature of the second person's response, especially behavioral.

This point can be appreciated by considering the following exchange between Prospero and Ariel that takes place in Act V of Shakespeare's *The Tempest* (1909). The magician Prospero, who seeks vengeance for past wrongs, has cast a spell on King Alonso and his brother Sebastian, as well as on Antonio, Prospero's own brother, the usurper of Prospero's dukedom. Ariel, a sprite who serves Prospero, enjoins his master to consider the plight of these three from the perspective of the remainder of the king's party, who appear "brimful of sorrow and dismay" as they witness the distracted state of their companions. He notes especially the apparent sadness of the kindly Gonzalo, a person who had been loyal to Prospero:

Ariel: His tears run down his beard, like winter's drops
          From eaves of reeds ... Your charm so strongly works 'em,
          That if you now beheld them, your affections
          Would become tender.

Prospero: Dost thou think so, spirit?

Ariel: Mine would, sir, were I human.

Prospero: And mine shall ...
Hast thou — which art but air — a touch, a feeling
Of their afflictions, and shall not myself,
One of their kind, that relish all as sharply,
Passion as they, be kindlier moved than thou art? (p. 95)

Prospero, overcoming his anger, decides to be forgiving; although he indicates that his kindness is based on having achieved his sole aim, their penitence, there is no evidence that they are penitent. Prospero appears to be acting in sympathy. Ariel, in contrast, denies the capacity for "tender affections" that a human might have, but understands empathically the emotional state of those he has observed.

Is sympathy, then, the more human response, dependent on the capacity for "tender affections"? If so, does it mean that empathy is by its nature dispassionate? *Webster's* defines dispassionate as follows:

Free from passion, emotion or bias; calm; composed; impartial; temperate; unmoved by feelings. (p. 528)

Compassion, on the other hand, is defined as:

A suffering with another; hence, sympathy; sorrow for the distress or misfortunes of another, with the desire to help; pity; commiseration. (p. 369)

These definitions leave us with a problem. If empathy is dispassionate, does it mean that the desire to help is based on something other than fellow feeling? Is the physician required to resist compassion? It appears that sympathy and empathy are rather closely related to each other, and the major distinction is not in the presence or absence of "fellow feeling" but how it is processed and managed.

The model for contemporary mental health care is increasingly a medical one. What can we learn from the medical literature about the distinction between sympathy and empathy? The great medical teacher, Sir William Osler, considered imperturbability to be an essential trait for the physician, but distinguished it from callousness:

> Cultivate then, gentlemen, such a judicious measure of obtuseness
> as will enable you to meet the exigencies of practice with firmness
> and courage, without, at the same time, hardening the human heart
> by which we live. (Halpern, 1993, p. 106)

Charles Aring (presumably no relation to Ariel), who also encouraged emotional detachment, pointed to the risks of sympathy in medical practice, calling for "reflective commitment" to another's problems while maintaining a sense of personal identity (1958, p. 448). Although he emphasized cognitive understanding, free of entanglement, his motive was presumably based on concern for the (perceived) needs of the patient. The separateness of the physician-observer from the patient corresponds to Rogers' "as-if" requirement (Rogers, 1980, p. 140). It is necessary, according to Aring, for the physician to be free to act in the patient's best interest. This is most likely to be achieved when s/he is interested but not enmeshed: appreciating but not experiencing the patient's pain.

In considering the matter of emotional detachment versus fellow feeling, Halpern (1993) took issue with the idea that empathy involves a detached, essentially inferential process based on projection. Halpern's view of empathy was that it is emotionally triggered and driven by the curiosity of the empathizer in search of something new. This position is reminiscent of Margulies' use of the idea of wonder as it drives the imaginative process of the empathizer (Margulies, 1989). Lewis Thomas (1983), in his wonderful essay, *On Matters of Doubt* (pp. 156–159), decried the polarization of the sciences and the humanities and made a similar point: that both stem from the experience he calls *bewilderment*; that we are, or ought to be, dumbfounded by how little we know about the world, and especially about ourselves and each other, and enjoy the process of considering what he termed "the ambiguity of being." Thomas suggested that the proper attitude is marveling and wondering, and the quest for clarity a game. Winnicott may have had something analogous in mind when he used the metaphor of play to characterize psychotherapy (1968).

Ellen More (1994) offered a historical hypothesis to account for the wariness of medical practitioners to characterize their attitudes toward patients as sympathetic. She postulated two overlapping considerations: first, that sympathy came to be regarded as a feminine attitude and was thereby devalued, and, second, that holistic ways of thinking about medical care were vague and subjective and were out of keeping with trends toward a medical discipline that was scientific, objective, and precise. Empathy, borrowed by physical medicine from psychiatry, became an alternative to sympathy in characterizing the attitude of the compassionate but detached physician toward his patients.

Much of the discourse about empathy has centered on making it compatible with scientific medicine. Within mental health practice in general, the feeling state of the observer has been deemphasized in favor of the cognitive activities designed to render affective resonance objective. Whether the process begins in some type of identification, projection, introjection, or any other way of experiencing something evoked by the patient, most theorists we have considered make the point that the therapist processes this experience cognitively in order to arrive at an understanding of the patient's mental state or perspective that is more or less objective. Although no one is likely to disagree with the idea that the entire process is driven by some motive on the part of the therapist, and most would contend that compassion or caring are desirable, few would use the term sympathy to characterize it.

I believe that sympathy, a form of compassion, is an essential component of therapeutic empathy, by which I mean that the therapist is drawn toward the patient in a positive way that sets the tone for an empathic transaction. The therapist must *care about* something as a precondition of accepting the *care of* the patient, for example, s/he may care about the patient's welfare. Sympathy, as stated above, is characterized by some form of behavior in response to fellow feeling; the offer of oneself as a treater may be understood as a behavioral response. Frank (1974) offered the following quotation from Freud to indicate the same point: "I cannot imagine bringing myself to delve into the psychical mechanism of a hysteria in anyone who struck me as low-minded and repellent, and who, on closer acquaintance, would not be capable of arousing human sympathy" (Breuer & Freud, 1895/1957, p. 265).

Shlien (1997) made the point that empathy in the absence of compassion may be used destructively. This point is illustrated by Dostoievsky in *Notes From Underground* (1943). The protagonist has encountered a prostitute, Liza, and is surprised to find her capable of thoughts similar to his own. Attracted by the prospect of exercising his power to affect her deeply, he belabors her with arguments about her state and her prospects. As she reacts with anguish, he thinks,

> I had felt for some time that I was turning her soul inside out and rending her heart, and — and the more I was convinced of it, the more eagerly I desired to gain my object as quickly and as effectually as possible. It was the exercise of my skill that carried me away; yet it was more than mere sport. I knew I was speaking stiffly, artificially, even bookishly; in fact, I could not speak except "like a book." But that did not trouble me: I knew, I felt that I should be understood and that this very bookishness might be a help. But now, having attained my effect, I was suddenly panic-stricken. Never before had I witnessed such despair! (p. 517)

Perhaps the major distinction to be made between sympathy and empathy is that the former refers to a caring emotional response in the observer to something assumed about a person or situation, while the latter represents a search for understanding that may be evoked by such a caring emotional response. Sympathy may precede or follow empathy; when neither is the case, empathy is not likely to be therapeutic and may even be harmful. On the other hand, sympathy alone, without empathy, signifies failure to process an awareness of an emotional state in another in order to understand its meaning *to the other*. Any action taken by the therapist, if it is to be helpful, must be based on the meaning to the subject observed rather than to the observer. Both empathy and sympathy are concerned with subjectivity, but the subject differs: sympathy concerns the responsive state of the observer, while empathy has as its target the state of the observed.

Olinick (1984), who made a similar point about the distinction between sympathy and empathy, considers sympathy to be an immature, imperfect form of empathy: nonobjective, personalized, and mainly affective in nature. On the other hand, Shlien (1997) takes the opposite point of view, regarding sympathy as the more highly developed function, in that it involves some form of commitment. Empathy, in Shlien's view, is a primitive capacity for spontaneous resonance that must be used wisely if it is to be of therapeutic value. Wise use includes a collaborative search for understanding what has been experienced, presumably by both parties, during the psychotherapeutic interaction. For Shlien, empathy is grounded not in affect or perception but in sensation, both mental and physical, and is reciprocal and interactive, requiring considerable commitment and trust on the part of both participants in order to be of therapeutic benefit.

If empathy is a reciprocal, interactive process, which requires trust and commitment on the part of the parties involved, then questions arise as to how the context shapes the transaction and makes it either likely or unlikely to occur. Using the dyadic relationship as a model, for simplicity's sake, we may ask the following questions:

1. What are the basic requirements for an empathic transaction to occur?

2. What factors are likely to enhance or encourage such exchanges?

3. What factors may interfere or make empathic transactions unlikely, inaccurate, or ineffective?

Magritte, *The Lovers* (1928).

THE PATIENT

Although other terms are used to characterize the seeker of help, I prefer the use of the term *patient*, and will use it throughout this book. The *American Heritage Dictionary of the English Language* (1969) traces this term, in its medical usage, to the Latin *pati* [to suffer] (p. 961). The patient comes to seek help because, in one way or another, s/he suffers. It is this suffering, which we have learned to characterize in terms of the associated symptoms (which are actually the hallmarks of suffering rather than the suffering, itself) or disease (as a diagnosis), that brings the patient to seek help. Furthermore, it is suffering, as it is experienced by the patient, that is the most important aspect of his/her presenting mental state—more important than the diagnosis that may be associated with it, more important even than the patient's stated reason for seeking help, which may or may not be related to it. A psychotherapist must find ways to appreciate this presenting pain, as early in the course of treatment as possible, preferably during a first session, often in the opening minutes of a first session. The key to doing so is empathy.

We will consider in a future chapter how the initial contact between a patient and a potential helper is shaped by the beliefs of the psychotherapist, and is a product of his/her school of psychotherapy, and how these variables affect empathy. For now, however, let us limit our attention to the core task shared by all schools: the patient brings a need to communicate personal pain to someone who will listen, and the psychotherapist's first job is to discern what that pain is. The motive on the part of the listener may vary but usually involves some combination of responsibility and compassion; personal motives, whatever they may be, are usually presumed to be subordinated to the professional ones (although I will have more to say about this shortly). The psychotherapist's predominant task at the beginning of a helping relationship is to understand the nature of the problem *as the patient understands it* so that the next steps in defining and addressing it therapeutically may be considered.

If the basic requirements for a therapeutic empathic transaction are that a person with a problem seeks to communicate with someone who wishes to help, then the person with the presumed ability to help must know what is needed and must listen as a first step in determining it. All forms of psychotherapy require, as a first objective, the establishment of a helping relationship (Bennett, 1989, 1997). Margulies and Havens (1979) have pointed to the importance of listening skills in an initial session and illustrated how the ways of listening might vary with the school of psychotherapy of the practitioner. The feature that does not vary is the need to understand the patient's communication and establish a frame of reference within which the problem and possible solutions might be addressed. Success in accomplishing this first step depends on the attitude of the two parties toward the task, and this attitude may be influenced by a number of factors. For example, the patient who cannot easily trust is likely to erect barriers to being understood and may distract the psychotherapist from the presenting pain, focusing instead on situational factors or theories of causation. Lesser degrees of this may be seen in patients who have a strong need to control the interaction or who are ambivalent about seeking help in the first place. Buie (1981) has commented on the suicidal patient who resists being understood empathically, perhaps in order to be able to carry out a suicidal act. The patient is likely to bring certain attitudes to the encounter: expectations that may be based on previous experiences with therapists, reading, hearsay, or perhaps an intellectual grasp of the process of psychotherapy but skepticism about its value.

In addition to the types of attitudes noted above, which may lead to the erection of barriers to being understood, receptivity to empathic transactions may depend on the patients' priorities and agendas: what, in particular, they wish to have understood. In addition to the specific request that serves as a rationale for seeking out a therapist, patients bring agendas to treatment that may not be immediately apparent. Sometimes, as Weiss and his colleagues have suggested (1986), the patient seeks to test the therapist to either confirm or disconfirm attitudes and beliefs about what will happen in therapy. Such attitudes or beliefs have their origin in the patient's past life experience, especially with key figures, and serve as templates for the as-yet-unformed relationship with the therapist. Attempts to test expectations are crucial to the development of a genuine, trustworthy relationship. The problem for the therapist is that testing may occur early in treatment, before the nature of the test is clear, and failure to pass the test may lead to premature decisions on the part of the patient to drop out or go elsewhere. An example of this is the patient who believes that the therapist will not value him/her and who therefore presents an exaggerated picture of bad behavior in order to test the limits of tolerance. Or, to consider another example, the patient may fear that the therapist will become angry and reject him/her, and may present in a provocative manner to test this. Often such fears are not in conscious awareness; commonly, behavioral patterns meant to keep certain fears at bay are repetitive, offering the opportunity for the therapist to perceive first hand what it is like for those close to the patient, but not necessarily, as yet, what it is like to be the patient.

These examples reflect an important feature common to the various psychotherapies: patients bring both explicit and implicit hopes, expectations, and fears. Discerning and appropriately responding to the suffering associated with this mixture of agendas requires what Reik referred to as "listening with the third ear" (1948/1983). The therapist must make choices in response from the very beginning of a treatment relationship, and such choices may shape what follows. Lacking data, the basis of such choices lies in the therapist's perceptions of what is likely to be most important to the patient in the material being presented: in other words, discerning the meaning to the patient of what is being presented. This is accomplished through the type of listening we have characterized as empathic.

Sometimes the patient's suffering must be separated from the diagnosis, as the following case illustrates:

Margaret R was a 58-year-old widowed attorney who presented on referral from her internist for symptoms related to an assault that had taken place three weeks earlier, and in which she was robbed at gunpoint and her life threatened. Her symptoms, which had failed to respond to reassurance from her friends and family, and to a course of benzodiazepines prescribed by her physician, included intrusive recollections of this event, nightmares in which she was chased, attacked, and killed, and severe anxiety when she was required to walk through the parking area where the attack had taken place. She had begun to avoid going to work, had felt blunted in her relationships with others, and was generally pessimistic and gloomy, in sharp contrast to her usual state of cheerfulness and optimism. Her sleep had become severely impaired; she was irritable and overly reactive and she had difficulty in concentrating. Her internist diagnosed an acute stress disorder.

When seen for the first time, the patient appeared haggard, pale, and anxious. She was dressed in a business suit and was well groomed. She shifted frequently in her chair, avoided direct eye contact and seemed uncomfortable. The therapist told her what information had been conveyed to him by her internist and asked her how she was feeling today.

Patient:	I have never felt so bad in my life.
Doctor:	What is your understanding of what is happening to you?
Patient:	I'm falling apart
Doctor:	You can't hold it together?
Patient:	Dr V said you could help ... you know about this sort of thing ... you'd take care of me ...
Doctor:	Ever see a therapist before?
Patient:	Probably should have, but no.
Doctor:	Why "should have?"
Patient:	I haven't been myself for a long time.
Doctor:	Before the attack?
Patient:	Years.
Doctor:	What allowed you to come now?
Patient:	No place else to turn ...
Doctor:	Desperate? What else did you try?
Patient:	To manage it myself ... I live alone ... now.
Doctor:	Now?
Patient:	[cries]
Doctor:	[handing a tissue] Is that part of the pain ... the "now" part?
Patient:	My husband died three years ago last week ...
Doctor:	You called for this appointment ...
Patient:	That day ... I always feel worse that day ...
Doctor:	It saps your usual strength.

This patient, who suffered from an acute stress disorder and who was referred for help, waited to make the appointment and did so on the anniversary of the loss of her husband, another traumatic event. Although her explicit reason for making the contact was her persisting symptomatology, the timing of her initiative suggested another motive as well, an implicit one. It also raised the question as to possible connections between the two events. All responses in psychotherapy are selective, that is, there are always many possible responses. Based on Ms. R's introduction of the word "now," it seemed she wanted to communicate how alone she felt, and the response was to this rather than to the disorder she had also brought with her to this session.

Ms. R went on to describe her efforts to come to terms with the death of her husband through "burying myself in my work." With the assault, her adaptation had been undermined, since going to work now involved feelings of aloneness and vulnerability similar to those she had been combating, leaving her feeling shattered and defenseless. The exact relationship between this subjective state of fragility and the constellation of symptoms that constituted her diagnosis was not apparent, but further work would reveal how her ability to cope with a traumatic event had been undermined by the previous loss, which continued to operate as a persistent source of pain.

While the disorder did exist, and was her ticket of entry into therapy (allowing her to overcome her reluctance to seek help), it was superimposed on the deeper, more meaningful trauma; it had compounded her problems by interfering with her adaptation. Her comment "I live alone now" evoked a sense of her isolation in the listener and was the key to an empathic understanding of her dilemma: she was all alone in a dangerous world. Her comment "you'd take care of me" suggested a wish deeper than her presenting one, treatment of her stress disorder.

As this case demonstrates, patients present for help with agendas, not all of which are explicit, and not all of which are accounted for by the disorder that they bring. Most commonly, it is not a traumatic event, per se, that brings a patient to seek help, but the failure of adaptation that may occur in response to such an event or series of events. Thus, while the patient brings a problem and a wish to communicate, the communication may be about something other than the problem that is the ticket of entry. This patient did not present a barrier to empathy, but she had tested the therapist (perhaps unknowingly, perhaps not) to determine whether he could and would tolerate her as the fragile and needy person she felt herself to be, which proved to be in contrast to her longstanding picture of herself as competent, strong, and independent. This latter picture of herself was the bedrock of her self-esteem or, from a self-psychological perspective, the integrity of her self, and its disruption was the basis of her experience of "falling apart." In this example, the ability of the therapist to empathize with the patient's shattered state led to an early rapport and the beginnings of a shared formulation, the basis of the work to come. When we consider the forms of psychotherapy that may be practiced in organized systems of care, we will have more to say about the importance of identifying a patient's agendas and the role of empathy in doing so.

THE THERAPIST

Therapist neutrality is a myth. In a speech to the American Psychiatric Association at its eighty-sixth meeting in May 1930, Sullivan characterized clinical detachment as a fancy of the clinician, in that it fails to take into account the "chiefly immeasureable [sic], imponderable interplay going on in and within the complex of physician–patient–and–others-relevant" (1931, p. 979). Despite the increasingly biological foundation of modern mental health theory and practice, the psychotherapist continues to operate as a variable in the clinical situation and, as with other variables, variably. This point is especially important when the current chaotic state of our health care system and the shifting nature of clinical practice is considered. Contemporary psychotherapists operate in an arena that is far less insular, far more scrutinized, far more shaped by intrusive external forces, than has been the case at any time in the past. These circumstances inevitably must impact on the therapist–patient complex.

In considering the vicissitudes of empathy, Greenson (1960) considered sharing to be a basic requisite of the empathizer, and commented on the difficulty the analyst who either found it difficult to share or who tended to share too much (i.e., to identify with his/her patient) might experience. In his version of the empathic process, Greenson believed that the psychotherapist (for Greenson, the psychoanalyst) must oscillate between attitudes of detachment and involvement, and may succumb to excess in either direction.

We speak of those who are "empathic" and those who are not, by which we usually mean a relative rather than an absolute distinction. The personality of the prospective empathizer is therefore always a relevant determinant of the potential for empathic exchange. In the *Diagnostic and Statistical Manual of Mental Disorders* (fourth edition; DSM-IV) description of a narcissistic personality disorder, one of the diagnostic features pertains to empathy; interestingly enough, the "lack of empathy" is defined in terms of unwillingness rather than inability "to recognize or identify with the feelings and needs of others" (American Psychiatric Association, 1994). Whether the matter is inability or unwillingness, however, such features of personality are likely to be present to varying degrees in normal individuals, including therapists.

Personality, as characterized in the DSM system, is manifested in behavior, which in turn may be shaped by context as well as a host of biological, developmental, and genetic factors. Even when empathic capacities are present, they must be evoked; further, as with patients, there are certain aspects of context that favor or oppose the type of personal risk-taking required of an empathizer. These might be considered analogous to such concepts as Winnicott's holding environment (1965) and Haven's (1989) notion of a safe place: situational factors in and beyond the dyad that we are considering, that support or undermine the psychotherapist's use of empathy.

The first of these, which I will call "triggers," can be illustrated by reference to a personal experience. Some years ago, when I first began practicing, I had occasion to see a young man, whom we will call Mr. X, who had been experiencing difficulties in his work relationships and who came to see me because he was on the verge of being let go following a bad performance review. After presenting the reasons for the consultation, he proceeded to describe salient parts of his current life situation. He was a rather isolated person, alienated from his family and with no close friends. He claimed to be good at his work, which involved sales, but to have a difficult time getting along with his bosses, one in particular, who had given him his recent review. As he spoke, he became progressively more animated, expressing anger and the conviction that he was being mistreated. When I asked for examples of what was angering him, he let loose a litany of complaints, all of which were rather vague and did not answer my question. I said nothing, hoping to learn where he wanted to take the discussion. Within minutes, he had moved from discussing his boss, who was Jewish, to revealing his anger at Jewish people in general, with considerable vehemence. I tried in vain to bring him back to his present impasse, but he had one further comment to make: that he had always admired Hitler, but felt that Hitler had "not gone far enough." As I tried to explore the basis of his hatred, I found myself distracted, uncomfortable, and irritated, and unable to engage with him or to accept the extent of his rage. I felt remote from him, my way of distancing myself from the anger his comment about Hitler had evoked in me. I felt obliged to inform him that I did not feel able to help him, since I found his anti-Semitism personally offensive. I thought it best that he be referred to a non-Jewish psychotherapist and offered to make the referral, which he accepted.

I have often wondered how I would handle such a situation today, some 30 years later, since I have seen several thousand patients since Mr. X and have never again had the need to disengage so abruptly. In reflecting on the experience, I am impressed by two features: first, the fact that I experienced his hatred personally, though it was not directed at me and, second, that I was unable to detach enough to consider what was going on between us and respond in a more helpful manner. I have since worked in prisons with convicted murderers and rapists, and have seen many patients with similar or comparable attitudes to those expressed by Mr. X. I have been spoken to abusively and even threatened on occasion, without having so strong and immediate a response. At the time that this event took place, I had recently returned from a trip overseas and, while in Germany, had visited the site of the death camp at Dachau. Although I had not personally lost anyone during the Holocaust, I had been raised during the war years and found myself profoundly affected by what I saw. I am certain that my response to Mr. X was shaped, at least in part, by this experience. Whatever the reason, however, the point to be made is that psychotherapists have their limits; at that time in my life, that was mine. I could not empathize with my patient and felt it best to refer him to someone else who might be able to do so.

Personal triggers such as those described are to be expected in any activity that demands use of the self to the degree required in psychotherapy; the tool is itself vulnerable. An initially compassionate or sympathetic response on the part of the therapist makes it considerably easier to respond to the affective or cognitive signals that initiate an empathic process, while the opposite may interfere. Attunement may be easier to achieve when the patient and the psychotherapist are similar with regard to life experiences, points of view, and values; when there are significant differences between patient and psychotherapist, more is demanded of each in order to engage empathically. When the therapist is not sympathetic, or the opposite, empathy may either be distorted (shaped by the caregiver's own attitudes) or lacking. If the psychotherapist is emotionally blunted for other reasons, the results may be the same. In contrast to personal triggers, the context within which practice takes place may exert generic effects on practitioners that either favor or militate against the likelihood of empathic transactions. This is of special relevance to the present environment in which practice takes place.

It is a well-recognized fact that powerful forces operating in the health care system have impacted adversely on health care practitioners. Menninger (1996), citing the fact that many clinicians who work in organized care settings are confronted with the need to treat more patients for shorter periods of time, saw practitioners as highly stressed and prone to burnout. Exposure to suffering on a regular basis, he stated, results in absorbing some of that suffering and may bring on what he terms "compassion fatigue" (p. 5). Menninger also referred to the personality makeup of many physicians (which may apply equally well to non-physician caregivers) who may be prone to high self-expectations and guilt when expectations are not met. The need of many practitioners for autonomy and a sense of control of their lives may also be a factor, in that these aspects of professional life have been adversely affected by changes in health care system ownership, reimbursement, and overall working conditions. For those who work in inpatient settings, more severely ill patients are often treated for briefer periods of time, placing great demands on practitioners to do their work more rapidly, often with less time to get to know patients and less inclination to take the time to assess the subjective aspects of illness. At times, the needs of patients may come into conflict with their own needs for respite, tolerable workloads, and a balanced lifestyle, again limiting their inclination to extend themselves in the manner that empathic transactions require. It is interesting to note that working conditions have recently become legitimate targets of activism in medicine, which has a history of neglecting such matters in favor of collective stoicism. Current trends toward unionization, spurred by such concerns, are an example of this phenomenon.

Physicians are expected to subordinate their own interests to those of the patient. A fiduciary obligation, which has legal implications, is assumed to exist, in which the physician has a duty to the patient, and his/her personal interests must be put aside if they interfere with it. When the caregiver's own interests clash too strongly with those of the patient, however, this task becomes more difficult. As an example from contemporary medical practice, physicians who own or receive income from diagnostic or treatment facilities may be inclined to refer patients to such resources, and there may be a conflict of interest in such situations, leading to patterns of professional behavior that are ethically suspect. Psychotherapists, although not yet involved to any major degree in such situations, may experience a variant: reimbursement rates may vary from patient to patient, for example, under case or episode reimbursement arrangements, making it financially advantageous to treat some patients rather than others. These problems may also be manifest at the systems level, where uninsured or otherwise unprofitable patients are less valued, leading to collective attitudes that may influence individual patient care. Rates of reimbursement may also vary from insurer to insurer, creating incentives for therapists to keep some patients in treatment longer than others. One way of accomplishing this is to develop treatment plans that require different degrees of engagement and a different level of commitment on the part of the psychotherapist. As already noted, commitment is a close relative of empathy. Additionally, in considering conflicts of interest and their relationship to empathy, Book has pointed out that empathy may not always be cost-efficient; when concerns about the "bottom line" become predominant, the caregiver can come to regard patients whose needs jeopardize profits as "sucking us dry" (1991, p. 26).

Many practitioners who were accustomed to solo practice have been forced to join groups, networks, or other organized configurations of care in order to survive professionally. They may be poorly prepared to do so. The new circumstances of practice may in fact require adherence to a system of rules and values in conflict with the psychotherapist's own. Many who were attracted to the profession because of the autonomy historically associated with mental health practice now find themselves confronted with the need to meet performance expectations that require skills they do not possess or possess to an insufficient degree (Bennett, 2000). An example of this is the demand to be expert in the brief psychotherapies. In consequence, practitioners may find their professional futures at stake unless they modify practice patterns and bring them into alignment with the expectations of their employers, colleagues, case managers, and others. This type of accountability and pressure to change may lead to both anxiety and resentment, both of which undermine the ability and willingness to be open to the patient in an empathic manner.

The term *managed care* has become the watchword for the forces that are reshaping the health care landscape and placing unprecedented pressure on health care providers to redefine, even reinvent, their roles, expectations and functions. This interpretation is oversimplified, in that it neglects the historical trends involved, focusing on the messenger rather than the message that the system of health care must be overhauled if it is to meet the needs of the population at a cost the population decides it can afford. Within the mental health arena, as in general medical care, practitioners often feel besieged and demoralized—attitudes they cannot help but bring to their work, adversely impacting on their ability to give to patients.

As Shakespeare's King Lear found himself exposed to "what wretches feel," changes in the circumstances of practice have left many practitioners not only demoralized, but at times subject to feelings of helplessness and hopelessness about their perceived losses. Depressed affect, whatever its source, deadens the heart. Camus (1948), describing the erosive effects of the plague on the overworked physicians who were helpless to prevent the decimation it was causing among the citizens of their town, said of his protagonist,

> It was now that Rieux and his friends came to realize how exhausted they were. Indeed, the workers in the sanitary squads had given up trying to cope with their fatigue. Rieux noticed the change coming over his associates, and himself as well, and it took the form of a strange indifference to everything. (p. 169)

Under such circumstances, protection against dysphoric affect may make even the most dedicated helper remote as a form of self-protection:

His sensibility was getting out of hand. Kept under all the time, it had grown hard and brittle and seemed to snap completely now and then, leaving him the prey of his emotions. No resource was left him but to tighten the stranglehold on his feelings and harden his heart protectively. (p. 172)

If these references appear to be overly dramatic exaggerations of the actual state of affairs, consider that Bursztajn and Brodsky (1999) have compared the plight of physicians and patients who find themselves "captives" of managed systems of care to the horrors of the Holocaust. Citing others who have drawn on this metaphor (pp. 246, 247), they made the point that involuntary restrictions placed on patients and physicians amount to a form of captivity that is reflected in adverse clinical consequences. Those responses that occur in patients were referred to as "transferential," while those in their caregivers were considered "countertranferential." These distinctions, which are based on psychodynamic theories about the shaping of behavior by unconscious determinants rooted in past life experience, are somewhat misleading, since they assume a fundamental distinction between the patients and their treaters and suggest a degree of irrationality. As the authors described the clinical consequences of feeling captured, however, they placed patients and their caregivers in a common boat. Patients, they stated, wish to see caregivers as omnipotent and it may increase their sense of despair to find them limited; clinicians, facing the confinement of a managed system of care, may give in to "the human tendency to forget, to look but not see, to deceive or anesthetize oneself as a protection against anxiety and pain" (p. 241). Both are dealing with limitations that are perceived as external. In the absence of strategies to accept and deal with such limits, demoralization is an expectable response.

The psychotherapist who believes that s/he cannot provide optimal care because circumstances prevent it is likely to experience anger as well as despair. At times, this anger may be turned against the patient, particularly if the caregiver feels burdened by excessive demand, by patients who are not responsive to treatment ("treatment resistant"), or patients who are assigned without consideration of the clinician's ability to provide the type of services they may require—for example, the clinician who finds his/her psychotherapy patient to be abusing substances but lacks the knowledge or skill to respond appropriately. Bursztajn and Brodsky pointed as well to the conflicted caregiver, who feels it necessary to choose between the demands of the patient and the demands of the organization that controls reimbursement, in some instances providing his/her salary. The result may be that the therapist distances him or herself through limiting the time spent with the patient or abandoning the role of patient advocate. Empathy is highly unlikely under such circumstances. A similar situation is likely when the therapist fears the patient, for example, when the patient has a history of suing professionals. Empathy requires trust, which is unlikely when therapists feel forced to protect themselves against their patients.

It is interesting in this regard to consider the work of James Mann, a pioneer in the development of brief psychotherapies. Mann's model of time-limited psychotherapy is existential in nature. The structure of treatment theoretically evokes the patient's problems involving separation as feelings about termination are processed. But it is not only the patient's feelings about endings that are evoked, for therapists have their own existential challenges to meet as well. In the course of the work, both patient and therapist must deal with the matter of limitations against the backdrop of a ticking clock, and settle for what is realistically possible. As Mann summarized, "What stands out vividly is the struggle around the refusal to relinquish infantile and childhood wishes in favor of the uncertain pleasures of adult reality" (Mann, 1973, p. 58). The vehicle for bringing about acceptance without excessive ambivalence is the relationship the patient has with a therapist who accepts the structure of the treatment. In contrast to the captive status suggested by Bursztajn and Brodsky, both patient and therapist are voluntary participants. When they are not, the empathic connection may be *against* the limits and, therefore, *countertherapeutic*. The matter of accepting realistic limitations, of course, is a contentious one in health care, where the definition of *realistic* is an ongoing matter of debate.

When mental health practitioners are forced to practice in ways they do not believe optimal, the conflicts between what is wished for and what is achievable are not addressed as therapeutic issues but as constraints that are imposed on them by an unempathic, even malevolent, other. Zealberg has referred to the "depersonalization" that results when business principles are introduced into the management of health care, focusing on the alterations of language that accompanies the cultural shift. He regards terms such as "consumer" or "customer" as indicative of a shift from Buber's "I–You" relationship to an "I–It" relationship, in which patients are seen as "mere objects." The suggestion is that clinicians' behavior toward their patients will be adversely shaped by abandoning traditional terminology; he likens this to activities of totalitarian regimes (Zealberg, 1999). Interestingly, he objects as well to use of the word "client," which is certainly not associated historically with this type of shift.

The most important point to be made with regard to empathic transactions in the clinical setting is that changes in the culture of health care practice are likely to lead to changes in behavior. Nadelson (1993) has called attention to the impact of collective discrimination based on gender (and the same point might be made about race or social class) on the ability of individual caregivers to empathize with patients whose interests are marginalized. This position assumes that the clinician participates in prevailing attitudes of the culture in which s/he participates, and brings such attitudes into the clinical setting. Empathy, for Nadelson, is important on both an individual and a broader, collective, social level, where it overlaps with the domain of ethics.

There is, among many mental health practitioners, fear that the change in the practice environment may undermine the relationship between physician and patient in fundamental ways, making the necessary subjugation of self-interest to that of the patient difficult or impossible (Bennett, 1988). Dyckman has characterized the psychotherapist placed in a managed care setting, where there are pressures to do the work quickly and efficiently, as "impatient." Because of the press of time, therapists may find themselves prematurely planning strategies of intervention based on limited understanding, on diagnosis alone, or on preconceived notions about what types of treatment similar patients may have required. The therapist who feels impelled to demonstrate that his/her patient is making progress may press too hard; may exit the treatment too soon; may avoid the deeper and more important aspects of the patient's problems in favor of quick fixes; or may limit the intervention to what s/he already feels competent to treat. Of course, none of this is new or limited to managed systems of care, but the constraints and pressures are widely experienced by therapists as beyond their control and not of their making: the important new factor. Dyckman (1997) anticipated three tendencies under such circumstances: aversion to the patient, over-attachment to particular forms of intervention, and confusion of the process of therapy with therapy as a product.

CONCLUSIONS

In considering the impact of context on the ability and willingness of psychotherapists to empathize with their patients, we have focused on an oversimplified picture of context. For many in our field, the change in culture is attributed to *managed care*, an external agent perceived as venal, powerful, and alien to the culture in which medicine has been practiced in the past. Neglected in this oversimplified view are the variety of factors that have shaped the new landscape from within medicine itself, which we will consider in the following chapter. The oversimplification and associated externalization of blame is unfortunate for two reasons: first, it leads to a sense of powerlessness and despair which is quite widespread, and, second, it relieves the mental health profession of the duty to reconcile evolutionary trends with core values. Empathy, as a crucial aspect of the relationship between clinician and patient, is such a core value; it becomes one of the victims when the environment, itself, is seen as unempathic. A vital point to keep in mind, however, is that the assumption of an adversarial posture with regard to the imperative to manage resources so that they are allocated across populations is not the only possible choice: the challenge may also be accepted. Such acceptance would change the perception of the environment and lessen the danger to humane care that current trends pose.

In considering the impact of extrinsic or environmental forces on patient–therapist relationships, and especially on the likelihood that empathic transactions will take place, I have tried to separate those aspects of context that relate primarily to patients from those that relate to clinicians. This is an arbitrary and somewhat unrealistic distinction, but one made for rhetorical reasons: to underscore the importance of attitude on the part of each participant in a clinical interaction, and the contribution of overlapping environmental and cultural variables in shaping how that interaction will unfold. As we have seen, empathic transactions occur when the participants are amenable to them and willing and able to take the risks they require. If either recoils, empathy becomes unlikely. In the present environment, rife with demoralized practitioners and disillusioned seekers of care, the empathic healer may be harder to find.

But is the situation necessarily this bleak? All psychotherapeutic interactions take place in a context—always have, always will. Context shapes, but does not fully account for, behavior; adaptation is always an alternative. In future chapters, we will consider the type of adaptation to the emerging practice context that may be made and how empathic transactions not only are compatible with the emerging delivery system but are essential to it. Before doing so, however, we must consider those *intrinsic* factors that have led us to consider the empathic healer as endangered: the belief systems that practitioners bring to the clinical encounter. In the following chapter, we will review the broader trends in medical and mental health culture that have shaped and continue to shape the way practitioners are educated, trained, and oriented to their work and, in particular, how such factors have affected the interpersonal dimension of health and mental health practice that are the source of empathic healing transactions.

REFERENCES

American heritage dictionary of the English language (1969). Boston: Houghton Mifflin Company.
American Psychiatric Association (1994). *Diagnostic and statistical manual of mental disorders* (4th ed.). Washington, DC: Author.

Aring, C. D. (1958). Sympathy and empathy. *Journal of the American Medical Association, 167*(4), 448–452.

Bennett, M. J. (1988). The greening of the HMO: Implications for prepaid psychiatry. *American Journal of Psychiatry, 145*, 1544–1549.

Bennett, M. J. (1989). The catalytic function in psychotherapy. *Psychiatry, 52*, 351–365.

Bennett, M. J. (1997). Focal psychotherapy. In L. I. Sederer & A. J. Rothschild (Eds.), *Acute care psychiatry: Diagnosis and treatment* (pp. 355–373). Baltimore: Williams and Wilkins.

Bennett, M. J. (2000). Retraining the practicing psychiatrist. *Psychiatric Services, 51*(7), 932–934.

Blumgart, H. L. (1964). Caring for the patient. *New England Journal of Medicine, 270*(9), 449–456.

Book, H. E. (1991). Is empathy cost efficient? *American Journal of Psychiatry, 45*(1), 21–30.

Breuer, J., & Freud, S. (1955). Studies on hysteria. In J. Strachey (Ed. and Trans.), *The standard edition of the complete psychological works of Sigmund Freud* (Vol. 2, pp. 30, 33–37). London: Hogarth Press. (Original work published 1895.)

Buie, D. (1981). Empathy: Its nature and limitations. *Journal of the American Psychoanalytic Association, 29*, 281–307.

Bursztajn, H. J., & Brodsky, A. (1999). Captive patients, captive doctors: Clinical dilemmas and interventions in caring for patients in managed health care. *General Hospital Psychiatry, 21*, 239–248.

Camus, A. (1948). *The plague.* New York: Basic Books.

Dostoievski, T. M. (1943). *Notes from underground.* In B. G. Guerney (Ed.), *A treasury of Russian literature* (pp. 442–537). New York: Vanguard Press.

Dyckman, J. (1997). The impatient therapist: Managed care and countertransference. *American Journal of Psychotherapy, 51*(3), 329–342.

Frank, J. (1974). *Persuasion and healing.* Baltimore: Johns Hopkins University Press.

Greenson, R. R. (1960). Empathy and its vicissitudes. *International Journal of Psycho-Analysis, 41*, 418–424.

Halpern, J. (1993). Empathy: Using resonance emotions in the service of curiosity. In H. M. Spiro, M. G. MCCrea, E. Peschel, & D. St. James (Eds.), *Empathy and the practice of medicine: Beyond pills and the scalpel* (pp. 160–173). New Haven: Yale University Press.

Havens, L. (1989). *A safe place: Laying the groundwork of psychotherapy.* Cambridge: Harvard University Press.

Mann, J. (1973). *Time limited psychotherapy.* Cambridge: Harvard University Press.

Margulies, A. (1989). *The empathic imagination.* New York: W. W. Norton and Company.

Margulies, A., & Havens, L. (1981). The initial encounter: What to do first. *American Journal of Psychiatry, 138*(4), 421–428.

Menninger, W. W. (1996). Practitioner, heal thyself: Coping with stress in clinical practice. *An occasional paper from the Menninger Clinic.* Topeka: The Menninger Foundation.

More, E. S. (1994). Empathy enters the profession of medicine. In E. S. More & M. A. Milligan (Eds.), *The empathic practitioner: Empathy, gender and medicine* (pp. 19–39). New Brunswick, NJ: Rutgers University Press.

Nadelson, C. C. (1993). Ethics, empathy, and gender in health care. *American Journal of Psychiatry, 150*(9), 1309–1313.

Olinick, S. (1984). A critique of empathy and sympathy. In J. Lichtenberg, M. Bornstein, & D. Silver (Eds.), *Empathy I* (pp. 137–167). Hillsdale, NJ: The Analytic Press.

Peabody, F. (1984). The care of the patient. *Journal of the American Medical Association, 252*(6), 813–818. (Original work published 1927.)

Reik, T. (1983). *Listening with the third ear: The inner experience of a psychoanalyst.* New York: Farrar, Straus and Giroux. (Original work published 1948.)

Rogers, C. R. (1980). *A way of being*. Boston: Houghton Mifflin.

Shakespeare, W. (1909). *The tempest* (Act V, Scene 1). In *The works of William Shakespeare* (Vol. 18, p. 95). New York: Bigelow, Smith and Company.

Shlien, J. (1997). Empathy in psychotherapy: A vital mechanism? Yes. Therapist's conceit? All too often. By itself enough? No. In A. C. Bohart & L. S. Greenberg (Eds.), *Empathy reconsidered: New directions in psychotherapy* (pp. 63–80). Washington, DC: American Psychological Association.

Sullivan, H. S. (1931). Socio-psychiatric research: Its implications for the schizophrenia problem and for mental hygiene. *American Journal of Psychiatry, 10*, 977–992.

Thomas, L. (1983). *Late night thoughts on listening to Mahler's Ninth Symphony*. New York: Bantam Books.

Webster's New Universal Unabridged Dictionary, Deluxe Second Edition (1979). (pp. 594, 1848). New York: Simon and Schuster.

Weiss, J., Sampson, H., and the Mount Zion Psychotherapy Group (Eds.) (1986). *The psychoanalytic process: Theory, clinical observation, and empirical research*. New York: Guilford Press.

Winnicott, D. W. (1965). *The maturational process and the facilitating environment: Studies in the theory of emotional development*. New York: International Universities Press.

Winnicott, D. W. (1968). Playing: Its theoretical status in the clinical situation. *International Journal of Psycho-Analysis, 49*, 591–599.

Zealberg, J. J. (1999). The depersonalization of health care. *Psychiatric Services, 50*(3), 327–328.

CHAPTER 5

Empathy and Ideology

> The most common criticism made at present by older practitioners is that young graduates have been taught a great deal about the mechanism of disease, but very little about the practice of medicine—or, to put it more bluntly, they are too "scientific" and do not know how to take care of patients.
>
> *Francis W. Peabody, 1927*

*I*n considering how context shapes both attitude and behavior, we have thus far focused on the external environment and those features that either facilitate or discourage practitioners from engaging with their patients empathically. This perspective, while of contemporary relevance, places the cart before the horse. Our immediate environment shapes us, beyond a doubt, but far less so than the frame of reference that we bring to it, which is largely a product of our times, the beliefs of those who have trained us, and the most basic elements in our personal and professional identities. Insofar as a collective frame of reference exists, a basic way of conceiving of our roles and functions, the orientation that is implied stems less from immediate circumstances than from the larger historical forces in which we participate. In order to appreciate the impact of such historical forces on our relationship with individual patients, we must step back from the angst that pervades our field and consider the broader issues at play: the trajectory of historical trends and the locus of our generation on that trajectory.

THE GREEKS HAD A WORD FOR IT

The practice of medicine is an ancient and honorable art that has aspired to become a science. This dynamic has been dichotomized for over two millennia, leading to sharp disagreements among health care practitioners about the legitimate content of health care and the importance of the interpersonal environment in which it takes place. During this time, medicine has evolved from its roots in philosophy and religion to its current status as a branch of science. Psychiatry, as the branch of medicine that specializes in the care of the mentally ill, has had its own evolutionary lines, which have often run counter to those of medicine. The evolution of the health care system and of psychiatry within it is more cyclical than linear, amounting to an ongoing dialectic that may be varyingly characterized as the debate between humanism and science, or between mind and brain as the legitimate organ of concern. Underlying these points of view is a persisting metaphysical dilemma: is the ultimate reality material or is it mental? Attempts to resolve this dilemma, for example, by considering either of these alternatives to be reducible to the other, have their counterparts in contemporary theories of brain and mind, leading some to question whether psychiatry is fated to be either brainless or mindless, both, or neither (Lipowski, 1989; Eisenberg, 1986; Szasz, 1985).

Therapeutic empathy, as we have conceived it, operates at an interpersonal level as a variable in the relationship between a caregiver and a recipient of care. Heretofore, empathy and the understanding that is associated with it have been prized because of their contributions to the healing process, a point of view that is shared primarily by treaters committed to a model of intervention that is based on the concept of mind, independent of, parallel to, or included as part of the biological realities involved. For those who place primary emphasis, however, on biological as opposed to psychological theories of causation and cure, or who see behavior as the key variable distinguishing the mentally healthy from the mentally ill, the attitude toward empathy may be different (or, more precisely, indifferent). If a practitioner has been trained to believe that mental illness is best treated by direct attention to altered biology or altered behavior, interpersonal variables will be diminished in importance, treated with skepticism, or disparaged as unscientific, unknowable, or lacking in the necessary degree of objectivity. Indeed, as we have seen, empathy has been considered primarily in connection with the art rather than the science of medicine, a means of attunement by one mind to the unique and subjective reality of another. Before considering how empathy may be rendered compatible with the current level of understanding of the way mind and brain are related to each other, it may be helpful to briefly consider the major barriers to such integration. In the following brief historical summary, I will focus on two that are closely related: dualism and determinism.

Scholars have traced ideas about brain and mind, which was originally conceived of as soul, to the earliest recorded times. Mind and brain were not understood to be distinct entities in Hindu and Buddhist teachings, nor are they polarized in Eastern philosophies (Stone, 1997); the idea of dualism is a Western creation, with its origin in the pre-Socratic Greek philosophers and its strongest advocate, Plato. The great philosopher's dualism represented a sharp departure from the earlier thinking of Thales, Anaximines, and Heraclitus, for whom the world was made of a single material element: respectively, water, air, or fire (Nahm, 1947, pp. 56–65). Empedocles introduced the notion that four elements could be distinguished—earth, air, fire, and water (p. 126)— an idea that was to find its later counterpart in theories about the body's internal humors as determinants of a person's basic nature. The categorization of personality disorders in Axis II of the DSM has much in common with such categorical thinking, as do contemporary theories about the inborn nature of temperament. It was Parmenides who introduced the notion of substance per se (pp. 102–105), which anticipated later ideas about mind and matter; Democritus and his followers introduced the idea that everything was made of indivisible atoms, always in motion—ideas that bear some similarity to contemporary science (Russell, 1945, p. 65) Anaxagoras understood mind, which he termed *nous*, to be a substance that distinguished living from nonliving things (Russell, 1945, p. 62), but it was left to Plato to place mind in the predominant position that it was to occupy for many years.

Plato and his student Aristotle elaborated the idea of dualism. Plato's conception of mind was based on the primacy of ideas in his hierarchy of being, with the body and the material world representing but shadows of reality. Plato disparaged knowledge acquired through the senses, with ultimate reality knowable only through the medium of thought. Furthermore, since Plato believed in preexistence, knowledge was essentially a matter of recollection rather than acquisition. The body, and all that is material, was for Plato a distraction from reality (Edman, 1928). For Aristotle, the senses were also a means to knowledge, especially vision, but he was also a dualist, or maybe a "quadracist" would be more accurate. The soul was itself dual, and only that part related to the mind was immortal. Although the soul was related both to body and mind, conferring essence to each, thinking was a pure activity of the mind and thinking was distinct from all body activities, including perception (Ross, 1938, pp. 203-215).

These ideas have had a profound and lasting effect on Western thought, and were to recur in various forms over the next two thousand years. Two features are especially relevant to psychiatry in general and to the importance of empathy in particular: the metaphysical and the epistemological. The first states that mind and matter are different from each other in a fundamental and essential way: they represent different levels of reality. Plato's version of the mind was to dominate Western thinking for hundreds of years, with a profound impact on health care in general and on mental illness in particular. Simon (1978) has reviewed Plato's ideas about mental illness in some detail and found similarities with those developed later by Freud, a neurologist-turned-psychologist, who was to become the major proponent of the transcendence of mind over matter.

The second important legacy of Greek philosophy was the idea that knowledge gained through the mind differs from knowledge gained through the senses, and that the former is superior. This idea has direct relevance to later theories about empathic communication from one mind to another. Much of scientific history may be understood as an attempt to legitimize perception as a means of acquiring data on which objective knowledge of the world may be based, in part as a reaction to the assumed primacy of mind over matter. Within medicine in general, and psychiatry in particular, there would be a persisting quest to establish scientific legitimacy without surrendering the humanistic underpinnings of health care.

DUALISM AND MENTAL ILLNESS

King (1999c) has suggested that the idea of catharsis as mental cleansing originated with Plato; it was to find later expression in the Freudian concept of abreaction. Mental illness was understood as an imbalance in the substances that were associated with the body: the four humours, as enumerated by Hippocrates (Jackson, 1994) as well as Plato (Stone, 1997) or related to vapors emerging from the heart (Aristotle) (Stone, 1997, p. 9). The brain was recognized to be the organ of thinking, and to play some role in mental illness, but the idea that it could be influenced by treatment was far distant. Although there were antecedents of modern psychotherapy and humane care for patients (Asclepiades, Epicureans), certain fixed characteristics of temperament or of the patient's nature were focused on rather than more remediable causes. Humane care, when it was advocated at all, referred to general measures to promote health and well-being. The soul remained a core consideration, but

Richard Stine, *Head/Heart* (1994).

the idea of soul gradually merged with that of brain (Stone, 1997). For Galen, as for Plato earlier, the soul consisted of a rational and an irrational part, but the brain was considered the site of mental activity. Determinism, the notion that mental illness was constitutionally based, was an implicit assumption that was to persist in one form or another to the present, where the equivalent of such ideas is the immutability of genetic inheritance or the determinism associated with early environmental trauma.

During the Middle Ages, with the dominance of the church, mental illness was considered a moral matter; aberrant behavior was related to demonic presence: possession (Elliott, 1986). The mentally ill were regarded as sinners who might recover through penitence, prayer, or punishment. Although determinism was implicit, the dominant attitude was severe rather than humane: distancing, not empathy, was indicated. The stigma associated with mental illness probably had its origins in such thinking, which lasted until the Renaissance. Empathy, which is based to a great extent on the ability to perceive commonalities between observer and observed, would have been inconsistent with the predominant picture of the mentally ill as alien.

Oddly enough, it was not idealism that rescued psychiatry from the ignorance and superstition of the dark ages, but a rebirth of materialism that accompanied the rise of science during the Renaissance. Discoveries in anatomy and physiology reawakened interest in the brain (King, 1999a). In France, Descartes rekindled the idea of dualism, proposing that the mind and body were made of different substances, while Hobbes proposed that both the mind and external world were composed of atoms. Knowledge, some said, was innate, while others, for example, Locke and Rousseau, argued that all knowledge comes from experience (Elliott, 1986). The picture of a largely passive individual, subject to the shaping influence of environment, was accentuated by Rousseau's vision of man as emotional and corruptible. Zohar (1990) has argued that the seeds of pessimism and alienation that persist into the twenty-first century have their roots in Cartesian dualism as well as in the mechanistic theories of Newtonian physics, both of which undermine our sense of being part of the natural world (p. 3). The mentally ill remained distant from those entrusted with their care and unknowable, though more diseased than demonically possessed.

During the eighteenth century, treatment of the mentally ill was dominated by Cartesian dualism. Hospital reform, usually associated with the work of Pinel, represented a more sympathetic attitude toward the mentally ill (King, 1999b), but the predominant theories about causation and treatment were shaped by materialism and a mechanistic view of the world. For example, Mesmer, whose lineage was to include Charcot and eventually Freud, based his work with hysterical patients on the notion of "animal magnetism." His technique for curing hysteria, which involved hypnosis, was based on the notion that a maldistribution of an electromagnetic substance was responsible for the illness (Stone, 1997, p. 59). Despite the dubious nature of his work, Mesmer's focus was on the individual patient, and the field of psychiatry benefitted from his successes. A spirit of optimism about treatment in general followed, setting the tone for the remarkable advances of the nineteenth century.

MONISM: THE DOMINANCE OF BRAIN

The nineteenth century saw a shift away from the level of pessimism that had existed about healing mental disorders, based primarily on discoveries about the brain and its functions. Although there were exceptions, such as the impact of German Romanticism, which placed the plights and rights of the individual center stage (Stone, 1997, p. 72), the development of psychiatry as a discipline was most strongly associated with its evolution as a science. The work of William Griesenger, which was based on the primacy of brain over mind, reshaped the identity of the nineteenth century psychiatrist, who became a neurologist or a neuropsychiatrist (Stone, 1997). Both determinism and monism, the reduction of mental phenomena to events taking place in the brain, were reinforced by discoveries about the brain. They were further confirmed

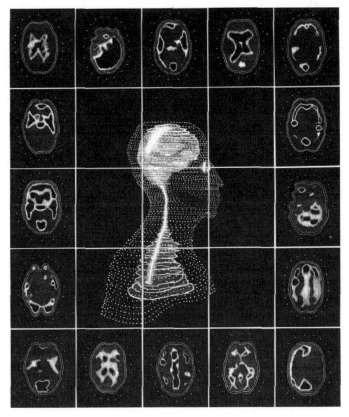

Joshua Simons, *16 States* (1987).

by the impact of Darwin's theories about evolution, which appeared to deprive man of his central and unique position in the universe and render him as subject to the forces of nature as are other life forms.

As an example of the principle that all movements contain their opposites, though in nascent form, the work of Charles Darwin presaged the swing of the pendulum that was to come at the end of the nineteenth century. Although Darwin's findings appeared to some to reinforce a fatalistic and mechanistic view of the universe, his theories embraced not only the evolution of species but also of subsystems, including the organs and their functions. For the brain and the neurons, these functions included consciousness, which must therefore have purpose and meaning. With respect to the communication of affect and its possible phylogenetic import, Darwin said the following:

> The movements of expression in the face and body, whatever their origin may have been, are in themselves of much importance for our welfare. They serve as the first means of communication between the mother and her infant; she smiles approval, and thus encourages her child on the right path, or frowns disapproval. We readily perceive sympathy in others by their expression; our sufferings are thus mitigated and our pleasures increased; and mutual good feeling is thus strengthened. (Darwin, 1979, pp. 385–386)

One is reminded of the work of Paget and Lipps, and the later application of the idea of *Einfuhlung* to psychology. These comments also presage knowledge about infant development and the types of preverbal communication between mothers and infants now believed to be the basis of identity.

In his gem of a volume *The Expression of The Emotions in Animals and Man* (1989), Darwin underscored the phylogenetic importance of the various affects and suggested that the relationship between emotion and the brain was a reciprocal one when he stated,

> the conducting power of the nervous fibres increases with the frequency of their excitement. This applies to the nerves of motion and sensation, as well as those connected with the act of thinking. That some physical change is produced in the nerve-cells or nerves, which are habitually used can hardly be doubted, for otherwise it is impossible to understand how the tendency to certain acquired movements is inherited. (pp. 29/30, 30/32)

These ideas about the linkage of structure and function and the plasticity of the nervous system, which included the tantalizing suggestion that the relationship between the brain and behavior was a reciprocal one, were to lie dormant for many years before reappearing and finding confirmation in the late twentieth century (Dalton & Forman, 1994).

The tensions inherent in dualism were mitigated during the nineteenth century by an almost universal commitment to a biological model of illness and its treatment. In this model, mind was incorporated into the idea of brain, a form of reductionism that was to reappear in cycles that were to follow. Beginning with Griesinger, who considered psychoses to be physiological disorders (Wortis, 1988), developments in the biological sciences dominated thinking about mental disorder and its treatment. Elliott (1986) has summarized the major developments that shaped medical and then neuropsychiatric practice, reducing mental phenomena to functions of the brain. These included the work of Hughlings Jackson, who incorporated mind into his physiology of neurological functions; Sechenov, who postulated that sensory stimulation was the origin of all mental activity; Goltz, whose animal experiments exploring the relationship between specific emotional states and specific areas of the brain led to the work of Cannon and Bard in the subsequent century; and Fritsch and Hiztzig, whose discoveries prompted the investigations in electroneurophysiology that eventuated in the development of electroconvulsive therapy. The brain became knowable at both a gross and histological level, and the promise of science, advanced by the discovery of organic diseases such as neurosyphilis, was that mental functions, and mental disorders, were explicable and might be treatable as disorders of the brain. Within this framework, a neuropsychiatrist of the late nineteenth century would have had little use for interpersonal skills. Once again, patients were defined not as suffering individuals, but as representatives of a class of people with disordered brains.

While there were exceptions to the organic emphasis of the nineteenth century, such as the paths taken by William James and John Dewey, who proposed psychological explanations for mental content (King, 1999a, p. 6), no major change in this trend took place until the threshold of the twentieth. Along with the emphasis on biological causation, there was a renewed attempt to categorize. The most famous nosologist was Emil Kraepelin, a monist who attributed mental illness to neuropathology, and who is often seen as the predecessor and model for contemporary descriptive psychiatry. Kraepelin's careful work was based on a neurophysiological foundation that used the idea of syndrome, defined earlier by Sydenham as *a group of symptoms having a common course and prognosis* (King, 1999a, p. 7), to delineate disorders. Models of treatment associated with these theories were largely supportive in nature, but with the advent of pharmacological agents that was about to change. For the most part, this phase of mental health history was dominated not only by a monistic focus on the brain, but also an associated determinism; little could be done to cure the disorders identified. It may have been this factor, more than any other, that caused the pendulum to swing. The catalyst for that swing was Freud.

Monism: The Dominance of Mind

Two factors drastically altered the landscape in the late 1800s and set the tone for a renaissance of psychologically based psychiatry that was to dominate for the next 50 years. The first of these was the evolution of psychiatry as a discipline in the United States, and especially in the increasingly humane nature of treatment provided in mental hospitals, and the second was the work of Freud, his direct predecessors, and his followers.

The situation in the United States in the early nineteenth century was not unlike that of Europe at an earlier time. Psychiatry was fledgling as a specialty. Research, training, and treatment were not well developed; hospitals remained unpleasant places offering largely custodial care. Under the influence of psychiatrists such as Benjamin Rush, and reformers such as Benjamin Franklin and Dorothea Dix, by the middle of the nineteenth century, the situation had begun to change (Stone, 1997). The causal influence of social and emotional issues began to be acknowledged, creating some balance to the impact of American neurologists such as Weir-Mitchell and Beard, who were very much in the European tradition. As an illustration of the polarization between American and European psychiatry, Eisenberg (1986) has cited a speech given in 1894 by Weir-Mitchell to the fiftieth annual meeting of the Association of Medical Superintendents of American Institutions for the Insane, which was to become the American Psychiatric Association, in which he chided them for having departed from science. Mental hospitals, like training centers, at that time lacked a coherent relationship with the science of brain. There were few academic links and little in the way of research, a situation that was to be remedied within the next twenty years.

The influence of Freud, himself trained as a neurologist, was immense. Stemming from his contact with Pierre Janet and his familiarity with hypnosis as practiced by Charcot, Freud moved psychiatry from its biological monism to one based on mind. It is noteworthy that he did this with considerable misgiving, and it may be his successors rather than Freud, himself, who can be held accountable for the rift with biological science that was to continue until almost the middle of the next century. In 1895, concerned with maintaining a relationship with the emerging science of brain, Freud proposed and began work on his Project for a Scientific Psychology. In his letters to his friend, Wilhelm Fliess, Freud chronicled his efforts to quantify the mental phenomena he was discovering and relate them to what he termed the "material particles" of the brain: neurons. This project occupied him for over nine months, at which point he abandoned and never returned to it. In his introduction to the paper describing this project, which was published only after his death, Freud expressed his intent:

> The intention is to furnish a psychology that shall be a natural science: that is, to represent psychical processes as quantitatively determinate states of specifiable material particles, thus making those processes perspicuous and free from contradiction. Two principal ideas are involved: (1) What distinguishes activity from rest is to be regarded as Q, subject to the general laws of motion. (2) The neurones are to be taken as the material particles. (Freud, 1895/1966, p. 295)

Although the project contains many of the ideas that were to be developed as a psychological framework associated with psychoanalysis, Freud failed to accomplish what he set out to do, largely, it appears, because of limitations in knowledge about neurophysiology and the unavailability of modern methods of studying the neurological substrates of mental functions. Psychoanalysis, both as a body of theory and as a method of psychotherapeutic intervention, was ultimately a monistic creation; one hundred years later, psychoanalytic theorists are engaged in attempting to bring about the type of reconciliation Freud envisioned. We will have more to say on this topic later.

The reasons for the shift from biological to psychological theories and therapies were many. Reich has pointed to the pessimism inherent in theories of brain disorder that is fixed, genetically or constitutionally based, and, with few exceptions (e.g., fever therapy for general paresis) resistant to extant methods of treatment (Reich, 1982). A therapy based on the notion of each individual as unique, shaped by the environment, and capable of change and a fuller life, was likely to be particularly appealing in the United States, where the rejection of things European and the quest for new frontiers was in vogue. As we have considered at some length, the return to a psychological model of health and illness, one that was based on a picture of the mind as a battleground of urges, constraints, recollections, defenses, and adaptations—a dynamic field of activity—placed demands on the treater to understand the patient. This, in turn, led to the adoption of *Einfuhlung* as a theoretical construct accounting for the analyst's ability to transcend interpersonal barriers.

As we have seen, it was not Freud who elaborated the theme of empathic understanding, but his disciples, while they gradually increased the conceptual gap between brain and mind. Although there were periodic attempts to forge links to science, psychoanalysis became progressively more sequestered from the fields of brain and psychological research. The emphasis was squarely on a two-person relationship, which held the key to recovery and health and operated by principles that did not vary with diagnosis, variable constitutional factors, or the influence of the constantly changing external environment. As we have considered, the empathic capacities of the analyst were largely related to his/her mastery of unconscious forces in self and other and accuracy of empathic knowledge was almost entirely a pragmatic question: did the patient get better as a result of it? Although attempts were made to differentiate between countertransference and empathy, there was little progress in separating subjective from objective phenomena. Analytic institutes developed rigorous methods to assess the capacity of a trainee to work within the model, placing great importance on personal characteristics. As Eisenberg has noted (1986), training in psychoanalysis was carried out in settings far removed from critical scrutiny (though internecine quarrels reminiscent of scholasticism were legion) and from academic settings.

In this climate, a psychotherapist who was not empathic or could not learn to develop such capacities was likely to be viewed as less than adequate. This matter was compounded by the trends that took place in general psychiatric education over the same time period. While psychoanalysts were not heavily represented in academic settings outside the United States (Lewis, 1953), by the early 1960s more than half the chairmen of departments of psychiatry in the United States were psychoanalysts.

Within psychiatric training programs, as in medicine in general, the lack of standardization remained a problem until well into the twentieth century. Adolph Meyer, a major force in bringing about the necessary reforms (Meyer, 1917), was also a critic of psychoanalysis for its abandonment of the science of the brain. Meyer coined the term "psychobiology" to characterize his approach to the care of the mentally ill and the core of his teaching philosophy. In an attempt to bridge the psychological and biological domains, he urged that we take account of "the mental working of the patient and his way of meeting the situation as well as the regulation of his physiological mechanism" (Rutter, 1986). This approach placed emphasis on the patient's disorder as a combination of constitutional and experiential factors, and urged that the treater take into account the person with the illness: his/her adaptive strengths and capacities as well as vulnerabilities. This philosophy made the patient an active collaborator in treatment, and focused attention on the patient's conscious experience rather than hypothesized unconscious determinants. Although Meyer did not speak of empathy, his insistence on appreciating the patient's perspective is consistent with an empathic posture. His work has reemerged in the current integrative environment, as we will see later.

Despite Meyer's warnings, over the years of its dominance in the United States psychoanalysis exercised the major shaping influence over psychiatric training. In the practice of psychoanalysis, which was based on a two-person relationship designed to elicit and amend unconscious mental content believed to be pathogenic, a practitioner valued empathic capacities as a basic tool of the art of practice. This value was reflected in the reliance on case-based supervision, which became the training norm, as well as the requirements for a personal analysis in order to develop the capacity to utilize this and other tools of the trade in an unbiased and presumably neutral fashion. Though the desirability or even the possibility of neutrality remains a contentious matter, even among psychoanalysts, there still is widespread agreement within this community that empathy is important in itself or as a prerequisite for interpretative work. Advocates of psychodynamic psychotherapy, a derivative of psychoanalysis, also consider this aspect of the treatment relationship to be important, and psychodynamically oriented training programs, especially in the United States, have produced a generation of practitioners who consider it an essential part of their healing arsenal. As Frank has taught us, empathy is widely regarded as one of the basic prerequisites for the psychotherapist. Frank, it should be recalled, was speaking mainly of those who practice within the psychodynamic tradition (Frank, 1974).

Thus, trainees bound for other corners of the profession were shaped by psychoanalytic thinking, with its emphases on the dyad as the basic unit of treatment, on unconscious determinants of symptomatology, and on corrective strategies based on the development of insight. Not only was it not encouraged, but interest in basic science was, in some instances, actively discouraged. Kandel (1998), in describing life in the 1960s at one of the nation's premier training programs, Massachusetts Mental Health Center, an experience that the author shared, had the following to say about the anti-intellectual attitude that prevailed:

> Much of this attitude came from our teachers, from the heads of the residency program. They made a point of encouraging us not to read. Reading, they argued, interfered with a resident's ability to listen to patients and therefore biased his or her perception of the patients' life histories. One famous, much quoted remark was that "there are those who care about people and there are those who care about research." (p. 458)

The values that were promoted stemmed from the transcendent training objective, which was:

> to develop better therapists—therapists prepared to understand and
> empathize with the patients' existential problems. (p. 458)

Wallerstein (1991), referring to a somewhat earlier time, the immediate
postwar years, and his experience as a resident in psychiatry at the Menninger
Clinic, said something similar:

> the theory of psychoanalysis and its application in psychoanalyti-
> cally informed and guided psychotherapy represented almost the
> totality of what was taught and learned. (p. 424)

Empathy, both with regard to the capacity to gain access to the patient's
mental state and to gain the understanding that proceeds from the type of
process we have considered, was a feature of such psychotherapy. Both the
selection of residents and the shaping effects of supervisors took place in an
environment that supported the full development and use of the therapist's
person in the work of treatment.

In addition to the orthodox form of psychoanalysis that evolved from the
work of Freud and his immediate successors, other schools of analytically
oriented treatment were spawned by the core mentalism that characterized
psychiatry well into the 1960s. The work of Kohut in America, the object-relations theorists such as Winnicott, Guntrip, and Balint in England, the schools
of brief psychotherapy that emerged from self-psychology and dynamic brief
psychotherapy, and the existential school all placed a premium on empathic
means of knowing the patient. Training programs thus produced a host of
psychotherapists whose attitudes were strongly slanted toward the models of
pathogenesis and treatment they had learned in their training. This is not to
say, of course, that such attitudes were universal; in fact, the seeds of the next
revolution were sown during the same time frame.

Thus far, we have focused on the pendular swing that took place in psychiatry at the beginning of the twentieth century, shaping practice until the
biological revolution of the 1950s. The situation in psychology was somewhat
different. Toward the end of the nineteenth century, psychology was primarily
concerned with mental content. Beginning with the experiments of Pavlov,
behaviorism, the belief that human behavior is determined by the shaping
influence of environmental factors, became a major force. With Watson and
Skinner, these ideas became predominant and affected the training and orientation of more than a generation of psychologists who saw their fundamental
concern as understanding and shaping behavior. Although there have been
major changes, so that classical behaviorism has been replaced by more flexible
models of learning, the role of interpersonal ambience and the importance of

empathy remain far less clear than they are for the psychodynamic practitioner. While psychiatry of the first half of the twentieth century was held in thrall by psychoanalytic thinking, which relied on hypothesized mental structures and internal representation of present and past events to apply its techniques to the resolution of conflicts between warring impulses, many of the advances that have come from the psychological community have concerned cognition. The questions raised there concerned what we know and how we know it, what the nature of consciousness is, and how we might quantify mental phenomena. Psychology, which has not defined itself historically as a profession of healers, and which has maintained its historical linkage to measurement and experimentation, has concerned itself largely with the processes of thought and learning as these could be explored in the laboratory, in child development, and through clinical experimentation. Models of treatment that have evolved from this tradition have been primarily concerned with identifying and modifying behavior and mental content. More recent developments, such as cognitive therapy, alone or in conjunction with behavior modification, owe their defining characteristics to this tradition.

THE PENDULUM SWINGS AGAIN

In the 1950s, several dramatic events took place and the pendulum in psychiatry swung away from psychoanalysis and back to biological psychiatry (King, 1999d). First, the mood-elevating properties of monoamine oxidase inhibitors, then of imipramine and amitriptyline, were discovered, and these drugs were introduced into practice in the mid and late 1950s. Chlorpromazine made its entry within the same time frame, providing the first significant pharmacological agent for the treatment of psychotic disorders. Lithium carbonate, though known to be effective as a mood stabilizer as early as 1949, was slow to be accepted by the Food and Drug Administration but made its entry in the early 1960s. These startling developments provided alternatives to psychotherapy, which had never proven itself effective in treating the major mental disorders, and complemented other somatic therapies already in use: insulin, then metrazol and then electroconvulsant therapy, and psychosurgery. Perhaps as a manifestation of the continuing quest for treatment that worked, and especially worked more rapidly than the process of analysis, somatic therapy was embraced. Antianxiety medication followed—meprobamate, then the benzodiazepines—offering an alternative for the treatment of anxiety.

Psychiatry has not only rediscovered its medical background but has renewed its relationship with neurology, causing some to recommend that the two fields be combined (Detre & McDonald, 1997). Citing the value of somatic therapies, the advent of new neurobiologic and neuropsychologic assessment tools, and the advances in genetics, epidemiology, and biochemistry, Yudofsky has suggested that the concept of neuropsychiatry should be resurrected (1987). The linkage with psychology has also been renewed. Theories of cognition, learning, and behavior have led to demonstrably effective forms of therapy and helped us to understand the ways in which the brain creates mental phenomena, leading to a new version of reductionistic thinking in which brain is conceived to be the organ of the mind. In this regard, some have argued that a new type of materialism may be possible, based on reductionism but still providing a place for psychological phenomena (Karlsson & Kamppinen, 1995).

The burgeoning science of psychiatry has been driven by advances in neurophysiology and especially by clarification of the mechanism of action of drugs, which have attracted important sources of funding for research. We have entered the era of designer drugs and, with completion of the map of the human genome, are on the threshold of gene therapy. In contrast to the situation in the 1960s, training directors and department heads in our major institutions are no longer psychoanalysts, but are more likely to be biological scientists; most large training programs have active research programs, and research dollars heavily favor biological approaches. Along with this, far fewer hours are allotted to the training of psychiatrists in psychotherapy, especially the dynamic form that has been most closely associated with the concept of empathic communication, causing some to fear that psychotherapists, themselves, may be an endangered species (Wallerstein, 1991). Time in a training program must now be shared among considerably more alternatives than was true in the past: briefer therapies, psychopharmacology, epidemiology, health care economics, research. The opportunity to sit with patients and to listen has been much reduced and, along with it, the role of imaginative thinking and absorption in the world of individual patients that is so central to empathic exchange.

The incentives for the profound shift in ideology that has occurred are understandable. The most apparent one is that the limitations of psychotherapy have driven us in these new directions in the hope that at last we will find cures for disorders that afflict millions and have resisted our efforts at cure. Reich (1982), in considering the shift, pointed to the quest for "optimism." Eisenberg (1986), though agreeing that a search for effective treatment is the driving force behind cyclical change, also suggested that psychiatry at last has succumbed to the pull of organized medicine, which was already firmly in the biological camp during the first half of the twentieth century, leaving psychiatry as the last holdout to the march of the biological sciences. Whatever the root causes, psychiatry made a dramatic shift away from a preoccupation with mind to an equally monistic investment in brain. This shift has grown over the ensuing decades, leading psychiatry back into the camp of science, renewing its identification with medicine, and, in the mind of some, risking the abandonment of what makes psychiatry unique: its position at the interface of the psychosocial and the biological factors related to mental health and illness. While some celebrate the reconciliation taking place between psychiatry and neurology, others, such as Szasz (1985), have perceived psychiatry as forced to choose between being "brainless or mindless," holding out little hope that the two can be reconciled. The biopsychosocial model proposed over a quarter of a century ago by Engel (1977) remains unrealized (Meyer, 1998, p. 49).

CONVERGING TRENDS

As a result of the dominance of biological models in mainstream psychiatry, a void has been created. Some claim that the public interest in complementary forms of medicine represents one attempt to fill this void (Campion, 1993). There is also evidence that both psychiatry and psychology are adapting to the biological environment and finding ways to reconcile with it. Psychoanalysts, for example, who have been marginalized by the shift from mental to material monism, have renewed their interest in empathy, as reflected in a spate of articles on the topic (Schwartz, 1987; Chessick, 1998; Tuch, 1997; Reiser, 1999; Meissner, 2000). This renewed interest is accompanied by fundamental shifts in the identity of the psychoanalyst (Stolorow, 2000). Much of this may be attributed to the influence of self-psychology in shaking psychoanalysis loose from its preoccupation with the unconscious and its insistence on therapist neutrality to consider the importance of the interpersonal domain. Some psychoanalysts have found evidence for the core concepts of psychoanalytic theory in new findings about the brain, and some are involved in research on memory, learning, and other aspects of brain function. Medical practitioners, having lived longer under the influence of a narrow biological frame of reference, are rediscovering the importance of the doctor–patient relationship and the requisite communication skills necessary to optimize that relationship in the service of healing (Spiro *et al.*, 1993; Emanual & Dubler, 1995; Emanual & Emanual, 1992).

While psychiatry has returned to the biological camp, psychology has continued to develop its ideas about learning, cognition, memory, and consciousness, overlapping with basic research in the brain sciences. Both infant and animal studies have contributed heavily to the advances in knowledge about human behavior and its relationship to brain physiology. Along with these trends, however, empathy has remained an important research subject. Much of the interest comes from the developmental psychologists, who have made enormous contributions to our understanding of the sequence of normal development. It should be noted that the view of empathy within this tradition favors its affective aspect and tends to downplay the idea of an empathic process that is directed toward understanding; this is in sharp contrast to the clinical use of the concept, but has contributed to our understanding of the social value of affective resonance, for example, in generating altruistic behavior, as well as in domains of ethics and morality (Bohart & Greenberg, 1997, p. 23).

From a clinical perspective, first gestalt and then the cognitive therapies have emerged to challenge the dynamic psychotherapies, with a considerable boost from the third-party payers and managers of care, whose bias is understandably toward the briefer forms of psychotherapy, and especially toward those that can and have been standardized and demonstrated to be effective. Behaviorism has been wedded with cognitive science, resulting in new forms of psychotherapy for the less severe disorders in particular, and complementing the use of psychoactive agents for the major mental disorders. Unlike classical behaviorism, which downplayed the importance of relationship, the quality and nature of the treatment milieu has been found vital to success with these newer forms of psychotherapy. Burns and Nolen-Hoeksema (1992), for example, have written about its importance in the practice of cognitive therapy, both with regard to the patient's willingness to follow required assignments (homework) and as a healing factor in its own right. Linehan's model of dialectical behavioral treatment also exploits empathic engagement in that it rests heavily on the therapist's appreciation of the patient's state of mind and the need to balance validation with the imperative toward change (Linehan, 1997). Thus, these newer methods of treatment, although oriented toward behavior, and based on careful protocols in research settings, do not overlook the power of relationship in achieving their aims.

For psychologists, as well as other non-psychiatrist mental health care practitioners, training in brain science as well as efforts to acquire prescribing privileges speak to the relaxation of boundaries and the broadened scope of basic necessary knowledge. In recent years, psychologists have increasingly directed their energies toward clinical practice, both on an outpatient and an inpatient basis, even while psychiatrists have rediscovered the research lab. Interestingly enough, psychology has softened its approach to the behavioral sciences, placing a new emphasis on the study of consciousness and the importance of the subjective aspects of human motivation, inner experience, and thought (Sperry, 1988). These trends, which are comparable to the psychoanalytic emphasis on hermeneutics, are compatible with the type of humanism advocated by Rogers fifty years earlier; they suggest a convergence of biological and psychosocial thinking and raise hope for more integrated approaches to care.

The past half century has seen a remarkable progression from gross anatomic knowledge about brain function, to cellular to molecular understanding. Progress in genetics as well as clarification of the mechanism of action of drugs and the development of sophisticated new methods of studying the relationship between brain and behavior have provided new and promising avenues to the treatment of mental disorder. At times, however, we seem to have become preoccupied with the patient's disorder while becoming oblivious of the person who suffers from it. While we are learning a great deal about neural circuitry and neurotransmission, intercellular chemical messengers, gene transcription, the relationship between stressors and humoral and brain alterations, and the importance of glial and neuronal cell biology (Coyle, 2000), some have cautioned that our flight to scientific respectability comes at a high cost. The development of a sound foundation in biology and the marvelous new technology that supports our work is not the problem, however; the problem is the risk of immersion in a reductionistic biomedical model (Pasnau, 1987). As Eisenberg has reminded us, "what brings patients to doctors is discomfort and dysfunction, not the pathology which may underlie them" (1986, p. 505). The argument continues.

The poet John Godfrey Saxe immortalized the Indian fable concerning six learned men of Indostan, who, though blind, sought to determine the nature of an elephant by making a set of observations, each from a single perspective. Each "sees" only what his perspective allows. The situation in psychiatry is analagous, and the level of contentiousness reminiscent. The last two verses summarize the problem, which in this case is not monism, dualism or reductionism but what, sexism?

And so these men of Indostan, disputed loud and long,
each in his own opinion, exceeding stiff and strong,
Though each was partly in the right, and all were in the wrong!

So oft in theologic wars, the disputants, I ween,
Tread on in utter ignorance, of what each other mean,
And prate about an elephant, not one of them has seen!
(Saxe, 1936)

CONCLUSIONS

The history of psychiatry and the allied field of psychology illustrates the cyclical nature of ideological shifts in the way that mental illness is understood and its treatment crafted. In considering the historical trends over two thousand years, I have focused on the tension between mind and matter, which has resulted in alternating periods of dominance of one over the other (monism), or reductionistic thinking, wherein one is conceived to be a subcategory of the other. Empathy, though associated most strongly with psychological theories of causation and treatment, and therefore less likely to be seen as important when treatment is based on a biological bias, may be understood as relevant to both frames of reference, especially as the two are integrated into a coherent biopsychosocial model: a point to which I will return in the next chapter. Fundamentally, as we have discussed earlier, the use of empathy in treatment represents a commitment to incorporating the subjective elements in the patient's presentation with those that are considered objective: the person with the disorder as well as the disorder afflicting that person. The first of these is based on the uniqueness of each individual while the second is created from commonalities found in populations of individuals. Empathy is an important pathway to the former, and it is abandoned when the path is.

Along with a discussion of dualism and its role in keeping mind and brain in separate silos, I have pointed to the role of determinism as it arises periodically, usually because a particular approach to healing proves less effective than it was initially perceived or hoped to be, leading to collective pessimism and an incentive to create a paradigm shift. The process is not linear, though in each era it is likely that theorists will perceive themselves as having benefitted from the mistakes of the past and being now on the right track. So goes the theologic war.

I have argued that the treaters who are trained, who define their professional identities and who practice within an environment dominated by a particular ideology, will be shaped by that environment. This is, of course, a psychological rather than a biological perspective except in one regard: that those who are attracted to the profession and who are accepted within it are likely to be constitutionally oriented toward the dominant motif. This issue is of particular importance when a capacity such as empathy is involved, since we have seen that empathic engagement places personal demands on the practitioner to be present and to take interpersonal risks. Those who are not so inclined may feel relief at being able to practice without this type of commitment. In our current iteration, too narrow a fascination with brain science threatens to undermine the knowledge we have attained about the influence of environment on health and illness; the role of conscious and unconscious factors and of historical events in shaping behavior; the vital importance of the family and social milieu to well-being, growth, and human fulfillment; and the flexibility and adaptability of the human organism faced with obstacles that must be overcome through acts of will and courage. There is nothing about brain science that requires abandonment of these aspects of psychiatric understanding, but, if we are to avoid perpetuating the problems created by dualism, then an integration of brain and mind must be forged. I will argue in the following chapter that not only is this possible, but recent findings make it highly feasible. Adolph Meyer, presenting his views on the training of psychiatrists in 1917, had the following to say:

> [W]e have to train the student of psychiatry and psychopathology to heed the structural facts, the toxic and endocrine and serologic facts, and the constitutional and psychogenic facts, and to learn to work with them, individually and in combination. (Meyer p. 862)

This point of view was echoed eloquently by George Engel (1977) fifty years later, when he questioned the adequacy of the biomedical model to medical care in general, and pointed to the irony in psychiatry's "subscribing to a medical model which some leaders in medicine already are beginning to question" (p. 134). Engel characterized the problem as follows:

> The biomedical model not only requires that disease be dealt with as an entity independent of social behavior, it also demands that behavioral aberrations be explained on the basis of disordered somatic (biochemical or neurophysiological) processes. (p. 130)

Engel, as others before him, lamented the reactive tendencies in psychiatry toward dualism, reductionism or what he referred to as "*exclusionism*" (the advocacy of removing psychiatry from the field of medicine entirely) and called for reforms that remain elusive as we begin the twenty-first century. Fortunately, the advances in science and those in psychology allow for a fresh approach to these problems, not yet possible in either the 1970s or earlier. This challenge, which we will consider in the following chapter, can be met by considering the use of capacities such as empathy as bridging constructs between two worlds perceived for over two thousand years to be polar alternatives.

REFERENCES

Bohart, A. C., & Greenberg, L. S. (1997). Empathy and psychotherapy: An introductory overview. In A. C. Bohart & L. S. Greenberg (Eds.), *Empathy reconsidered: New directions in psychotherapy* (pp. 3–31). Washington, DC: American Psychological Association.

Burns, D. D., & Nolen-Hoeksema, S. (1992). Therapeutic empathy and recovery from depression in cognitive–behavioral therapy: A structural equation model. *Journal of Consulting and Clinical Psychology, 60*(3), 441–449.

Campion, E. W. (1993). Why unconventional medicine? *New England Journal of Medicine, 328,* 282–283.

Chessick, R. D. (1998). Empathy in psychotherapy and psychoanalysis. *Journal of the American Academy of Psychoanalysis, 26*(4), 487–502.

Coyle, J. T. (2000). Mind glue: Implications of glial cell biology for psychiatry. *Archives of General Psychiatry, 57,* 90–93.

Dalton, R., & Forman, M. A. (1994). Mind, brain, and psychiatry. *Harvard Review of Psychiatry, 2,* 133–141.

Darwin, C. (1979). *The origin of species.* New York: Gramercy Books.

Darwin, C. (1989). *The expression of the emotions in man and animals.* In F. Darwin (Ed.), *The works of Charles Darwin* (Vol. 23). New York: New York University Press.

Detre, T., & McDonald, M. C. (1997). Managed care and the future of psychiatry. *Archives of General Psychiatry, 54,* 201–208.

Edman, I. (Ed.) (1928). *The philosophy of Plato.* New York: Simon and Schuster.

Eisenberg, L. (1986). Mindlessness and brainlessness in psychiatry. *British Journal of Psychiatry, 148,* 497–508.

Elliott, F. A. (1986). Historical perspectives on neurobehavior. *Psychiatric Clinics of North America, 9*(2), 225–239.

Emanual E. J., & Dubler, L. L.B. (1995). Preserving the physician-patient relationship in the era of managed care. *Journal of the American Medical Association, 273*(4), 323–329.

Emanual, E. J., & Emanual, L. L. (1992). Four models of the physician–patient relationship. *Journal of the American Medical Association, 267*(16), 2221–2226.

Engel, G. L. (1977). The need for a new medical model: A challenge for biomedicine. *Science, 196,* 129–136.

Frank, J. (1974). *Persuasion and healing.* New York: Shocken Books.

Freud, S. (1966). Project for a scientific psychology. In J. Strachey (Ed. and Trans.), *The standard edition of the complete psychological works of Sigmund Freud* (Vol. 1, pp. 281–397). London: Hogarth Press. (Original work published 1895.)

Jackson, S. W. (1994). Catharsis and abreaction in the history of psychological healing. *Psychiatric Clinics of North America, 17,* 471–492.

Kandel, E. R. (1998). A new intellectual framework for psychiatry. *American Journal of Psychiatry, 155*(4), 457–469.

Karlsson, H., & Kamppinen, M. (1995). Biological psychiatry and reductionism: Empirical findings and philosophy. *British Journal of Psychiatry, 167,* 434–438.

King, L. J. (1999a). A brief history of psychiatry: Millennia past and present, Part 1. *Annals of Clinical Psychiatry, 11*(1), 3–12.

King, L. J. (1999b). A brief history of psychiatry: Millennia past and present, Part 2. *Annals of Clinical Psychiatry, 11*(2), 47–54.

King, L. J. (1999c). A brief history of psychiatry: Millennia past and present, Part 3. *Annals of Clinical Psychiatry, 11*(3), 99–107.

King, L. J. (1999d). A brief history of psychiatry: Millennia past and present, Part 4. *Annals of Clinical Psychiatry, 11*(4), 175–185.

Lewis, A. (1953). Letter from Britain. *American Journal of Psychiatry, 110*, 401–405.

Linehan, M. M. (1997). Validation and psychotherapy. In A. C. Bohart & L. S. Greenberg (Eds.), *Empathy reconsidered: New directions in psychotherapy* (pp. 353–392). Washington, DC: American Psychological Association.

Lipowski, Z. J. (1989). Psychiatry: Mindless or brainless, both or neither. *Canadian Journal of Psychiatry, 34*, 249–254.

Meissner, W. W. (2000). On analytic listening. *Psychoanalytic Quarterly, 69*(2), 317–367.

Meyer, A. (1917). Progress in teaching psychiatry. *Journal of the American Medical Association, 69*(11), 861–862.

Meyer, R. E. (1998). *Between mind, brain, and managed care: The now and future world of academic psychiatry.* Washington, DC: American Psychiatric Association Press.

Nahm, M. C. (Ed.) (1947). *Selections from early Greek philosophy.* New York: Appleton-Century-Crofts.

Pasnau, R. O. (1987). The remedicalization of psychiatry. *Hospital and Community Psychiatry, 38*(2), 145–151.

Reich, W. (1982). Psychiatry's second coming. *Psychiatry, 45*, 189–196.

Reiser, M. (1999). Memory, empathy and interactive dimensions of psychoanalytic process. *Journal of the American Psychoanalytic Association, 47*(2), 485–501.

Ross, W. D. (Ed.) (1938). *Aristotle selections.* New York: Charles Scribner's Sons.

Russell, B. (1945). *A history of western philosophy.* New York: Simon and Schuster

Rutter, M. (1986). Meyerian psychobiology, personality development, and the role of life experiences. *American Journal of Psychiatry, 143*(9), 1077–1087.

Saxe, J. G. (1936). The blind men and the elephant. In H. Felleman (Ed.), *The best loved poems of the American people* (pp. 521–522). New York: Doubleday.

Schwartz, A. (1987). Drives, affects, behavior, and learning: Approaches to a psychobiology of emotion and to an integration of psychoanalytic and neurobiologic thought. *Journal of the American Psychoanalytic Association, 35*(2), 467–506.

Simon, B. (1978). *Mind and madness in ancient Greece: The classical roots of modern psychiatry.* Ithaca: Cornell University Press.

Sperry, R. W. (1988). Psychology's mentalist paradigm and the religion/science tension. *American Psychologist, 43*(8), 607–613.

Spiro, H. M., McCrea, M. G., Peschel, E., & St. James, D. (Eds.) (1993). *Empathy and the practice of medicine: Beyond pills and the scalpel.* New Haven: Yale University Press.

Stolorow, R. D. (2000). From isolated minds to experiential worlds: An intersubjective space odyssey. *American Journal of Psychotherapy, 54*(2), 149–151.

Stone, M. H. (1997). *Healing and the mind.* New York: W. W. Norton and Company.

Szasz, T. (1985). Psychiatry: Rhetoric and reality. *Lancet, ii*, 711–712.

Tuch, R. H. (1997). Beyond empathy: Confronting certain complexities in self psychology theory. *Psychoanalytic Quarterly, 66*(2), 259–282.

Wallerstein, R. S. (1991). The future of psychotherapy. *Bulletin of the Menninger Clinic, 55*, 421–443.

Wortis, J. (1988). The history of psychiatry. *Biological Psychiatry, 23*, 107–108.

Yudofsky, S. C. (1987). Neuropsychiatry: An idea whose time has come—again. *Hospital and Community Psychiatry, 38*(7), 701.

Zohar, D. (1990). *The quantum self.* London: Bloomsbury Publications.

CHAPTER 6

Empathy and the Brain

Some strange commotion
Is in his brain: he bites his lips and starts;
Stops on a sudden, looks upon the ground,
Then, lays his finger on his temple; straight,
Springs out into fast gait; then, stops again,
Strikes his breast hard; and anon, he casts
His eye against the moon; in most strange postures
We have seen him set himself

William Shakespeare

For reasons reviewed in the preceding chapter, the reconciliation of our ideas about the brain and those about the mind is undermined by the problem of dualism. Classical science, on which much of biological psychiatry has been based, argues that a few simple principles underlie the world's complexity, and the problem of mind–brain duality may best be solved by assuming that what we call mind is really the activity of the brain. Within such a reductionistic framework, "emotion, aesthetics, and religious experience can be reduced to biological instinct, chemical imbalances in the brain, or the rules governing genetics and physics" (Zohar, 1990, p. 308). Therapeutic empathy, because of its historical association with the art of health care, comes to be regarded as nonscientific; therefore, in an era such as the present one, empathy is likely to be relegated to a peripheral role in the care of patients who are understood to be biologically deranged. This means that therapies dependent on empathic communication or therapists who draw on data acquired through such means will be suspect. The decline of psychoanalysis and with it the dynamic psychotherapies is partly a product of such an environmental shift. The dominance of descriptive psychiatry is more compatible with the ideas of Griesinger and Kraepelin than with those of Kohut and Rogers, for whom diagnosis was of questionable value and for whom the therapeutic relationship was central to healing. Nietzsche, reflecting on the future of the physician in the late nineteenth century, a comparable era of scientific dominance, stated:

> There is at present no profession that could be so greatly enhanced as that of the physician; especially since the spiritual physicians, those described as ministering to the soul, no longer have public approval to engage in their conjurer's arts and cultivated people avoid them. (Nietzsche, 1878/1995, p. 166)

Perceiving that a science that casts suspicion on "the comfort provided by metaphysics, religion and art" may deprive humanity of "almost all it means to be human," Nietzsche proposed that

> A higher culture must therefore give people a dual brain, two compartments of the brain, as it were, the one to experience science, the other to experience nonscience: lying next to each other, without confusion, separable, each able to be closed off from the other; this is a requirement for health. (Nietzsche, 1878/1995, p. 171)

Nietzsche's trenchant suggestion anticipated contemporary thinking about a bicameral brain, composed of two cerebral hemispheres differentiated as to function, but also indicated a dichotomy between emotion and reason. The idea that science and passion are alternatives, however, is far from the truth. Damasio has argued persuasively that emotions and the feelings that alert us to their presence are derived from biological mechanisms that subserve survival, and that it is only when normal emotional capacities exist that rational behavior is possible. He put the matter as follows: "Emotions are part of the bioregulatory devices with which we come equipped to survive" (Damasio, 1999, p. 53). When brain damage impairs emotional capacities, the individual who has suffered such a loss is at a great disadvantage both in adapting to the external environment appropriately and in managing internal body mechanisms that facilitate such adaptation.

Nietzsche's suggestion for a firewall between two competing demibrains, a metaphor for dualistic thinking, is inconsistent with contemporary brain science and with science in general. Not only does new knowledge about how brain and mind are related call for nonlinear models of health and illness, but the fundamental shifts that have occurred in scientific paradigms, themselves, demand them. The scientific revolution of the twentieth century has replaced mechanistic and deterministic models of the universe with the dynamism and uncertainties of relativity, quantum, and chaos theory, all of which oppose the linear thinking that underlies dualism. Advances in neuroanatomy, neurophysiology, genetics, and cellular and molecular biology, coupled with a better understanding of learning, memory, and consciousness, are providing us with new ways of thinking about health and illness. As a result of such advances, we are now in a position to reconsider interpersonal phenomena such as empathy from a biological perspective. Within the scientific community, perhaps as a form of backlash (dare we say "frontlash") to the erosion of humanism from the psychiatric scene, new questions about the purpose, biological foundation, and mechanisms associated with empathy are now being raised. We will consider these questions in this chapter.

We have seen in previous chapters how the concept of therapeutic empathy originated and developed parallel to rather than as part of the scientific tradition, leading to its devaluation in the current era. One of the central messages of this book is that empathy is not only consistent with mental health care that is based on scientifically established premises, but that it is crucial to it. This premise requires a far more dynamic picture of our mental function than the mechanistic one of the past. Such a picture emerges as we begin to understand that the brain is a dynamic organ that both shapes and *is shaped by* experience, and the mind, as a manifestation of brain activity, is in a state of constant becoming.

This picture of the brain as plastic rekindles interest in the quality and nature of personal experience as a clinically relevant variable, and especially on its *unique and subjective aspects*: the meaning of events as well as the fact that they have occurred. The belief that personal meaning should be taken into account as a factor in development is true with regard to both our ontogeny, those features that are associated with our individual development, and our phylogeny, the continuing evolution of our species. Therapeutic empathy, which finds its greatest utility in bringing to light those subjective elements of personal meaning that derive from our interpretation of experience, becomes relevant only to the extent that subjective factors are considered relevant to illness and healing. For reasons that will be presented in this chapter, it is my belief that we are witnessing a backlash to dehumanized health care and that that backlash is being spearheaded, of all places, in the scientific community.

In pursuing this line of argument, we will consider three domains of enquiry: the development of early and largely unsuccessful attempts at integrating mind and body, as reflected in the history of psychosomatic medicine; the contributions of neo-Darwinism to an emerging model of genetics that emphasizes the reciprocity between nature and nurture; and the identification of neural pathways, sites, and cellular processes that are associated with emotion and memory and relevant to the genesis and treatment of mental disorder. Throughout, we will continue to center our attention on the phenomenon of empathy in order to make three points: first, that empathic forms of communication are one of the hallmarks of the healthy human brain; second, that empathy is one of the clinical variables required to correct the aberrant patterns of learning that underlie mental disorders; and, third, that there is a scientific basis for limited clinical interventions that are designed to *strengthen the environment in which healing may take place* as an alternative to attempts on the part of therapists to *constitute* such a healing environment. The purpose of making these points is to pave the way for the clinical chapters that follow.

PSYCHOSOMATICS

In the previous chapter, we considered trends that indicate convergence of monistic lines of development. Another example of such efforts can be found in the subdiscipline of psychosomatic medicine, which addresses the relationship between body and mind and seeks to find linkages. Antonio Damasio (1994), in what might be considered a neurophilosophical critique of dualism, referred to "the abysmal separation between body and mind," which he further qualified as "the separation of the most refined operations of mind from the structure and operation of *a biological organism*" (italics mine). As others have done, he traced this trend to Descartes. For Damasio, the matter of integration of psyche and soma requires more than reconciling brain with mind, since he regards the body, as it is represented in the brain, as the appropriate frame of reference for "the neural processes that we experience as the mind" (1994, p. xvi). In other words, it requires consideration of the whole organism, brain and body in entirety, connected through humoral and neural activities, in a reciprocal relationship with environment. The mental phenomena that emerge as a result of this interaction constitute what we call mind. This holistic vision contrasts not only with Cartesian dualism, but with conventional thinking about reconciling mind with brain. As we will see in a later chapter, when we consider the relationship between empathy and healing, observations about the beneficial impact of relationships on the integrity of the immune system support this broad frame of reference.

The origin of psychosomatic medicine was not in unifying psyche and soma but linking them and, more specifically, in the belief that somatic and emotional factors overlap in the genesis of certain physical illnesses. The term was first used by Johann Christian Heinroth in 1818, who applied it to insomnia (Kaplan *et al.*, 1994), and it was seized on as a way of reconciling two sets of variables (physical and mental) that were seen as separate. Over the years, the term has been used varyingly to characterize specific disorders—disorders in which stress appears to play a precipitating role (consistent with the work of Selye and others)—and as a general principle of dual causality, as advocated by Meyer or Engel (pp. 752–754). Dunbar, in the 1960s, related the various disorders thought to be caused by psychological factors to personality variables, suggesting vulnerability based on psychodynamic factors (Stone, 1997).

It is interesting to note that the DSM system has modified the psychosomatic concept several times (Kaplan *et al.*, 1994). DSM-I, which appeared in 1952, categorized physical disorders understood to be reactions to psychological factors as *psychophysiological reactions*, consistent with the thinking of Meyer that mental disorders were reactive; in 1968, DSM-II characterized *psychophysiological conditions* as synonymous with *psychosomatic*; DSM-III, published in 1980, shifted from the idea of *reaction* as too vague and used the medical concept of *disorder* instead; the term, *psychosomatic* was dropped. DSM-III (American Psychiatric Association, 1980) and DSM-IIIR (APA, 1987) moved away from terms that suggested etiology, toward a more descriptive stance, while increasing the number of diagnostic categories. By the time that DSM-IV was published (APA, 1994), various conditions that were regarded as "psychosomatic" in the 1960s were now diffusely listed as *somatoform, conversion,* or *psychological factors affecting medical condition*, with the latter no longer considered to be a mental disorder. The trend, therefore, has been away from the unifying notion of *psychosomatic* or *psychophysiological*, terms that suggest a causative linkage, toward a system that is more purely descriptive. In other words, the holistic idea that the mind shapes an illness of the body has been abandoned in favor of one that says only that a medical condition may be affected by a variety of nonsomatic factors, which is a monistic position.

Despite its association with the ideas of Meyer and Engel and its suggestion of holistic thinking, psychophysiological research has been dominated by largely behavioral thinking. This fact is reflected in the shift from interpersonal or psychodynamic methods of treatment to those that are based on cognitive and behavioral strategies. As with any trend, however, its opposite resides someplace nearby. In her presidential address in April of 1973, the then president of the American Psychosomatic Society, Margaret Singer (1974), called attention to the importance of assessing the subject's current and customary level of engagement and involvement with self, others, and the environment as an important variable both in the lab and in practice. Noting a series of studies that related changes in physiological parameters to the nature of the relationship established with the interviewer, Singer called for reframing the research situation to include its transactional aspects. Attention to this dimension allows the interviewer to "make interview–observational ratings within a transactional model, rather than within a stimulus–response, interactional model" (p. 2). Although Singer did not refer to empathy as an evaluative tool, her definition of involvement as "a quality of directness, intensity and immediacy in the transactional pattern shown by the subject" (p. 5) would seem to call for the type of activity we have previously defined as empathic.

Carek (1987), in considering the manner in which a biopsychosocial model might be implemented, pointed to the importance of empathy, and especially of what he termed "affective exchanges" in assessing the meaning to the patient of the psychological and social variables assumed to be associated with the development of a psychosomatic disorder. He noted the risks of communications that lack empathy, as well as tendencies to lump presumptive causal factors and think of them in generic terms (i.e., as stressors) rather than in terms relevant to an individual patient; the former leads to what he termed "a facade of empathy" (presumably nongenuine or feigned rather than felt), while the latter results in an overly cognitive or intellectual appraisal that may overlook the patient's real needs. Carek warned of the danger of reductionistic thinking when either the physical or the psychological dimension are overemphasized and empathy is lacking. Although he focused on affective attunement, which we have considered only one aspect of empathic transactions, his reason for doing so appears clear: to warn about the danger of overly cognitive appraisals.

The contributions of psychosomatic medicine to our topic lie in the gradual movement of this field toward dualism, through consideration of the mechanisms that link body and mind in health and illness. With the improvements in techniques that allow us to study the brain directly, we are now in a position to pursue our interest in integrating mind and matter into the cranial vault. Our central question, which concerns the relevance of empathic healing to the treatment of mental disorder in the present environment, leads us to ask whether a biological basis for empathy can be found in the brain, and, if so, what its ontological and phylogenetic purpose may be. In our quest, we turn again to the remarkable work of Charles Darwin.

Neo-Darwinism and Genetic Plasticity

As have seen, Darwin's contributions to the study of empathy were consider-able. Although his insistence on the struggle for survival has been seen by some as too narrow an emphasis in explaining evolutionary phenomena, the idea that certain capacities have value beyond survival of the species is not incon-sistent with his findings. A resurgence of interest in evolution is associated with discoveries about the reciprocal nature of the relationship between genes and the environment. Not only is there a discrepancy between the genetic capacity of an individual cell and the actual level of genetic activity in that cell, which accounts for the specialized capacities of groups of cells subserving some common function, but we now know that genes are capable of turning on and off in response to a variety of environmental factors. Environment, of course, is a dynamic rather than a static variable, so that genetic expression constitutes a response to the demands of evolution as well as adaptation at any given point in time. As our understanding of the human genome increases, we will be able to track genetic expression and perhaps influence it as a method of preventing and treating disease. The question that concerns us now, however, is whether empathic capacities are inborn as part of our genetic makeup and, if so, what purpose such capacities may be designed to serve.

Teleology, the belief that there is order and intent in the universe, is closely associated with Darwinism. In considering the development of a capacity such as empathy, Gierer (1998) posited one of two sequences leading to the estab-lishment of this capacity, which he considered to be a basic human one. Either, he reasoned, the capacity developed cumulatively through small increments in the neural network, or it occurred as an innovative event, which then endured because of its value to the species; choosing the latter possibility, he went on to suggest a mechanism by which a rare genetic event might be introduced and, if it proved beneficial to fitness, might lead to a new evolutionary path.

How might empathy be of value? Gierer proposed that empathy is a cogni-tively based, genetically encoded capacity that came into being because it contributes positively to well-being. In making his argument, he focused on the social rather than the derivative (therapeutic or clinical empathy) that we have been considering. According to Gierer, data acquired empathically allows us to predict the current and likely future states of our selves and others, so that we may anticipate behavior and plan accordingly. Such an ability consti-tutes an asset in strategic planning. In other words, empathy enables us to select behaviors that will benefit us and avoid those that may harm us. Gierer saw the evolution of empathy as a byproduct of the capacity for strategic thinking that is dependent on our ability to develop and sustain internal representations. This ability, in turn, is encoded in the human genome. His hypothesis takes into account both the affective and cognitive dimensions of empathy, since internal representation in the brain can enlist centers of emotion as well as those associated with cognitive activities. The ability to assess and predict is enhanced by comparison of one's own behavioral propensities with those anticipated from and later experienced from others, leading to new learning: another contribution to long-term well-being. Gierer also considered that altruistic behavior, though not always evoked by empathy, is more likely in its presence, and that such behavior promotes collective well-being. Others have suggested that the ability to engage empathically may confer additional social benefits, for example, affective attunement as an aid in the mating behavior known as courtship.

Drawing on Darwin's original observations that we respond sympathetically to expressed strong emotion, Leslie Brothers (1989) has proposed a biological substrate to empathy that centers on the processing of visual sensory information that is affect-laden and socially relevant. She suggested, like Gierer, that empathic capacities may improve fitness, by presenting evidence that primates respond selectively to facial features associated with strong emotion and reasoning how such capacities might be beneficial—for example, the ability to read social signals offers a competitive edge as well as protection against being manipulated or outsmarted by rivals. The ability of infants to read the mother's face and attune to her affect has been linked to neurological development in specific areas of the brain and may be a precursor of empathic abilities later in life (Stern, 1985).

Brothers (1989) also hypothesized that the impaired empathic ability found in certain neurological conditions, for example, in autism or certain right-hemisphere cortical lesions, suggests that this capacity has a neuroanatomical and/or neurophysiological origin. Certain types of brain damage have been found to interfere with social awareness and impair interpersonal decision-making (Adolphs et al., 1996, 1998; Bechara et al., 1997). Citing single-neuron studies in primates that involve the superior temporal sulcus of the temporal lobe and the amygdala, Brothers (1989) reported that the animals were responsive to facial features, and possibly to facial expression, and she was able to track these phenomena anatomically. She argued that the amygdala imparts emotional tone to the analysis of data entering through the senses, through its connections to the sensory association cortex. In addition, she speculated that projections to brainstem areas that subserve autonomic and endocrine functions allow for a coordinated response to socially meaningful input. This mechanism, she suggested, has been honed through evolution. Her characterization of empathy focuses on its affective component and favors speech and facial expression, possibly involving somatic mimicry as means of implementation. The similarity to the ideas of Violet Paget is striking.

Grattan and Eslinger (1989) have taken issue with Brothers' emphasis on the affective aspect of empathy and pointed to the involvement of other areas of the brain (e.g., the prefrontal areas) when the cognitive aspects of the empathic sequence are considered as well. In considering the range of brain lesions associated with impaired empathy, Eslinger (1998) posited that the ability to mentally assume the roles and perspectives of others may be as important as the affective aspects of empathy, and that these require the type of flexible thinking associated with intact frontal lobe function; he distinguished between the types of lesions (dorsolateral frontal systems) that might impact primarily on the cognitive element and those (orbitofrontal) that might exert their major impact on emotional processing.

Others have also used the fact that certain disorders involve a deficiency in empathic capacities, and such deficiency constitutes a functional disadvantage, as an argument in favor of empathy as a sign of a healthy brain. Damasio (1994), although he did not discuss empathy per se, argued for the essential role that normal emotional responsiveness plays in guiding rational decision-making. He described patients with damage to the prefrontal lobes who lost their ability to experience emotional states, and consequently could not experience the feelings such states produce in a normally functioning individual. As a result of such damage, the sufferer became unable to respond adaptively to the environmental stimuli that were present and would evoke such response otherwise. Damasio's injured subjects were severely compromised in their ability to make planful and rational decisions as a result of such damage. What we can conclude from findings such as these is that events taking place in various brain sites shape the phenomenon that we know as empathy, and that a healthy and undamaged brain is capable of producing the necessary neural sequence while certain types of damage interrupt that sequence.

GENETIC PLASTICITY AND EMPATHY

The various psychotherapies all address the relationship between individuals and their environment. We have seen that empathy, by extracting the unique from the generic, allows such interventions to be tailored to the individual patient. With the more severe, chronic, and/or recurrent mental disorders, psychosocial interventions have an uncertain place. Generally, they are seen as secondary to somatic forms of treatment (Bennett, 1996). Genetic risk factors, which heretofore have concerned a small number of disorders, have been considered unmodifiable, that is, a genetic predisposition to develop an illness such as schizophrenia or bipolar disorder has been regarded as a fixed risk. As the role of genetic factors in bringing about or perpetuating mental disorders is discovered for an increasing number of conditions, the idea that biology is fate has tended to make psychosocial interventions of dubious or limited value in general. This attitude, which is based both on determinism and dualism, is called into question by new information about the dynamics of gene expression.

Kendler (1995) has written about the reciprocal relationship between environment and gene expression with regard to the development of psychiatric disorders. In a departure from traditional approaches, he made the point that genetic influences are likely to be overshadowed by environmental (largely familial) factors early in life but become progressively more important as the life cycle unfolds. Parenting, which has been assumed by dynamic psychiatry to be crucial to mental health, appears important by virtue of the unique features of individual parent–child relationships rather than some overall measure of adequacy of the home environment, an observation that supports individualized relationships early in life and may support corrective relationships that are *tailored to individual need* later. Reiss and colleagues (2000), in differentiating the impact of environment from that of genetics on developing adolescents, made the same point and also suggested that the impact of parenting on development declines with time. We will return to this point when we consider how learning takes place in psychotherapy.

New information about the variable expression of genetic vulnerability has reshaped genetic epidemiology. The progressive importance of genetic factors is not necessarily immutable. Kendler (1995) made the point that self-selection, the tendency to shape one's environment and bring it into alignment with one's genetic proclivities, may be responsible for the increasing risk as the life cycle unfolds, especially under the influence of certain types of stressors that may be hazardous for the individual in question. With the discovery that genes may turn on or off, our genetic makeup may be regarded as a risk factor instead of immutable fate. These developments offer the promise that tailored interventions, particularly those that operate in tandem with healing forces in the environment, may be capable of reprogramming the brain.

The work of Eric Kandel on gene regulation illustrates changes in thought about the biological basis of behavior. Kandel (1998) proposed a new intellectual basis for psychiatry that is founded on five principles: (1) all mental processes derive from brain activity; (2) genes and combinations of genes contribute to the pattern of connections and the function of brain cells; (3) gene expression is shaped by learning, which is a product of experience; (4) alterations in gene expression as a result of learning produce changes in brain architecture and function; and (5) psychotherapy exerts its healing effects through inducing new learning at a cellular level. These principles are based on new understanding of genes as exerting two types of functions: the first, which Kandel termed *template function*, is replicative, allowing the passage of genetic material from one generation to the next with a high degree of consistency: altered by mutations but not by life experience; the second, to which he referred as *transcriptional function*, allows cells to differentiate so that they may perform the tasks required of them: their phenotype. Since each body cell contains all the genetic material present in all the other cells, but only a small number are turned on (transcribed) in a given type of cell, this function is a regulated one.

But what are the regulatory agents? Kandel suggested that the environment can affect gene transcription. Since interpersonal interactions constitute one important feature of the environment, they may be regarded as one of the potential shapers of biological functions *not only at the beginning of life, but throughout it*. If this is the case, and there is evidence that supports such an assumption, biological change may be brought about through psychosocial means. Although psychotherapy is one such means, there is no reason to construe it as the only one or even the most important: a point to which we will return in chapters on psychosocial interventions that follow.

The plasticity of genetic function leads us away from a rigid determinism in our understanding of mental illness by linking the psychosocial and the biological aspects of our nature. As Kandel (1998) has asserted, the historical distinction between organic and functional mental disorders is outdated, since all disorders may be assumed to be organic in nature, though shaped by psychosocial factors. For those disorders with strong patterns of inheritance, the template function may be partly at fault for determining vulnerability, while the transcription function may account for timing of onset and course and provide opportunity for remediation. Some defects in gene expression, either related to a single gene or to genes acting in concert, may be reversible, while others may be modifiable—assumptions that fit well with clinical experience. To pursue this idea further, the architecture of the brain, itself, including the pattern of interconnectivity among neurons, may be a product of pathogenic processes, but such changes may be at least partially reversible through psychosocial interventions.

Robert Post and his colleagues at the National Institutes of Mental Health have expanded our understanding of gene transcription and its relationship to the course of mental disorder through the discovery that persons who suffer from major affective disorder share certain tendencies that have been observed in the natural history of seizure disorders, where the threshold for seizure activity may decline over time (Post *et al.*, 1986). Patients with recurrent episodes of affective illness may become sensitized over time both to the types of stressors commonly associated with such disorders and to the impact of episodes of illness themselves on the brain. Using kindling, the phenomenon observed with seizure patients, as a model, Post (1992) has suggested that episodes of illness leave behind memory traces that render the individual more susceptible to stressors, and that intracellular chemistry may be altered in ways that impact on gene transcription. This conception of recurrent affective disorder is a dynamic alternative to one that presumes discrete changes in neurochemistry at the point of illness that are then corrected by chemical means. Such a static view may ignore the mounting evidence that neuroendocrine abnormalities often persist during periods of presumed remission, making relapse or recurrence more likely; this may be the case in a variety of disorders that have been considered in the past to be subject to full remission. These findings may correlate with the well-recognized persistence of psychosocial deficits in function that frequently follow symptomatic recovery from a mental disorder.

The therapeutic implications of this work are considerable. First, the choice of clinical interventions should take into account the phase of an illness (Post, 1997); second, the need for environmentally based corrective influences may continue beyond acute recovery; and third, there may be common pathways affected by biological and psychosocial interventions. We will return to these three points in chapter seven, when we consider the relationship between recovery and healing as well as that between the phase of an illness and the appropriate clinical focus. We turn now to consider how brain architecture is involved in mental disorder and what the locus of healing influences, including empathy, may be.

FROM CIRCUITS TO BRAIN MAPS

In 1937, James Papez proposed a corticothalamic mechanism for the experiencing of emotion that later bore his name. The Papez circuit, which enumerated and characterized the various structures of what became known as the limbic system, was proposed as the anatomical substrate for emotion. As Papez described, "An attempt has been made to point out various anatomic structures and correlated physiologic symptoms which, taken as a whole, deal with the various phases of emotional dynamics, consciousness, and related functions" (1937, p. 111). Nautag and Feirtag have characterized the limbic system as "a determinant of the organism's attitude toward its environment" (as quoted in Brothers, 1989, p. 15). Although the concept of the limbic system is being replaced by more and more specific linkage of function to site, the idea that coordinated neurological activity involving various brain locations underlies complex emotional experience was a major contribution.

Neural circuits are subject to the strengthening effects of repeated patterns of stimulation, an observation that provides a biological basis for learning and memory and offers clues to the pathogenesis of both acute and chronic mental disorders. Using an animal model, the marine snail *Aplysia californica*, Kandel (1979) studied short-term learning. He was able to demonstrate altered transmission at a single neuron synapse, depressing it in response to an experimental design that produced habituation and enhancing it through one that created sensitization. In these experiments, the functional effectiveness of transmission was altered (by modulating calcium influx in the presynaptic terminal) and could then be restored by changing the nature of the experimental conditions. Based on these findings, Kandel suggested that one way that experience may act to alter brain chemistry is through effects on the strength of impulse transmission. This idea, which had been theorized by Darwin over a hundred years earlier, carries implications for treatment as well—for example, some (Reiser, 1984; Mohl, 1987) have suggested that psychotherapy may exert its mitigating effects by altering the strength of transmissions shaped by early life experiences. As Mohl indicated, the types of interventions that might accomplish this and where and how they might exert such effects remain a matter of speculation. The role of memory in mental disorder adds a new twist to the nature-versus-nurture debate on causation: nature provides the template, and nurture shapes it.

While studies of single neurons or neural circuits are suggestive of a biological basis for mental activity, one persisting problem lies in the complexity of mental phenomena. From quantum theory, we learn about *non-locality*, the potential for events at a distance from each other to occur simultaneously and without clear causal linkage (Zohar, 1990). Brain function presents the same problem in that diverse activation of brain sites apparently takes place in a coordinated fashion simultaneously. The phenomenon appears multicentric. Damasio has theorized that this apparent coordination is a "trick of timing" (1994, p. 95) in which diverse regions of the brain are activated and respond in synchrony, leading to an integrated mental experience, but that there is no single structure in the brain that brings together these diverse activities in a synthesizing fashion. The idea that neural circuits are involved—functional pathways that link diverse areas—has to be interpreted in this light. If pathways are involved, how are they organized? To what extent are there actual connections between neurons and what is the role of humoral substances? When is there coordination but no physical connection? The gestalt psychologists who preceded the behaviorists as a dominant force in psychology developed a model of thinking holistically about sensory experience: they spoke of configuration (gestalt), assuming that when we perceive we do so in wholes rather than in parts, a metaphor which now finds biological verification in the concept of neural grouping: coordination of neural activity taking place at diffuse sites, linked functionally but not necessarily structurally.

Several models have been proposed to account for neural groupings. First, there is the idea of brain maps. Gerald Edelman (1992) advanced a theory of group selection that presented a dynamic picture of brain mapping sensitive to experience as well as to genetic and evolutionary factors. He theorized that all conscious activity takes place in the brain according to three principles. The first, established genetically, is a general scheme of wiring which allows for variation according to natural selection, that is, neurons compete with each other for linkage: a form of neural Darwinism. Connections among neurons are then strengthened or weakened as a result of perceptions and experiences (neural plasticity), leading to functional circuits which shape memory and learning. These functional circuits then link with each other to produce an organized replica of the environment in the form of a dynamic memory. Sensory organs are thereby connected widely with internal maps that are linked with each other, as well as with sensory organs. Connections with the limbic system allow decision-making that incorporates sensation with values as well as with memory, allowing for coordinated, adaptive responses to the environment. Dalton and Forman (1994), in considering how Edelman's theory applies to the concept of attachment, suggest that attachment experiences are stored as maps, allowing matching between current and past experience regarding relationships.

The implications of brain mapping theories for empathy, though not specifically addressed, are apparent: the empathic sequence would involve maps that are recalled in response to the stimulus of an interpersonal exchange, bringing to bear all of the mental faculties previously described as part of the empathic sequence. As Dalton and Forman (1994) state, comparison of present with past involves efforts to reconfigure the present to bring it into alignment with the existing template. Although they do not mention empathy, they state that "this is central to several concepts, including transference, repetition compulsion, projective identification, and attachment, itself" (p. 137). One intriguing question that is raised by the idea of brain maps is whether they constitute the architectural substrate of the familiar psychological concept of internal representations.

EMPATHY AND THE BIOLOGY OF MEMORY

Cognitive science has offered alternatives to the type of mapping described by Edelman. One model is the computational one, which is associated with computers and artificial intelligence. This approach compares the brain to a computer, a mechanistic model that ignores the interpersonal sphere and has little to say about subjective meaning as a factor in shaping brain maps. Psychological theories such as those that posit internal representations, a central concept in object relations theory, generally lack a biological foundation, but Kandel (1983) has suggested one at a cellular level. Using the sea snail *Aplysia*, he developed an animal model for understanding the genesis and perpetuation of two types of acquired anxiety states: anticipatory and chronic anxiety. Both states, according to Kandel, are associated in humans with internal representations of environmental events that allow for adaptive action. Postulating that something analogous may occur in lower life forms, Kandel conditioned the snail to withdraw in response to two types of aversive conditioning: classical conditioning leading to a behavioral state resembling anticipatory anxiety, and long-term sensitization, leading to a state reminiscent of chronic anxiety. He then assessed the consequences at a cellular level and found defensive arousal was facilitated through strengthened connections made by sensory synapses on interneurons and motor neurons. Intracellular adenosine monophosphate was found to increase, leading to increased release of neurotransmitters. Further study indicated that this enhancement was related to intracellular alterations in protein behavior and ultimately to changes in cellular morphology. Kandel speculated that these intracellular changes brought on by learning are manifestations of altered genetic function within the cell.

These animal experiments provide a model that links learning and cellular biology and moves us further toward an understanding of mental phenomena at the molecular level. Moving in the other direction, extrapolations to disorders in more complex creatures are also becoming possible. One key to this progress is the work that has been done on clarifying how we remember. It is now known that important distinctions exist between *conscious* or *explicit memory*, which pertains to factual knowledge and recollection of events, and *unconscious* or *implicit memory*, which involves certain types of habitual motor behavior. The former depends on the hippocampus, and persons with lesions affecting this structure lack the ability to retain information about events or facts while being able to learn and perform activities dependent on perceptual and motor skills. The locus of unconscious memory is unknown. The unconscious nature of implicit memory should not be confused with Freud's use of the term, which was based on his theory of the instincts, on conflict and repression, but it may have much in common with Jung's broader version.

Kandel's work with invertebrates and a variety of other animal studies suggest learning and memory operate in various life forms to promote adaptation to the environment and to support evolutionary fitness. The role of memory in the pathogenesis of mental disorder and the reversibility of maladaptive learning provides another important link between the psyche and the soma. In an earlier chapter, we considered that emotional memory is a reservoir drawn on by the empathic psychotherapist. Stanislavski, whose methods have influenced generations of actors, developed exercises to evoke and strengthen the capacity for emotional recall. But what is emotional memory and how does it relate to memory in general?

LeDoux (1993) suggested that the limbic system concept may have outlived its utility and should be replaced by more precise models that describe the circuits associated with specific types of emotional experience. He subdivided implicit or unconscious memory and called attention to a subsystem he called the "emotional memory system," which depends primarily on the amygdala. LeDoux proposed that affectively laden experience leads to storage in the hippocampus and the amygdala, and retrieval requires coordinated activity of the two. Although this would ordinarily lead to conscious recollection, LeDoux also considered that the amygdala may be associated with unconscious affective content as well. His research with rodents tracked the inculcation of fear responses through behavioral conditioning and indicated plasticity in glutamate-mediated synapses from the thalamus to the amygdala. This work supports the hypothesis that certain types of emotional memory may be activated without hippocampal participation, and be outside of conscious recall.

The concept of implicit memory carries profound implications for psychotherapy, reminiscent of and perhaps equal in magnitude to the original discovery of the unconscious. Post (1992), for example, has suggested that the locus of disordered memory traces associated with a mental illness may change over time, and the optimal intervention may vary as a result. Thus, while psychodynamic therapies may be useful in addressing early stages of affective disorders, where explicit memory systems alone may be involved, cognitive and behavioral therapies may be more effective if multiple recurrences have placed the illness on "automatic." The important question is whether or not we can access and affect the locus of a disorder and, if so, how best to do it. Post contrasted limbic with striatal systems, the latter involving habit (a later consequence in the natural history of a disorder), but it is also possible that encoded memory traces do not follow his suggested pathway from explicit to implicit but bypass explicit memory entirely. When this is the case, attempts to retrieve pathogenic memories may prove fruitless at any phase of a disorder, and treatment strategies based on such approaches are likely to fail. The idea that treatment interventions should be tailored to phases and particular characteristics of an illness is a significant departure from the usual state of affairs in mental health treatment, where such specificity is a rarity, and argues for eclecticism.

Amini et al. (1996) proposed a related learning-based approach to psychotherapy that targets implicit memory through the power of a healing relationship, but is based on attachment theory. He postulated that the sequence by

Picasso, *Mother and Child* (1901).

which we respond to socially important and affect-laden events in the environment begins with perception which then leads to limbic activity. Related memories, attitudes, and values are then retrieved, so that an appropriate behavioral response may take place. We experience this emotionally, which he considered a subjective phenomenon. But affects are more than subjective states; they must also serve functions that benefit the organism (a teleological perspective based on Darwinian thinking and consistent with Damasio's position, which was noted above). What is the benefit? According to Amini, the benefits accrue from being able to accurately read communicative signals from others in the social environment. Drawing on infant studies that demonstrate early responsiveness to nonverbal communication with the mother, the antecedents of attachment, Amini proposed that the quality and nature of these experiences is internalized gradually, thereby shaping both the structure and function of parts of the brain involved in the response to social stimuli. The implications for treatment follow from the pathogenetic theory.

Citing recent departures in attachment theory from Bowlby's original assumptions, Amini *et al.* (1996) proposed that the maintenance of a state of neurophysiological homeostasis is dependent not only on good early experiences, but on continuing input from attachment figures throughout life. This theoretical construct, which supports Kohut's convictions about the continuing need for narcissistic reinforcement, similarly posits that the need will vary depending on the quality of early life experience and the degree of vulnerability (in the case of attachment variables, to separation and loss) that is encoded in memory as a result. Experience not only shapes and limits the individual's capacity for self-regulation, but also influences his/her social interactions because of the tendency to bring current experience into alignment with patterns imprinted in implicit (unconscious) memory. Because this type of memory is assumed to be operative early in life, while explicit memory is not, its impact may be largely shaped by developmental experience, and because it connects with structures that are not associated with recall, affective processing may take place entirely outside of consciousness. This is consistent with the work of both LeDoux and Post.

The idea of implicit memory, therefore, provides a way of understanding the mechanism by which a person with early attachment trauma might unconsciously repeat the trauma through maladaptive responses to current real or prospective attachment figures. Psychotherapy, it is proposed, is a form of biological intervention in such circumstances since it provides a functional attachment relationship that aims to reestablish homeostatic regulation. This approach to treatment appears to place demands on the psychotherapist to be a corrective figure, a proposal that is consistent with the thinking of Alexander, Rogers, or the later Kohut, and very much in the tradition of contemporary self-psychology and the various interpersonal psychotherapies. Insight, per se, which is dependent on the recall of explicit memory, is deemphasized in favor of corrective experience, which represents new learning.

The model of therapy recommended by Amini requires the type of personal commitment, affective availability, and sensitivity to context that is the essence of active as opposed to passive empathy. One problem with Amini's suggested treatment model is that it appears to underestimate the corrective potential of an environment that is always in flux and therefore appears to represent a form of environmental determinism: you are what you have been shaped to be, and in the absence of an extensive corrective experience, will continue to be. As Reiss (2000) and others have suggested (Bennett, 1983, 1984, 1989; Budman & Gurman, 1988; Cummings & Sayama, 1995), this position may underestimate the potential for healing outside a two-person treatment relationship while overestimating the tendency to repeat old traumas despite changing life circumstances. We will have a great deal to say about this "all-or-none" approach to healing in the chapters that follow.

Schwartz (1987) explored the role of empathy in reversing neurobiological deficits caused by developmental insults that have become encoded in memory, writing from a traditional psychoanalytic perspective and directing attention to conscious rather than unconscious memory. His thinking was based on the primacy of affective experience. He regarded affects as the prime motivators of human behavior and saw affect as a type of internal sensation generated in the limbic system. When experienced, affect generates motor behavior, including facial expression, which Schwartz saw as the key to empathic awareness and exchange. Drawing on the concept of signal affect, Schwartz presented a model of relearning through psychotherapy in which the patient readjusts his/her responsiveness to affective signals and learns to interpret them in a more adaptive and realistic fashion. Greenberg and Paivio (1997), in the experiential tradition of Rogers, made the same point. Motoric responses to affect are inbred (genetically), and are mediated through the extrapyramidal system, but they can be controlled, suggesting that for Schwartz explicit memory houses the programmed response pattern. Citing the same type of neural plasticity referred to by others, Schwartz posited that disorders of affect are conditioned by life experience, leading to efforts on the part of the patient to avoid discomfort by controlling "the neural substrates of attention, cognition, memory, behavior, and affect generation itself" (p. 485). Such distortions may be perceived by a therapist empathically, which becomes the key to initiating a corrective intervention. Schwartz saw the preferred interventions as those of orthodox psychoanalysis, because this theory, which places emphasis on explicit rather than implicit memory, favors the use of interpretation. It is interesting to note that Schwartz's recommendations also neglect the wide variety of environmental shaping influences that may exercise a similar corrective function, and either complement treatment or promote healing without it.

CONSCIOUSNESS: IS IT OVERRATED?

Empathy, which in the analytic tradition involves intersubjective communication between the unconscious of the therapist and the unconscious of the patient, may be a key to understanding what Kandel has termed "the neural basis for a set of unconscious mental processes" (Kandel, 1998, p. 468). The theme of consciousness, which is introduced when we ponder the relative influence of conscious versus unconscious pathogenic memory on the development and treatment of mental disorder, remains problematic in that it resists definition. In our earlier review of the history of empathy, we considered that intersubjective exchanges were the essence of the psychoanalyst's art, and the concept of the dynamic unconscious a central tenet of their theories of treatment. In this chapter we have considered the phenomenon of unconscious memory, which presents a far different rationale for treatment and challenges our strategies for accessing pathogenic material of which the patient may be unaware. How important is consciousness in the work that we do and what is its relationship to empathy?

In discussing the neurobiological basis of consciousness, Young and Pigott (1999) characterized alertness, awareness, and memory, which are aspects of consciousness, but not consciousness, itself. They made the interesting suggestion that consciousness is bound to the information elements in explicit memory and is recovered along with the memory. This would suggest that consciousness is an intermittent phenomenon, which appears to ignore the distinction between consciousness, itself, and its contents. The question that this raises is whether there is something more to consciousness than its contents. Damasio (1999) suggested that there was. He viewed consciousness hierarchically, with core consciousness emerging through the repeated experience of knowing. While that experience leads to the development of a core self, it is only through the use of reason, language, and well-developed explicit memory that human beings achieve extended consciousness, through which they are enabled "to reach the very peak of their mental abilities" (p. 230). Among the capacities made possible by extended consciousness is empathy. For Damasio, empathy proceeds through awareness, observation, inference. Its target is the consciousness of another, but this is knowable only through its "public manifestations" (p. 83) and never directly.

In our present state of knowledge, we have no positive way of tracking the body of information that does not reach conscious awareness or knowing how to access it. I have suggested that empathy may be a bridge between psyche and soma. Now I would like to suggest that empathy may also be a bridge between conscious and unconscious memory. Of course, this does not sound new or remarkable, since psychoanalysts have been talking about attunement with the patient's unconscious for a hundred years. But the new biology presents us with something quite different from Freud's unconscious, to be understood and used in a different way: procedural memory. A clinical example may illustrate what I mean.

❖   ❖   ❖

Mary V was an unmarried 36-year-old woman who had been a competitive skier until a career-ending injury forced her to retire. She had no college education and could not decide on how she would support herself. She was unmarried, rather a loner. Depression had slowed her convalescence, and the prospect of chronic pain demoralized her. She was referred for consultation to discuss the career impasse and to determine whether antidepressant medication was indicated. When seen, she was surprisingly cheerful without evidence of clinical depression. She was resistant to exploring her problems and angry at having been referred. Having recently learned that the patient of a colleague had suicided under similar circumstances, I was suspicious of her mood and puzzled that she had bothered to come to the appointment at all. Surely, there must have been a motive to come, operative at least until her arrival. As she sat in her chair, I noted a subtle rocking movement, so that she would lean a bit toward me and then backward, moving her trunk only slightly. She held her hands in her lap while doing this. Although her eyes were directed at me for the most part, she glanced over my shoulder from time to time and it was at these times that the rocking took place. I guessed that she might be looking at the picture of my infant granddaughter, which was on the bookcase behind me. Rather than ask her, however, I decided to act on a "hunch." I asked if she had considered child care as a line of work. To my surprise, she began to cry. At that point, our conversation became possible.

The patient in this case had communicated to me through her body movements something about which she had no conscious awareness. Perhaps because my new granddaughter was so close to consciousness for me much of the time, I readily associated to the picture, thinking her rocking might be a sign of need on her part to be held as a baby. Since we lacked an alliance, there was no way to explore this hypothesis at that point; rather, I made an overture that remained within the bounds of her reason for coming to see me: her problem in taking the next steps with regard to changing her line of work. I learned that the patient had been the oldest of six and had literally raised her siblings, a source of pride to her. She had "forgotten" how able she was at such work, perhaps because of her frustration at not yet managing to have her own children. In this case, empathic awareness led to a recovery of memory, but, in a deeper sense, it was not insight that was important, but her "recollection" of an important part of her personal repertoire that was there to be drawn on. Shortly thereafter, she began work in a day care center.

The Danish physicist Tor Norretranders, in his book *The User Illusion* (1998), has provided us with yet another perspective on the conscious mind. Norretranders compared implicit memory with subliminal perception, stating that the content of the former was at one point conscious while the latter never were. By "consciousness," Norretranders meant self-awareness, which he suggested was a relatively new phenomenon in human life, something which was also suggested by Julian Jaynes in *The Origin of Consciousness in the Breakdown of the Bicameral Mind* (1977). Norretranders (1998) suggested that consciousness may be overinvested, that is, that we may underestimate just how much of our behavior proceeds outside of conscious awareness. Antonio Damasio has made the same observation (1999, p. 228). Moreover, because of the limited capacity of consciousness to encompass the full extent of what we perceive, our conscious minds must select only a small percentage for our awareness. Norretranders (1998) estimated that the ratio is approximately one million to one! Consciousness acts as a gate or filter, and its *primary function* may be to reduce the large volume of incoming data (quantified as "bits," where a bit is defined as the smallest unit of information: the answer to a yes/no question) to a manageable level.

The filtering function is affected not only by limited capacity, but two other factors must be taken into account. First, that the second law of thermodynamics requires that some cost is incurred in the brain activity involved. Work must be done, energy expended. Erasure (of previous conscious content) must also occur. Time is required. Norretranders referred to experiments that have quantified the time involved: an interval of 0.5 seconds between perception and awareness. What happens during that time? He proposed the following challenge:

> [H]alf a second to play with. Half a second with the most powerful computer in the world (the brain), where we have to reduce eleven million bits of sensation to ten-fifty bits of consciousness—and erase the traces. Surely that is plenty of time. A brilliant theoretical challenge to the field that calls itself computational neuroscience. We have a thousand billion neurons and half a second, and the task is to reduce eleven million bits to sixteen bits so that the sixteen bits can be used as a map of the eleven million. (p. 242)

Not only does the conscious mind limit what we can focus on, but when we seek to communicate our thoughts to another we incur new limitations and must again edit in the course of putting our thoughts into words and articulating them. We have now reduced what we know, both consciously and unconsciously, to a much more limited and edited version. In considering how the richness of our available data can retain its flavor while being so dehydrated, Norretranders came up with an intriguing solution: *exformation.* This category includes all of the thoughts we had but chose not to convey. The argument is made that communications lacking the richness of context which lies behind our words will be barren, two dimensional. What gives information its value is all *that is not said but that is implicit.* This idea links the two participants in a dialogue to the extent that they share a common frame of reference. Our most basic frame of reference, that we are of the same species, is shared with all.

Norretrander's concept of *exformation* suggests another way of thinking about the basis and the importance of empathy as a mode of apperception or holistic grasp. He suggested that we, as social beings, have learned nonverbal means of communicating *exformation* and that we are attuned to send and receive the full array of *what we might have communicated* while in fact saying less. These theories have great relevance for psychotherapy in general and for empathy in particular. Though he does not use the term, I wonder if empathy can be considered the means by which *exformation* is exchanged. Consider, for example, the following description of the interpersonal transaction involved:

> A good communicator does not think only of himself; he also thinks about what the receiver has in his head. It is not enough for the explicitness of the information to refer to some information in the sender's head if that information does not somehow lead to the correct associations by the receiver.

And

> The idea of transmitting information is to cause a state of mind to arise in the receiver's head that is related to the state of mind of the sender by way of the exformation referred to in the information transmitted. The idea of sending information is that the mind of the receiver must contain some inner information related to the exformation the sender has in his head. The information transferred must elicit certain associations in the receiver. (p. 93)

What Norretranders suggested underscores the power of the unarticulated portion of any communication to affect the listener, which depends on the reciprocity of the effort made by each party in a dialogue. In earlier chapters, we considered the various means by which the content of one mind might be grasped by another. As we have considered the biological purpose, value, and nature of empathic communications in this chapter, we have incorporated the role of the listener into our concept of the healing environment. It is important to remember, as we prepare to move into the final portion of this book, where the function of clinicians will be explored in some detail, that the human environment operates at multiple levels to exert its palliative effects. Norretranders reminds us that a communication that is limited to the exchange of information will always fall short of sharing the essence of the sender's message, not because that essence was once present and has been repressed, but because of the limits of verbal exchange, itself. Much of what we wish most to share with another human being is the mental content that vivifies the words spoken: content that may be beyond or completely independent of recall, but knowable empathically.

CONCLUSIONS

The march of science has created both new problems and new opportunities for those who diagnose and treat the mentally ill. On the one hand, familiar trends toward materialism threaten to either reduce mind to chemical reactions taking place in the brain or to perpetuate parallel ways of thinking about mind and body by adherents who don't talk to each other. I have suggested that, not only does new knowledge about the brain allow better understanding of what we mean by mental activity, but that bridges can be built between brain and mind that do not require abandoning the important discoveries that have been made about each. I have suggested that empathy is a phenomenon that may be used in this manner.

In considering how a more holistic frame of reference may contribute to our understanding of mental function, embracing both health and illness, I have focused on discoveries about the brain and how it works and, in particular, the advances from gross to microscopic fields of enquiry. The new biology provides a dynamic alternative to deterministic theories of health and illness. Genetic plasticity, the reciprocal relationship between brain structure and function and the environment, and the cellular and molecular events that shape health and illness all permit a new vision of the role of professional helper. We will have much to say about that role in the concluding chapters, as we consider how to reconcile the complexity of aberrant brain structure and function with the limited time available to meet the treatment needs of populations.

Through the advances in brain science, mysteries of the mind are beginning to unravel. Learning theory and its structural and functional correlates in the brain lead us to consider new ways of regarding mental disorder and carry the potential to tailor our treatment to the phase of a disease process, its specific content and effects, and the potential of the sufferer for recovery and healing. The idea that our conscious selves represent but a small component of our mental activities is not new; that it can be accounted for somatically, is. The concept of habit memory opens the path to understanding a variety of common observations about unconscious processes; the idea that our conscious mind selects, filters, and erases—functioning as a kind of internal file manager—points to the importance of the mental content that is discarded: what Norretranders called exformation. Most fascinating are the suggestions from Kandel, Amini, Kendler, and others that we are shaped at a structural level by our experience and that plasticity may be exploited therapeutically. Empathy, as a biopsychosocial phenomenon, may help us to know so that we may come to understand. We will come back to this idea in the following chapter, when we consider how an informed biopsychosocial model of psychotherapy utilizes empathic communication as a way of enhancing focus and tailoring treatment.

How is empathy related to the new sciences? Contemporary science is expanding both outward, with new and startling discoveries about the universe, and inward, with equally remarkable insights about the smallest units of matter and energy. When we consider the new physics, it is striking to note that we find a level of spontaneity, unpredictability, ambiguity, and mystery that is reminiscent of where we began several chapters ago: with the atomistic theories of the ancients and the impact on individual minds of universal forces. The major tenets of quantum theory and the ideas of Heraclitus about a world in constant flux, where wholes emerge from competing parts, are eerily analogous.

We also learn from quantum theory that the activities of the observer and the method of observation shape the findings (Zohar, 1990). A similar shaping occurs with psychotherapy when the therapist uses his or her self actively as an instrument of appraisal and intervention. The nature of the relationship configures the field of enquiry and introduces bias into the process of problem appraisal: subjectivity is a fact of treatment life. If not understood and compensated for, it may subvert the effort to heal; empathy assists us in evaluating the subjective realities and taking them into account as we plan and conduct treatment.

A second consideration has to do with the need to balance diagnosis with the personal dimension of illness. Eisenberg (1986) warned that our diagnostic categories fail to take individual variations into sufficient account, especially with regard to the way that illness is experienced. The type of attunement that we have associated with listening is essential to extracting the unique from the general, the personal from the categorical. We will consider at some length how the therapist may do this.

Third, and perhaps most important, chaos theory teaches us that there will always be variations, and even small ones undermine our ability to predict. As psychotherapists, we function on the edge of chaos, in the sense of being present in the patient's life at a point of destabilization. Such a point offers opportunities for creative resolution of the life impasses that bring our patients to our attention, provided that we resist the temptation to bring premature closure in the form of oversimplified remedies. Nietzsche, who ushered in this discussion, said the following about chaos:

> One must still have chaos on oneself to be able to give birth to a dancing star.

Said less poetically, the ability to sustain an inductive posture as well as a high degree of tolerance for ambiguity favors both good science and good therapy. As Margulies (1989) argued, the essence of the empathic posture is in the therapist's sustained sense of wonder and receptivity to the unexpected. Our theories serve us best when we regard them as provisional: every hypothesis a stepping stone, useful only until we have a better one.

REFERENCES

Adolphs, R., Damasio, H., Tranel, D., & Damasio, A. R. (1996). Cortical systems for the recognition of emotion in facial expressions. *Journal of Neuroscience, 16*(23), 7678–7687.

Adolphs, R., Tranel, D., & Damasio, A. R. (1998). The human amygdala in social judgment. *Nature, 393*(6684), 470–474.

American Psychiatric Association (1980). *Diagnostic and statistical manual of mental disorders* (3rd ed.). Washington, DC: Author.

American Psychiatric Association (1987). *Diagnostic and statistical manual of mental disorders* (3rd ed., rev.). Washington, DC: Author.

American Psychiatric Association (1994). *Diagnostic and statistical manual of mental disorders* (4th ed.). Washington, DC: Author.

Amini, F., Lewis, T., Lannon, R., Louie, A., Baumbacher, G., McGuinness, T., & Schiff, E. Z. (1996). Affect, attachment, memory: Contributions toward psychobiologic integration. *Psychiatry, 59,* 213–239.

Bechara, A., Damasio, H., Tranel, D., & Damasio, A. R. (1997). Deciding advantageously before knowing the advantageous strategy. *Science, 275*(5304), 1293–1295.

Bennett, M. J. (1983). Focal psychotherapy—terminable and interminable. *American Journal of Psychotherapy, 37,* 365–375.

Bennett, M. J. (1984). Brief psychotherapy and adult development. *Psychotherapy, 21*(2), 171–177.

Bennett, M. J. (1989). The catalytic function in psychotherapy. *Psychiatry, 52,* 351–364.

Bennett, M. J. (1996). Is psychotherapy ever medically necessary? *Psychiatric Services, 47,* 966–970.

Brothers, L. (1989). A biological perspective on empathy. *American Journal of Psychiatry, 146*(1), 10–19.

Budman, S. H., & Gurman, A. S. (1988). *Theory and practice of brief therapy.* New York: Guilford Press.

Carek, D. J. (1987). The efficacy of empathy in diagnosis and therapy. *The Pharos, 50*(1), 25–29.

Cummings, N., & Sayama, M. (1995). *Focused psychotherapy: A casebook of brief, intermittent psychotherapy throughout the life cycle.* New York: Bruner/Mazel.

Dalton, R., & Forman, M. A. (1994). Mind, brain and psychiatry. *Harvard Review of Psychiatry,* 2(3), 133–141.

Damasio, A. (1994). *Descartes' error.* New York: G. P. Putnam's Sons.

Damasio, A. (1999). *The feeling of what happens.* New York: Harcourt Brace.

Edelman, G. (1992). *Bright air, brilliant fire.* New York: Basic Books.

Eisenberg, L. (1986). Mindlessness and brainlessness in psychiatry. *British Journal of Psychiatry,* 148, 497–508.

Eslinger, P. J. (1998). Neurological and neuropsychological bases of empathy. *European Neurology,* 39, 193–199.

Gierer, A. (1998). Networks of gene regulation, neural development and the evolution of general capabilities, such as human empathy. *Zeitschrift für Naturforschung,* 53(7–8), 716–722.

Grattan, L. M., & Eslinger, P. J. (1989). Letter to the editor. *American Journal of Psychiatry,* 146(11), 521–522.

Greenberg, L. S., & Paivio, S. C. (1997). *Working with emotions in psychotherapy.* New York: Guilford Press.

Jaynes, J. (1977). *The origin of consciousness in the breakdown of the bicameral mind.* Boston: Houghton Mifflin.

Kaplan, H. I., Sadock, B. J., & Grebb, J. A. (Eds.) (1994). *Synopsis of psychiatry* (7th ed.). Baltimore: Williams & Wilkins.

Kandell, E. R. (1979). Psychotherapy and the single synapse. *New England Journal of Medicine,* 301(19), 1028–1037.

Kandell, E. R. (1983). From metapsychology to molecular biology: Explorations into the nature of anxiety. *American Journal of Psychiatry,* 140(10), 1277–1293.

Kandell, E. R. (1998). A new intellectual framework for psychiatry. *American Journal of Psychiatry,* 155(4), 457–469.

Kendler, K. (1995). Genetic epidemiology in psychiatry. *Archives of General Psychiatry,* 52, 895–899.

LeDoux, J. E. (1993). Emotional memory systems in the brain. *Behavioural Brain Research,* 58, 69–79.

Margulies, A. (1989). *The empathic imagination.* New York: W. W. Norton & Company.

Mohl, P. (1987). Should psychotherapy be considered a biological treatment? *Psychosomatics,* 28(6), 320–326.

Nietzsche, F. (1995). *Human, all too human: A book for free spirits.* Stanford: Stanford University Press. (Original work published 1878.)

Norretranders, T. (1998). *The user illusion.* New York: Penguin Putnam.

Papez, J. W. (1937). A proposed mechanism of emotion. *Archives of Neurology and Psychiatry,* 38(4), 725–743.

Post, R. M. (1992). Transduction of psychosocial stress into the neurobiology of affective disorder. *American Journal of Psychiatry,* 149(8), 999–1010.

Post, R. M. (1997). Molecular biology of behavior: Targets for therapeutics. *Archives of General Psychiatry,* 54, 607–608.

Post, R. M., Rubinow, D. R., & Ballenger, J. C. (1986). Conditioning and sensitization in the longitudinal course of affective illness. *British Journal of Psychiatry,* 149, 191–201.

Reiser, M. F. (1984). *Mind, brain, body.* New York: Basic Books.

Reiss, D., Neiderhiser, J. M., Hetherington, E. M., & Plomin, R. (2000). *The relationship code.* Cambridge: Harvard University Press.

Schwartz, A. (1987). Drives, affects, behavior—and learning: Approaches to a psychobiology of emotion and to an integration of psychoanalytic and neurobiologic thought. *Journal of the American Psychoanalytic Association, 35*(2), 467–506.

Singer, M. T. (1974). Presidential Address. Engagement–involvement: A central phenomenon in psychophysiological research. *Journal of the American Psychosomatic Association, 36*(1), 1–17.

Stern, D. (1985). *The interpersonal world of the infant.* New York: Basic Books.

Stone, M. H. (1997). *Healing the mind.* New York: W. W. Norton & Company.

Young, G. B., & Pigott. S. S. (1999). Neurobiologic basis of consciousness. *Archives of Neurology, 56,* 153–157.

Zohar, D. (1990). *The quantum self.* London: Bloomsbury Publications.

CHAPTER 7

Treaters and Healers

Which of us has known his brother?
Which of us has looked into his father's heart?
Which of us has not remained forever prison-pent?
Which of us is not forever a stranger and alone?

Thomas Wolfe

The highest spiritual training of a physician has not yet been reached
when he knows and has practical experience in the best and newest
methods and understands how to make those rapid deductions from effects to causes for which diagnosticians are famed: he must in addition
possess an eloquence that adapts itself to every individual and addresses
itself to the heart.

Friederich Nietzsche

*O*ur journey thus far has led us to a picture of mental disorder inscribed
in brain circuitry and amenable to corrective influences that heal only
with the grandest expenditure of time and effort. Given the ubiquity of
mental disorder in our population (Kessler *et al.*, 1994; Regier *et al.*, 1993) and
the extent of unmet need, such thinking would represent a step backward. It
would incline us toward the type of pessimism we find, oddly enough, in a
book about love.

In *A General Theory of Love* (2000), Thomas Lewis and his colleagues Fari Amini and Richard Lannon argued eloquently that the problems psychiatrists treat are caused by neural patterns established early in life through faulty parenting and that are correctable only through prolonged contact with a psychotherapist of good breeding: one whose own development did not leave a residue of relationship problems (a position reminiscent of the early psychoanalysts' rosy assumptions about the health of the analyzed psychoanalyst). The mechanism of healing, these authors claimed, is resonance with the patient's limbic system followed by stabilization of that system through the power of relationship, and then correction through a process they termed, "limbic revision." In a successful outcome, "a patient doesn't become generically healthier; he becomes more like the therapist" (p. 186). This is a dangerous misconstrual. The paradigm is derived from Paul MacLean's theory of a tripartite brain, which Lewis and his colleagues dubbed reptilian (brainstem), limbic (Broca's "limbic lobe"), and neocortical. The sequence of treatment depends on the premise that these areas operate more or less independent of each other, which, as we have seen in the previous chapter, is questionable. One implication of the presumed triune brain is that treatment strategies aimed at the cortex will fail, since the source of aberrant relationships is in neural patterns located in the limbic system, and therefore beyond the recall of explicit memory. The extreme point of view advanced by these authors, if used as a basis to allocate psychotherapy resources to a population in need of them, would limit the availability of qualified treatment services considerably while turning out a small number of healed persons who resembled their psychotherapists. Is such thinking a necessary consequence of accepting the premise that mental disorder is associated with structural problems in the brain? I will argue in the remainder of this book that it is not.

As we have seen in the previous chapter, the reciprocal relationship between brain infrastructure and experience is a dynamic one: it is not unchanging. In the light of evidence that experience alters both function and structure in the brain, Mohl (1987) has raised the question of whether psychotherapy should be considered a biological form of treatment. Michael Balint, who spoke of "the drug, doctor" (Balint, 1957, p. 5), had a similar perspective in mind, though, writing in the 1950s, he may have been using the term less literally. If we believe, along with Lewis, Mohl, and Balint, that doctors (or psychotherapists) target the neurons when they access the mind, then questions arise as to how the prescription for "doctor" ought to be written. How should the drug be used? How often? In what dosage? And for what duration of time? Can we differentiate among the various types of doctor-drugs that might be used and find a rational basis for our selection? Is there a generic form, or must it all be brand name? Also, if there are many who need such drugs and the supply is limited, how can we make the resources go farthest?

Magritte, *The Therapist* (1937).

Such questions underlie the thrust of the remainder of this book. In the not-so-distant past, psychotherapy was the primary mode of treating mental disorders; chemical agents, if used at all, were adjunctive: they contained the symptoms while "real" healing took place. Today, the situation has been reversed, and it is psychotherapy that is considered adjunctive while real healing is promoted by altering chemistry at the synapse (Bennett, 1996). Both positions represent dualistic thinking and therefore may be seen as anachronistic. How, in a holistic frame of reference, should the drug "doctor" be best used?

The idea that the brain is shaped by early life experience is indisputable; that the shaping, however, is immutable in the absence of a relationship with a therapist is not a justifiable bias. We have seen, in the previous chapter, that the brain is a dynamic organ, responsive to a variety of environmental, biological, and genetic influences, all of which continue to operate throughout the life cycle of the individual. David Reiss and his colleagues (2000), in an elegant summation of their twelve-year project to determine the respective importance of genetic and environmental factors in the course of adolescent development, have written of the diminishing effects of adverse parenting over time, as their subjects matured, adapted, and engaged in alternative forms of relating with the many others who entered their lives. Because gene transduction continues, in balance with the constantly changing environment, neither genes nor bad parenting will inevitably fix behavioral patterns. These findings argue against both biological and environmental determinism, and raise consideration of how people grow and change over the course of their lives under the influence of what life brings (Viederman, 1986). Only one of the things that life may bring is a psychotherapist.

The treatment required by a patient who suffers from a mental disorder is not purely a product of its etiology. Reiss *et al.* (2000) have pointed to three sets of factors that determine severity and treatability: the etiological ones such as risks (e.g., unempathic parenting), the lack of mitigating or protective influences, and the immediate precipitants of a disorder; the perpetuating ones (such as jailing a misbehaving teen); and those associated with treatment itself, such as the patient's willingness to participate in treatment, the nature of the treatment, and the personal characteristics of the treater (pp. 39–40). I have referred elsewhere to the first two of these, respectively, as *pathogenic* and *pathostatic*, and elaborated the third to take into account factors that may promote healing but are not treatment per se: corrective influences that exist within the environment of the sufferer, which I have termed *patholytic* (Bennett, 1997). This framework establishes treatment as but one possible patholytic influence and, in some situations, not the most important. It also provides a rich set of alternatives to two-person psychotherapy, which has historically been most directed toward reversing presumed causes and either underestimated or neglected the other two sets of variables.

In the following chapters, we will consider the psychotherapist to be an effective and powerful change agent if used in proper dosage, at the proper times, and primarily in support of the patient's own thrust toward health. The working assumption is that *treatment*, as provided by a psychotherapist, is but one step in the process of *healing*; this step, sometimes but not always the first one taken by the patient, is directed both toward promoting recovery and mobilizing the resources in the patient's own environment that will catalyze the process of healing. In the discussion that follows, we will be particularly interested in the role of empathy when psychotherapy is used parsimoniously.

The distinction between treatment and healing is an important one. By treatment I mean those activities performed within the formal health care system, and to some degree by practitioners who operate at the border of that system (the so-called *complementary* therapies), which are designed primarily to mitigate the barriers to healing and allow it to proceed, but are not capable, in and of themselves, of producing healing. Most commonly, illness constitutes the first barrier and therefore becomes the first target of the treater. The distinction made between treatment and healing is not a polar one, since the two may overlap. Some treaters, but not all, are healers; some healers, but not all, are treaters. Rachel Remen has characterized healing as "the leading forth of wholeness in people" (Moyers, 1993, p. 344). Healing, therefore, goes considerably beyond recovery from illness and must be differentiated from the common notion of cure. In distinguishing healing from curing, Remen underscored the spiritual nature of the former. This distinction carries the counterintuitive implication that some people who die from a disease die healed. The following case is an example.

Clarissa O was a 60-year-old school administrator who presented with severe anxiety following an episode of angina pectoris. After being seen and evaluated in the emergency room, Ms. O was thoroughly evaluated by her primary care physician, who was also a highly qualified cardiologist. Despite reassurance that all her tests of cardiac function were normal, Ms. O persisted in her certainty that she was about to die of a myocardial infarction. In her evaluation, she indicated that her anginal episode had followed an argument with her mother, with whom she lived, over her decision to take a new job in another city. This was Ms. O's first episode of chest pain, but she had a strong family history of heart disease: both her father and two paternal uncles had died at an early age of infarctions. Ms. O had no previous psychiatric history. She had lived with her family for most of her adult life, leaving only to attend college and briefly during a marriage in her late twenties that had ended in divorce. Her decision to "leave home" had led to recurrent arguments and left her feeling guilty that she was abandoning her mother. Mother, though in good health at the age of 82, had become increasingly demanding of her time, and Ms. O felt as though she were being "strangled." The metaphor was not lost on either Ms. O or her evaluator, and psychotherapy began with a focus on how she might learn to breathe in a healthy manner again.

Over the course of the next two months, the patient made excellent progress. She was able to deal effectively with her conflicted wish to leave home and provide alternative arrangements for her mother's care that involved help from her two younger siblings, and for the first time in many years began to feel hope for a better phase of life. She accepted the new job, found a place to live, and sold her condominium. Her symptoms disappeared and her anxiety and certitude of imminent death remitted. In good spirits, she terminated her psychotherapy and prepared to move. Two days prior to her move, she died suddenly of a myocardial infarction.

When her psychotherapist, shocked and saddened by her death, attended her funeral, he was greeted warmly by Ms. O's family. Her brother thanked him for helping Ms. O die a peaceful and happy person.

Although treaters may contribute to healing, for example, by facilitating recovery—I have suggested elsewhere that *catalyzing* may be a more apt term (Bennett, 1989)—most healing takes place outside the formal health care setting, enabled by the preparatory work that goes on in that setting. For Ms. O, her healing required that she take the steps she was taking at her death. An important aspect of the sequence implied is the handoff: guidance provided by a treater who helps the patient to identify or develop healing resources in his or her own environment. A transition is required. The anxiety that such a shift of the healing locus produces in some patients leads them to attempt to perpetuate a treatment relationship well beyond the bounds of necessary care. In some instances, this takes the form of wishing the therapist to become a permanent part of the patient's life structure, for example, fantasies of a personal relationship with the psychotherapist in order to retain the unique and seemingly irreplaceable bond that has been experienced. One patient, whose life had been characterized by a series of unsuccessful romances, and whose early history had involved a psychotic and abusive father and a passive mother who failed to protect her from his cruelties, expressed her apprehension thus: "What if there aren't any men out there like you?" The narcissistic gratification a psychotherapist may receive from such a communication often tempts him or her to *be for the patient* what the patient needs. There is no appropriate end-point to this choice. In the case of the patient referred to, the termination work took this statement as its point of departure, examining with the patient what the particular features of the relationship were that she found most important and what she could do to look for it in her life outside the office. Not surprisingly, she identified his willingness to listen to her. This particular patient, a professional philosopher and writer, had spent a great deal of time in therapy revising her personal narrative. What she failed to realize was that she had a much more coherent story to tell the next listener. She found one and, two years later, made what appeared to be a solid marriage; her healing continued in that context.

Empathy is no less important in treatment than it is in any other phase of the healing process. When treaters have too narrow a view of their role in the patient's life, they may limit their interventions to the disease and therefore may fail to guide the patient properly into healing aftercare. The impact of such myopia is destructive not only for the patient but for the treater as well. Rachel Remen (1996), in her evocative and personal account of her life as a "wounded healer," pointed to the importance of human qualities to the well-being of the practitioner. In an exercise that involved hands-on healing, a woman described as an "intimidating surgeon" found herself engaged empathically through touch with a colleague who was in pain because of a divorce. When he wept, she was "touched" as well. Remen described her reaction:

> Jane was close to tears herself. In a halting voice she began to talk about all that she felt she had lost through her medical training— her softness, her gentleness, her warmth. About how there was no approval for these things in the masculine world of medicine and so in an effort to succeed as a physician she had cut them off. (pp. 240–241)

In what way can treatment address structural alterations of the brain? There are many routes to the brain, but only one effective route to the mind: the interhuman. Psychotherapy is founded on the interhuman interaction; to treat with psychotherapy is to approach the brain through the mind. Whether or not such treatment includes biological agents, as we have seen in the preceding chapter, it has a biological impact. The psychotherapist becomes, for a time, a representative of the environment and a catalyst for necessary change. She or he operates at a point of destabilization in the patient's life, but the transcendent aim is not always to stabilize; insofar as destabilization is necessary to change, a therapist may seek to promote it as a means of opening up the prospect of stabilization at a higher level of function. In Greenberg and Paivio's model of "emotionally focused-therapy," for example, which is based on the experiential model introduced by Carl Rogers, the objective of an intervention is to enhance the patient's level of self-acceptance while promoting more adaptive ways of managing emotion (Greenberg & Paivio, 1997). For these writers, as for Lewis and his colleagues, the targets of the intervention may lie outside the sphere of conscious awareness, within the brain centers that are responsible for emotion and its modulation. When this is the case, the experience of *being with* a validating person may set corrective forces in motion.

Greenberg and Paivio's (1997) concept of "schemes," which they defined as the meaning that the patient gives to the experience of a bodily state as well as the incentive toward action that such meaning generates, appears analogous to Lewis *et al.*'s (2000) term "attractors": preferred neural patterns that may be remodeled only through loving interactions. For these writers, behavioral inclinations that are beyond awareness, perhaps because they rely on brain centers that bypass consciousness, must be addressed through the power of a healing relationship, without which they are prone to repetition and therefore create interpersonal impasses. For Lewis and his colleagues, treatment is a lengthy process that is most likely to take place in a psychotherapist's office because there is a fixed and compelling nature to the patterns they describe. Greenberg and Paivio, in contrast, although depending like Lewis on empathic attunement to access the relevant brain activities, appear to envision a self-corrective capacity that may be evoked by acknowledging an emotional state. The patient, having been helped to tolerate the painful emotion, is able to shift attention from a habitual explanatory scheme, and allow previously inaccessible alternative schemes to emerge (Greenberg & Paivio, 1997, p. 82).

The idea that our patients carry within them the capacity to self-correct is important if we are to consider psychotherapy as a limited form of treatment that can be used to *mitigate barriers to* healing rather than as a dyadic milieu that is designed to *be the vehicle for* healing. As the previous chapter indicates, our brains continue to reshape throughout the life cycle, and there is evidence of persistent tendencies to improve adaptation. When it is used in the service of the brain's self-healing potential, psychotherapy is not unlike an antibiotic that works by interfering with the agent that is challenging the body's immune system, thereby creating an opportunity for the body's own healing capacities to restore homeostasis. The biological agents that we use in psychiatry may have a similar mode of action, in that they help to stabilize aberrant neurochemical activity and allow a restoration of function. It is only through our ability to rejoin the functional world—to work, to relate to others—that our healing potential can be fully exploited. It follows from this line of argument that this limited use of psychotherapy depends on the identification and mobilization of healing resources that may be drawn on to exploit the preparatory work of treatment. Sometimes such resources are overlooked or lost from conscious awareness, and it is the job of the psychotherapist to find them, as the following case example illustrates.

Amanda B was a 32-year-old marketing executive who presented for psychotherapy complaining of longstanding symptoms of mild depression that met criteria for the diagnosis of dysthymic disorder. Although treatment had been recommended to her and previously considered, she had elected to take the step after her younger sister had delivered her first child and, more specifically, when she found herself experiencing the fantasy of dropping her niece while holding her. Although she denied that the fantasy was important to her, preferring to focus instead on her persistent dysphoria, she acknowledged that babies made her angry and she was adamant in volunteering that she would never consider becoming a mother.

Taking her at her word, her psychotherapist attempted to delve into her depression. She traced it back to her earliest childhood, which she described as bleak. Her life began with a prolonged separation from her mother, who had fallen ill and been hospitalized shortly after her birth. Things did not improve much after her mother returned home. Her parents, who were Holocaust survivors, were both described as chronically depressed. They had owned a grocery store and had worked hard, spending most of their time in the store and having little time for their children. Neither parent, it seemed, had much interest in relating to the patient or her sister, and a series of nannies were hired for combined housekeeping and babysitting. As Ms. B told her story, she did so in a tedious monotone. An attractive and well-dressed young woman, she described a colorless life: few friends, little dating and sexual experience, few interests beyond her job. Like her parents, she had made work her life.

Over the next few months, the patient became progressively more depressed. She refused medication. Her depression had an empty, anaclitic nature to it, suggesting that she was reexperiencing with the therapist some earlier period of deep despair. She seemed unable to engage. Always a conservative dresser, she began to appear dressed perpetually in black, with no adornments. She was asked about this, but had no explanation. Because he sensed the patient slipping away from him, the therapist decided to seek to come closer. Psychotherapy was increased to twice weekly, at which point the patient became more animated. She expressed surprise that the psychotherapist had so much interest in her, since she had been afraid she was boring him, and she began to talk more easily of her feelings of lack of worth, despair, and loneliness. As the connection deepened, she found herself recalling one nanny in particular, Louise, by whom she had felt loved. This allowed her to begin to grieve. She was invited to bring a picture of this woman who had been fired by her mother for suspected theft, but with whom the patient had been secretly corresponding for the past twenty years. Louise, who was black, was now in Barbados. Ms. B planned and carried out a visit to her and returned looking and sounding quite different. She was amazed to find that Louise had a picture of her in her bedroom, alongside pictures of her own children. Her mood began to improve as she was able to recall happy experiences in her early childhood that were connected with Louise. Shortly thereafter, the frequency of sessions was decreased at the request of the patient and termination followed.

Ms. B had a job opportunity that involved a move to the Caribbean, where she took up residence. In occasional letters to her previous psychotherapist, she indicated that she had developed a love relationship with a male colleague and soon thereafter she married. Two years later, Ms. B wrote to indicate she had become a mother. Her second child arrived two years after that.

This patient's recollection of her nanny was preceded by her regression and heralded by her clothing herself exclusively in black. Her therapist empathically perceived that her blandness covered fears that he would lose interest in her and abandon her after having made himself important in her life. The increase in the frequency of their meetings conveyed the opposite, allowing her fears to emerge and be voiced. She was able to recall her earlier loss, but it was the activation of this motherly figure that proved the turning point in the treatment. Her own attitude toward mothering was never explored, but her move to the Caribbean suggested and her motherhood confirmed that the barriers to loving a child were gone. The role of the psychotherapist in this case, as in most, was catalytic; interpretation played no significant role.

A similar dynamic was observed in the case of Ms. P, described in chapter three, who was able to recall a loving relationship with her grandfather's mistress that she had "forgotten" for many years, when the husband who had rescued her from lifelong depression was in the final portion of his life and less available to her as a result of illness. As with Ms. B, Ms. P had resurrected this empathic figure at least in part as a consequence of an empathic relationship with her psychotherapist. These cases illustrate the overlapping relationship of treatment with healing, and the possibility of effecting basic change through activation of resources locked within the patient's neural circuitry or in some instances available within his or her current life context. Not only does such use of context capitalize on the healing potential inherent in each of us, but it allows a more limited use of a precious resource: the time of the psychotherapist. As we will see when we consider how psychotherapy may operate within the type of organized systems of care that are becoming more prevalent, the distinction made between treatment and healing has profound implications.

There is a tendency among some psychotherapists to keep patients in treatment until they heal. Sometimes, however, the patient fails to reveal the significant obstacles to healing until the prospect of termination challenges him or her to mobilize adaptive capacities. James Mann has made this point in his writing about time limited treatment (Mann, 1973). In the following case, a brief course of psychotherapy failed to identify the barriers to healing until the patient had to face losing the therapist.

Elaine Y was a 24-year-old flutist who was referred for psychotherapy by her internist because of symptoms of anxiety and depression that followed an assault by a suitor who would not accept "no" as an answer to his amorous advances. Although she was not physically injured, she was traumatized and found herself unable to play at her usual level of performance. She met criteria for an acute stress disorder, which responded to a short course of benzodiazepines. Because her recovery was incomplete, however, a course of brief psychotherapy was begun to help her mitigate her sense of shame and guilt and express and accept the underlying anger. Eight sessions were scheduled.

The patient presented the following history. She had lost her loving and admired father suddenly at age 12, following which she had experienced repeated verbal and physical abuse at the hands of her mother, much of it around pressure to succeed in her music. Her current teacher, a demanding musician who expected full dedication from his students, had unwittingly reinforced her resultant ambivalence about her instrument, and she acknowledged to her therapist that she was actively contemplating giving up music.

Over the next month, the patient worked to clarify, express, and come to terms with her feelings about her mother. Nothing further was said about her music. Despite anxiety, which was treated with lorazepam, Ms. Y was able to assert herself with her mother and say "no" to her for the first time. Her longstanding fantasy that her mother's power would overwhelm her if she asserted independence proved illusory, and she experienced great relief. As she grew stronger, she decided to discontinue her medication and was referred to a stress reduction program, which further reduced her symptoms. Although still somewhat symptomatic, Ms. Y was willing to keep to the scheduled date of termination. At the next to last session, she announced that she had decided to leave the country for a year and study music abroad, separating at the same time from the dependent relationship she had developed with her caring and attentive boyfriend, as well as her teacher, her therapist, and her mother. Although the plan sounded somewhat impulsive, she was determined and her therapist supported her decision. She left on schedule.

Letters from Ms. Y over the next year reported that she was doing well and had no remaining symptoms. She reported that she felt strong and in control of her life. On her return, she and her boyfriend were seen together once and then he was seen alone for a single session. It was clear that their relationship had been renegotiated and was a strong one that was interdependent and mutual. They later married and had two children while she went on to develop her musical career.

Ms. Y's ability to shed her dependent relationships and strike out on her own was crucial to her development. Her inability to commit earlier to her boyfriend reflected ambivalence about their relationship as well as her musical career, and it was not until she was able to separate and manage herself independently that she could commit herself to both freely. In fact, she had to say "no" not only to her mother but to all the others who had expectations of her. Her boyfriend was a devoted and loving person who appeared similar to her father in that his acceptance of her was unequivocal. Father, however, remained buried for this patient until she was able to emerge from Mother's dominant shadow. Although her boyfriend was placing no immediate demands on her, she experienced such demands as implicit. She was therefore not able to say "yes" to him until she had established "self-ownership," which required leaving all ties behind (though she burned no bridges). It was only in the context of her feelings about letting go of the therapy that these issues of separation–individuation arose for resolution. In retrospect, Ms. Y's presenting problem involved a failed attempt to say "no," which proved to be the focus of her treatment.

THE EMPATHIC TREATER

If treatment is understood to be but one step on the pathway from illness to health, then the treater plays an important role in guiding the process. The first aim in restoring health is to treat the illness: to promote recovery. The second, no less important, is to identify the barriers to healing that remain. Like a cartographer who seeks to map an unknown landscape, the treater is an explorer, open to discovery, curious at the prospects of unimagined terrain, but pressed to commit to a provisional plan. The attitude with which the task is approached is central to its ultimate success.

In the cases described in this chapter, all of which involved a treatment experience that opened the door to healing, empathic knowing, and its derivative, empathic understanding, guided the clinical sequence. The empathic process as it applies to the role of the treater is furthered by certain attitudes. Perhaps the most basic of these is curiosity. Faith Fitzgerald, in her lament about the forces that undermine curiosity in contemporary medical training, said the following: "I believe it is curiosity that converts strangers (the objects of analysis) into people we can empathize with." She went on to say, "Both the science and the art of medicine are advanced by curiosity" (Fitzgerald, 1999, p. 24). The treater who is curious resists the temptation toward linear thinking and premature closure, and manages to sustain an inductive posture in the face of complex and contradictory data. But curiosity alone, which implies neutrality, may not be enough. For Carl Rogers, empathy was an attitude, one feature of the therapist's commitment to the treatment process. Kohut, when he spoke of vicarious introspection, was referring to a sustained attitude; for Margulies, the attitude was one of wonderment.

In an earlier chapter, we considered the attitude of the empathic healer as one of caring and compassion, and I suggested that the therapist's subjective responses furnish the fuel that drives the empathic process. The important point to be made here is that the attitude of the treater must be one that draws him or her into the world of the patient and conveys to the patient that there is genuine interest as well as receptivity. Only when this is the case is the patient likely to respond by venturing forward, toward the interpersonal boundary, and offering access to the inner world that is the source of both pain and healing potential. The manner in which this may be accomplished expeditiously will be the topic concerning us in the next two chapters.

CONCLUSIONS

As the health care system evolves, treatment methodology must be reconciled with models of health and illness that are consonant with scientific progress. Brain science points to the importance of chemical processes and structural configurations that may underlie the behaviors and affects associated with mental disorders, in a dynamic and constantly changing milieu in balance with the external environment. At an elementary level, genes turn on and off in response to a variety of intrinsic and extrinsic forces, impacting on health, state of mind, and adaptive capacities. Beneath or outside of conscious awareness, memory shapes complex patterns of behavior while the conscious mind seeks to contain, manage, modulate, and adapt. All of this takes place against the backdrop of a constantly changing social environment that supports, threatens, and challenges body and mind to maintain health, survive and thrive.

Somewhere within this dynamic complex the impairment of mental health that we term illness originates, exerts influence, and either waxes or wanes depending on circumstances. One of the circumstances is the presence of caregivers within the environment of the sufferer: but one more influence among many, seeking to exert a palliative influence. The challenge is to identify what has gone awry and set the forces in motion that will restore or improve health.

Despite burgeoning knowledge of how the brain operates, we still know very little. The basic unit of our treatment armamentarium remains the same: a person who offers him or herself as a helper to someone in pain. We offer treatment. But our patients do not seek treatment; they seek healing, a process that occurs largely from within. Our job is to determine what impedes healing and begin the process of addressing it. We do this largely by implementing strategies that will interrupt the destructive course of an illness, and free up the forces of healing.

The start of a healing process is appraisal, which involves some tools and certain techniques, but depends largely on skillful and attentive listening. If appraisal is to make sense to the patient, it must take as its point of departure the subjective experience of being ill and not the disease that underlies it. That fact means that helpers must be prepared to rapidly orient to the patient's reason for being there and attune to his or her perspective on what is wrong and what must be done about it. The fact that we expect our health care resources to go farther is of little concern to the person who suffers. A plan of treatment that begins with the patient's subjective sense of distress must also accommodate to the presumed sources of that pain: the pathological processes that reflect impaired brain health. The biology of unhappiness, apprehension, frustrated longings, and grief, and the activation of neural pathways repeatedly trod are the entities we must confront if we are to help our patients. To do so expeditiously serves their interests best. Our methods are often inelegant. Perhaps the mapping of the human genome will add new corrective or even preventive methods to our arsenal, but that remains in the future. For now, we rely on the human interaction that is the foundation of our science as well as our art.

The distinction made in this chapter between treaters and healers directs our attention to two sets of questions. First, how does the psychotherapist determine which piece of work is most essential to the recovery of the patient? Second, and related to the first question, how is the assessment process enhanced by the use of empathy? A separate question involves the healing process: how and where does it take place, and what is the relationship of the treater to it?

In chapter one, I offered a series of predictions about the health care system we are most likely to see in the coming years. To this point, we have introduced and weighed the circumstances in which the practice of psychotherapy is likely to take place, but we have not yet addressed how the clinician may manage these. We turn our attention in the final chapters to this important matter. How can the psychotherapist maintain an attitude of compassion, employ the requisite listening skills, utilize the power of empathic communication to understand and to promote healing, and yet provide limited interventions to the many who require them? I have suggested that the distinction between treatment and healing is vital to meeting the challenge. In the following two chapters, I will elaborate on the distinction made between treatment and healing by looking more closely at the way in which psychotherapy may be used as part of an organized system of care without losing the personal dimension that makes it an interhuman experience. The importance of a clear focus, which is derived from the patient's reasons for being there at the time, the development of a rationale for the treatment intervention, and the establishment of clear objectives for treatment are the hallmarks of such practice. Whether we frame our interventions in psychodynamic, cognitive, experiential, existential, behavioral, or cognitive/behavioral terms, or in any of the other terms used by practitioners to account for their activities and explain their behavior with their patients, the core activity remains engagement with another human being. The key to such engagement, regardless of treatment strategy, is the use of empathy.

REFERENCES

Balint, M. (1957). *The doctor, his patient and the illness.* New York: International Universities Press.

Bennett, M. J. (1989). The catalytic function in psychotherapy. *Psychiatry, 52*(3), 351–365.

Bennett, M. J. (1996). Is psychotherapy ever medically necessary? *Psychiatric Services, 47*(9), 966–970.

Bennett, M. J. (1997). Focal psychotherapy. In L. I. Sederer & A. J. Rothschild (Eds.), *Acute care psychiatry: Diagnosis and treatment.* (pp. 355–373). Baltimore: Williams & Wilkins.

Fitzgerald, F. (1999). Curiosity. *Annals of Internal Medicine, 130,* 70–72.

Greenberg, L. S., & Paivio, S. C. (1997). *Working with emotions in psychotherapy.* New York: Guilford.

Kessler, R. C., McGonagle, K. A., Zhao, S., Nelson, C. B., Hughes, M., Eshleman, S., Wittchen, H. A., and Kendler, K. S. (1994). Lifetime and 12-month prevalence of DSM-III-R psychiatric disorders in the United States: Results from the National Comorbidity Survey. *Archives of General Psychiatry, 51*(1), 8–19.

Lewis, T., Amini, F., & Lannon, R. (2000). *A general theory of love.* New York: Random House.

Mann, J. (1973). *Time-limited psychotherapy.* Cambridge: Harvard University Press.

Mohl, P. (1987). Should psychotherapy be considered a biological treatment? *Psychosomatics, 28*(6), 320–326.

Moyers, B. (1993). *Healing the mind.* New York: Doubleday.

Regier, D. A., Narrow, W. E., Rae, D. S., Manderscheid, R. W., Locke, B. Z., and Goodwin, F. K. (1993). The de facto U.S. mental and addictive disorders service system: Epidemiologic catchment area prospective 1-year prevalence rates of disorders and services. *Archives of General Psychiatry, 50*(2), 85–94.

Reiss, D., Niederhiser, J. M., Hetherington, E. M., & Plomin, R. (2000). *The relationship code*. Cambridge: Harvard University Press.

Remen, R. (1996). *Kitchen table wisdom*. New York: Riverhead Books.

Viederman, M. (1986). Personality change through life experience, I: A model. *Psychiatry, 49*, 204–217.

CHAPTER 8

Empathy and the Focus
of Psychotherapy

The good listener is strong, the talker weak.
The talker talking drains away his strength.
It fills the listener to hear a speaker speak.
He is a calm always of the greater length,
Receiving the turbulence into his own peace
Where it sinks like a slow stone, and rests,
And the rings round where it plunged widen and cease.

John Holmes

*S*tanley K was a 58-year-old man with a history of paranoid schizophrenia dating back to his twenties. He had come to the city by bus, for reasons unknown, and when he presented at the hospital was psychotic and infested with lice. Though college educated and highly intelligent, he had never held a job, but had survived on the streets, drifting from city to city, occasionally to other countries as well, accepting only acute care when forced to. With the exception of one sustained two-year period of treatment some years earlier, he had repeatedly rejected psychiatric aftercare and discontinued medication when discharged. On this occasion, he achieved a state of partial remission after court-mandated treatment with olanzapine and was discharged to the day hospital, spending his nights in a supervised inn run by the hospital. He made progress: got a haircut, bought some new clothes, began to relate to staff, appeared to enjoy his therapy meetings. He related particularly well to his resident psychiatrist, Dr. A, and was able after several weeks to be transferred to a lower-intensity day program (a clubhouse) several blocks from the hospital. After undergoing a brief orientation and tour of the facility, he was noted to be sitting by himself, rocking, refusing to talk to anyone, visibly hallucinating. Dr. A was summoned and informed that her patient had regressed and probably required rehospitalization. Dr. A elected to visit Mr. K at the facility and, after observing him, asked him to join her in repeating the tour. During the repeated orientation, Mr. K was largely silent but attentive while Dr. A asked many questions. Following the tour, Mr. K appeared more comfortable and was allowed to remain. He was observed shortly afterward having lunch with another patient, an unusual event for him. He continued his recovery over the following weeks without incident.

In her supervision, Dr. A was asked about her response to Mr. K's regression. Why had she identified the tour as the likely cause? She responded that she had asked herself, "What must it be like to be psychotic and in a new environment?" She elected to repeat the tour because it had preceded her patient's regression and, when she approached it by trying to ask the questions that her patient might want answered (drawing on her knowledge of what was important to him), he appeared to reintegrate. When I asked her whether she had any basis for understanding what it would be like to be psychotic, she said that she did not, but "could imagine it." I pressed her further. She then recalled how Mr. K had had a similar problem on his transfer to the day hospital, suggesting that transitions in general appeared to be a problem. I pressed further. Did she know from her own experience how a person might become disorganized in a new environment? She thought for a while, and then shared with me that she had moved frequently as a child and had often found herself in new schools, feeling alien and "as though in a foreign country." Unlike her patient, however, she had benefited from the fact that her mother, a teacher, prepared her for such transitions, and there was a great deal of attention paid in the family to rehearsal and preparation. She was somewhat surprised to make the connection with her mother, and volunteered that she had not thought about it before.

Therapeutic empathy requires a careful and attentive listener; furthermore, it is not only the patient who must be perceived, but voices that emanate from within the therapist as well. Dr. A's assumption about her patient's state of mind was based on two considerations: the timing of his behavioral regression and her previous observations of his response to transition. She did not mention, nor was there any evidence of, affective resonance, but she sensed in his psychotic behavior that he no longer was in control of his mind. As Basch (1983) has suggested, empathy does not depend on a linear process that begins with affective resonance and proceeds to ideational content, but is helical or cyclical in nature. As was the case in this example, entry into the cycle may begin with an idea or interpretation. Dr. A generated a hypothesis that she chose to test behaviorally, by repeating the tour, this time lending her own executive function to her patient in an effort to provide him with the type of information she believed most important to him. For example, she knew that Mr. K had artistic interests and some skills and made a point of asking in detail about opportunities to paint. She drew on her imagination, but may also have dipped into her personal reservoir of experience without being consciously aware of it, possibly drawing as well on her identification with her teacher mother. It might be speculated that her unconscious was attuned to Mr. K's, but the matter can be stated in another way as well: perhaps Dr. A's procedural (implicit) memory was leading her. She knew how and what to teach. No declarative (explicit) memory of childhood experiences was evoked, though she was able to recollect relevant data with some prodding. It is likely that reflection might have evoked these memories had there been a reason for such reflection at the time. As is often the case with empathic knowing, Dr. A knew more than she understood; understanding came later.

PSYCHOTHERAPY IN ORGANIZED SYSTEMS OF CARE

In addition to illustrating the therapeutic use of empathy, this case illustrates features of treatment that reflect the contemporary environment of practice. As a patient insured through federal and state sources of funding, Mr. K's treatment was in essence prepaid; in theory, treatment had to be allocated across an eligible population in order to meet the demands of a limited budget. His ability to be treated at progressively less intensive and costly levels of care reflected one consideration in planning his treatment. Documentation of his need for services included an ongoing assessment of his progress measured against not only his diagnosis, but his baseline state as well. Although Dr. A was not constrained in her choice of treatment, her selection of methods might have been questioned by a reviewer had it not correlated with his documented needs—for example, referral of Mr. K to intensive psychotherapy, something that might have been considered as an appropriate treatment mode fifty years ago, would have raised eyebrows. His care was collaborative, involving caregivers other than his psychiatrist, who was charged with the responsibility to oversee and coordinate it. Because of his baseline state as well as his diagnosis, treatment was geared toward goals such as recovery, relapse prevention, and rehabilitation rather than cure.

At first blush, these features appear to reflect the fact that Mr. K was a patient with a major mental disorder who was being treated in the public rather than the private sector. This is misleading, however, since the boundary between public and private sector is fast disappearing, and since the core aspects of Mr. K's care system reflect neither chronicity nor public sector membership; they reflect, instead, population-based care. Along with the biological revolution, prospective payment, which assigns a budget to the anticipated needs of a defined population and therefore mandates selective allocation, has become the major shaper of treatment paradigms. As shown in Table 8.1, a shift in values has taken place with regard to the allocation and objectives of treatment interventions. In the emerging culture of practice, the patient's life context is considered central to the process of healing, and treatment is a collaborative enterprise that may involve various caregivers rather than an insular two-person relationship with a healer. The major changes in culture carry implications for contemporary paradigms of treatment:

TABLE 8.1   Changing Values and Changing Paradigms

Aspect of treatment	Traditional frame of reference	Emerging frame of reference
1. Service allocation	Prioritizes the individual patient	Prioritizes needs of a population
2. Treatment objective	Cure	Recovery
3. Relationship to context	Establishes a healing context	Utilizes the patient's own context
4. Function of therapist	Artisan-healer	Catalyst
5. Treatment milieu	Dyadic	Collaborative

In the present practice environment, where a population of clinicians is responsible for providing services to a population of eligible recipients, service allocation for any patient must take into account the current and prospective needs of all. For many patients, perhaps most, the notion of "cure" is an anachronism. As with Mr. K, many patients suffer from disorders that are not amenable to cure, and for which goals such as recovery, relapse prevention, and rehabilitation may be more appropriate. Historically, schizophrenia has always been viewed in this manner, as has bipolar disorder and a handful of other diagnoses. By contrast, many of the disorders that mental health professionals treat were understood in the recent past to be acute and resolvable through limited interventions. Psychotherapy, when used to treat a patient beyond the point of recovery from acute illness, was directed toward preventing recurrence: prevention, by addressing the patient's propensity to develop the disorder. For the most part, psychotherapists who offered extended forms of treatment were seeking to modify the character structure presumed to underlie symptoms with the rationale that continuing treatment would avert recurrence and lead to a fuller life for the patient. In an unmonitored, unmanaged environment, this promise was accepted on faith. With the shift from an unmanaged to a managed environment, the situation has changed considerably.

The nature of psychotherapy provided within such a "population-based" framework (Bennett, 1996, 1993a, 1993b) differs sharply from the old, dyadic model. First, many of the disorders that mental health professionals treat are now regarded as likely to be recurrent in nature. This is true for most types of depression, panic disorder, generalized anxiety disorder, and the major forms of eating disorder, to name a few. Second, various forms of brief or intermittent psychotherapy, used alone or in combination with medication, have demonstrated efficacy in promoting recovery and preventing relapse and recurrence from the most common disorders. Third, exploratory forms of psychotherapy are regarded by payers as costly alternatives lacking in convincing evidence of efficacy.

If more patients require services over longer periods of time, and if access to the underserved is to be improved within the cost constraints society demands, the way in which professional time is used becomes a matter of pressing concern. There are only four ways that a limited budget can be used to provide for the service needs of a population: much service to the many who need it (which becomes rapidly unaffordable); much service to only a select few (an unjust and unpopular solution which characterized the unmonitored old system); limited service to a few (the cheapest but most shortsighted approach, and also very poor public relations); or limited service to the many. The latter is the most ethical though probably the most difficult to implement because it requires the greatest change in behavior from the practitioner. As the managed care backlash suggests, fundamental changes in the culture of service delivery are strongly resisted and unpopular. Attempts to modify professional behavior are especially likely to be mismanaged and die a rapid death if costs are too tightly constrained, a common problem in today's capitated environment.

Despite such concerns, the democratization of mental health care in the face of budgetary constraints has markedly reshaped the clinical landscape and promoted cultural change. A rapidly proliferating variety of brief psychotherapies has emerged from research settings, offering evidence-based alternatives to the use of biological agents alone. What these methods have in common is their reliance on the patient's ability to continue the healing process outside and beyond the clinical intervention. Treatment planning, therefore, must take into account not only diagnosis and short-term prognosis, but creation of an optimal healing environment in support of longer range goals: one in which these goals are supported and reinforced by significant figures in the patient's own life setting.

If the patient's life context is pivotal to healing, then it is one of the factors that must be taken into account during the process of assessment and treatment planning. This consideration makes treatment a systems matter, reshaping the relationship with the therapist from an insular, dyadic one to one with many partners, present and prospective. Psychotherapists come to occupy an important but not necessarily central place in the sequence, where they function as catalysts and facilitators of healing rather than as healers per se. The empathic healer has therefore become a treater. This shift in professional aims amounts to a cultural revolution, but one which lacks an agreed-on conceptual basis; hence the widespread demoralization and chaos. One casualty of this evolutionary change is the empathic healer. If empathy is to retain its central role in the healing process, then its value as a *treatment variable* must be established. In addition, if the empathic healer is to be replaced by the *empathic treater*, then the site and nature of the healing process must be reconceptualized. These two questions will occupy us in this and the next chapter.

THE CONCEPT OF A FOCUS IN PSYCHOTHERAPY

If we return to Mr. K, we note that Dr. A's empathic understanding helped her to focus her psychotherapeutic intervention. Said differently, she had *a focus*. The idea that psychotherapy should have a focus, a defined and delimited piece of work to be done by its participants, is not new. Historically, however, the idea of a focus has been more associated with brief and intermittent forms of psychotherapy than with extended variants. Psychoanalysts, psychoanalytically oriented psychotherapists, existential and experiential therapists usually have little to say about focus, articulating their objectives in terms that are less specific and therefore less measurable. For this reason, strategies that fail to specify achievable aims within a limited time frame may be viewed by payers with suspicion: as supplements rather than complements to targeted treatment.

But what is a focus? The vignette involving Mr. K suggests that a focus can be defined relative to a stage of treatment and therefore the idea of a focus need not be limited to brief therapy. At the stage of treatment described in the clinical example, Mr. K was moving from one service site to another, and the intensity of services offered was being reduced; in common parlance, not only the *site of care* but also the *level of care* was changing. A greater degree of self-management by Mr. K would be necessary in the new setting. Among other demands, he would have to contain his persisting psychotic symptoms so that he might interact appropriately in a setting where the goal was rehabilitation rather than acute care. His continuing recovery from the most recent acute exacerbation of his chronic illness would depend on his ability to make the transition without a substantial regression. As his caregiver, Dr. A's treatment objective was to facilitate the transition. Recognizing that her patient was operating at the margin of his adaptive capacities and had encountered a barrier to the transition, she intervened with the explicit aim of *helping him to transcend the barrier*. This was her focus.

The situation faced by Dr. A and her patient portrays two common antecedents of a therapeutic focus: first, that persons are likely to become patients in circumstances that involve or are expected to involve transitions; and second, that a request for professional help occurs because barriers to such transitions are either present or anticipated. The request, in this case, was expressed nonverbally. This assumption, that patients seek help because of a failure in adaptive capacities relative to a demand for such adaptation, is familiar to those who provide acute care. Its applicability to nonacute care is not immediately obvious. In the era of descriptive psychiatry, it is often (erroneously) assumed that patients seek out therapists because they suffer from a disorder; the distinction made by Kleinman between a disease (or disorder) and an illness is important: patients seek help because they are ill. They suffer; a disease may or may not be present (Kleinman, 1980). As Kleinman stated the matter, "Illness includes secondary personal and social responses to a primary malfunctioning (disease) in the individual's physiological or psychological status (or both)" (p. 72). By this definition, Mr. K's disease (paranoid schizophrenia) and his illness (regression in the face of his inability to negotiate a difficult transition) overlapped. The focus, which was discerned empathically, was not the key to curing his disorder, only to helping him move on toward an improved state of health.

In an era of diminishing resources and expanding need for service, it is no surprise that labor-intensive methods of treatment such as psychotherapy are regarded by payers with skepticism. This unfortunate situation stems in large part from the lack of clarity about how psychotherapy ought to be optimally used: for which patients, and for what purposes, is it necessary? Additionally, there is a growing gap between treatment methodologies that can be tested according to prevailing standards for demonstrating efficacy and those that are more difficult to assess, especially the psychodynamic forms that are based on the healing power of relationship. As we have seen, rightly or wrongly, the importance of empathy is most associated with these types of "relationship" treatment. At its core, the skepticism about the use of psychotherapy that exists among payers relates to a presumed lack of specificity, standardization, and replicability; doubt, in other words, about its scientific worth. Ironically, a similar bias against psychodynamic therapies has developed within the psychiatric training community; hence, we are witnessing a generation of psychiatrists whose training in the latter is sparse or nonexistent. Similar trends are apparent in the other mental health professions as well. Clinical psychologists, for example, are considerably more likely to be trained in and employ cognitive and behavioral techniques than psychodynamically based methods. Lest we lose the humanizing value of dynamic psychotherapy in mental health care and in medicine in general, this situation must be addressed.

The distinctions that have been made between therapies for which an experimental basis of validity exists ("evidence-based treatments") and those for which such proof is either insufficient or lacking may be more apparent than real. As Frank (1974) noted some years earlier, generic factors are always at play, exerting their effects though they may not be central to the therapist's frame of reference. With regard to the brief methods now in vogue, two stand out for the degree of interest they have produced and for their common pairing with biological treatments: cognitive-behavioral treatment and interpersonal psychotherapy. Although neither of these places the type of emphasis on the relationship between the therapist and the patient that dynamic psychotherapy does, there is evidence that a positive working relationship contributes to their successful use. Castelnuovo-Tedesco has stated the matter generically: "If there is no relationship, there is no treatment" (Roback et al., 1999). The nature of the therapeutic alliance has been related to outcome when patients with depression are treated with cognitive therapy (Castonguay et al., 1996). In the National Institute of Mental Health Treatment of Depression Collaborative Research Program, which included four study conditions (interpersonal and cognitive-behavioral psychotherapy and active and placebo pharmacotherapy), the therapeutic alliance was found to have a significant effect on all (Krupnick et al., 1996). Burns and Nolen-Hoeksema, who also reported on the use of cognitive-behavioral therapy to treat depressed patients, specifically attributed the beneficial effects of the treatment relationship to therapeutic empathy (1992).

Psychodynamic theorists who fail to distinguish between the power of relationships and the power of specific techniques that employ such relationships may unwittingly contribute to payers' skepticism about psychotherapy in general. Robert Michels, in a presentation to the American Psychiatric Association, characterized the three core activities of the psychotherapist as talking, listening, and thinking, distinguishing these generic features from the specific strategies that may then be employed to treat the patient—for example, interpretation of conflict (Michels, 2000). Understanding the patient, therefore, though it may not be healing in and of itself, sets the stage for it. When considered in this manner, psychotherapy is inseparable from the art of the treater and also compatible with the science of whatever treatment method is used. Proceeding from this line of reasoning, it may be possible to consider a generic form of psychotherapy that is suited to population-based care: one that establishes a focal objective that then may be achieved through using one or more treatment procedures, psychological or somatic, that are tailored to the situation and to the person who is being treated.

There are good reasons to integrate the practice of psychotherapy with the biological treatments of persons with mental illness. First, the promise of biological psychiatry is far from being realized. Although medications and other somatic treatments are effective, significant problems are associated with their use and especially with reliance on them as the core of treatment. Glenmullen (2000) has summarized the problems associated with serotonin-enhancing drugs: partial rather than complete response, loss of responsiveness over time, potentially dangerous side effects and symptoms of withdrawal. Perhaps the best evidence that drugs have provided only partial success in treating mental illness is the fact that pharmaceutical firms continue to spew out new ones at an ever-accelerating pace. The message in this is clear: the magic bullet is yet to be found. A second point to consider is that reliance on somatic treatments neglects important aspects of mental illness and has proven inadequate to treat many of its associated functional impairments, those that limit the patient's ability to operate effectively within the social environment. Attention to the psychosocial domain remains the province of psychotherapy. It behooves us, therefore, to render psychotherapy compatible with the evolving science rather than allowing it to languish as an undervalued alternative. Finally, the humanistic ripple effect on medical practice, a consequence of the psychoanalytic movement during the first half of the last century, is more needed than ever to balance the march of scientific medicine and the increasingly technical nature of health care practice: to preserve the heart at the heart of medicine.

When psychotherapy is used as a component of an organized system of mental health care, by which I mean a care system that has established linkages among the various service resources a population might require to meet its mental health treatment needs, certain assumptions underlie its use. First, commitment to a single ideological framework or a single method of treatment is incompatible with the service orientation such a system ought to have. Eclecticism, by which I mean adaptation on the part of the caregiver to the patient's preferred means of learning, and use of the most efficient and effective clinical means to get the job done, is the preferable orientation. Second, psychotherapy should be used as a component of a plan of treatment that is designed to promote recovery from illness in the shortest time possible.

Psychotherapy used in such a fashion will have certain properties. First, it will have a specified focus; second, the focus will be derived from the patient's own goals; third, both the objective and subjective dimensions of illness will be taken into account in planning and carrying out an intervention; and fourth, treatment should identify and seek to maximize those elements of the patient's own life context that will further the healing process. In this chapter, we will consider the conceptual basis of this type of "focal psychotherapy" and, in the next, examples of its use. It should be clear to the reader that we are not describing a method, per se, but the use of a helping relationship to establish a focus, lay the groundwork for a treatment intervention, and set the stage for healing activities that will follow.

FOCUS AND COMPLEX DISORDERS

Perhaps the best place to begin our consideration of focal psychotherapy as a generic approach is with the subset of the population for which focal methods of treatment might be considered most questionable: the persistently or recur-rently ill. A legitimate criticism of managed behavioral health care has been its common failure to assume a longitudinal perspective on service need for those patients whose problems do not fall neatly into the category of acute illness, such as Mr. K. Since his care involved multiple helpers and overlapping systems over time, the focus could be expected to evolve with the status of his illness, reflecting the continuing biological and psychosocial barriers to his progress. Though his care was *continuing*, psychotherapy as part of that care was not likely to be *continuous*, that is, psychotherapy was likely to be important at certain times and for certain discrete purposes. Continuity would be an impor-tant dimension of his care, but that continuity was not necessarily vested in the person of a psychotherapist. A case manager, a group home counselor, or others selected because *they already are part of the patient's life context* might play such a role. The assumption is not only that such persons are part of the environment but that they are part of *the healing environment*. While it did not occur in the example provided, it was entirely conceivable that Mr. K would enter a state of remission (return to baseline) that would limit the formal health care role to support of rehabilitation and medical maintenance. In such a situation, continuity takes a different form, and relapse prevention becomes the focus. Severely ill patients such as Mr. K have been helped by community-based programs that carefully monitor clinical and psychosocial status and intervene preventively, thereby seeking to limit the need for the formal health care system. This form of aftercare, the Assertive Community Treatment (ACT) model (Santos, 1997; Test & Stein, 1976), in fact constitutes part of a healing environment, representing a sharp contrast with episodic care in which only acute illness is addressed, and the patient left to his or her own devices when an episode ends.

Episodic care for the chronically or recurrently ill patient, for example, care that provides only for biological stabilization, may unintentionally overlook the lingering psychosocial impairments associated with many mental disorders, and thus prove inadequate to patient need. Even worse, disengagement from the formal health care system without provision for ongoing needs may inadvertently add to the cycle of recurrence. Guiding principles such as *medical necessity* may limit interventions to the restoration of biological homeostasis and fail to take rehabilitative needs into account. The care of the chronically and recurrently ill need not be unfocused, but the focus should reflect the barriers being addressed at a particular point in the sequence of care. This principle guided Dr. A in her response to Mr. K's needs: the shift in locus called for a shift in focus.

The idea that treatment may be sequenced, and that a focus will vary with the stage of recovery, is supported by a number of theorists. Liberman (1988) has postulated four stages in the care of the chronically mentally ill, encompassing the domains of neuropathology, functional impairment, social role performance, and handicap. The types of interventions called for vary with the stage. The implications of Liberman's model are that a natural history is involved and interventions must be sequenced. Such interventions are targeted to the phase of illness as well as the nature of impairments caused by disordered brain function. Sequential care involving multiple helpers should be expected, and a series of transitions (rather than cure) would represent the markers of progress. The barriers to such transitions would be found in the biological, psychological, and social functions affected by the disease and the focus would vary accordingly.

Considering patients who are less severely ill than Mr. K, some have proposed a multistage model that shares some of the features presented above. Howard and his colleagues (1986a,b) have divided psychotherapy into three phases: remoralization, remediation, and rehabilitation. The first two of these involve stabilization of the acutely ill and return to function, goals often achievable in a relatively short time frame within the formal health care system, while the third may take many years and occurs primarily outside that system. Linehan (1993) has developed a sequential model for the treatment of patients

172 The Empathic Healer

diagnosed with borderline personality disorder, targeting the most severe impairments first. Herman (1992), writing about victims of abuse, posited three stages of healing: the establishment of a safe environment, remembrance of and mourning the trauma, and reconnection with others. She pointed out that this way of thinking is in the tradition of earlier sequential models proposed by Janet for hysteria, Curfield for combat-induced trauma, Brown and Fromm for post-traumatic stress disorder, and Putnam for multiple personality disorder (Herman, 1992, p. 156). In each of these examples, stabilization is followed by the processing of memories and then reestablishment of the patient's place in the broader social environment. The focus would clearly have to vary. Each model assumes the need to mitigate barriers to reintegration in a social context from which the individual has been distanced and each therefore involves a transition from formal to informal care contexts. A barrier can be defined both biologically and psychosocially. The boundary line between formal health care and a healing social context is often ill-defined and may be a matter of fierce disagreement among theorists, particularly those who consider it the role of the psychotherapist to *constitute* the healing milieu.

While there is no easily defined boundary between treatment and healing, the demarcation of phases in recovery and the restoration of a state of health implies a handoff; more properly, there is a sequence of handoffs, first within the formal health care system (among concurrent and sequential treaters) and then between that system and the informal healing context without. How should that handoff be accomplished? When? By whom? If the provinces of treaters and healers overlap, one objective of those who labor in the former is to ready the patient for the latter. This means considering, as one of the objectives of a treatment intervention, what will follow it: in ordinary clinical parlance, a discharge plan. While discharge planning is common in high-intensity treatment sites (e.g., a hospital), the concept is not commonly applied to outpatient treatment. If the prospect of a handoff is considered from the outset of a treatment intervention, the way must be paved throughout that intervention by identifying and facilitating changes that must take place in the patient, the healing milieu, or both. This is best accomplished through including discharge planning in the assessment process.

FINDING THE FOCUS: THE IMPORTANCE OF A FORMULATION

If a focus can be defined in operational terms as the specific work that must be done in psychotherapy in order to mitigate or transcend the barrier(s) to necessary change, then the most complete understanding of the nature of such barriers is required, both at the point of entry into treatment and continuingly as treatment proceeds. Such an understanding is suggested by the term *formulation*, a clinical hypothesis that embraces both the patient's disorder and his/her illness: the objective and subjective data that must be systematized in order to provide a rationale for treatment. In contrast to formal diagnosis, such as that provided by use of the DSM system, formulation addresses causation and implies what must be done. Dr. A's formulation of Mr. K's presenting state might have been phrased in the following way:

> Mr. K, who suffers from paranoid schizophrenia, is in a state of partial recovery from his most recent exacerbation of illness. While attempting to make the transition from a high to a lower service intensity, he has experienced an impasse that has caused him to regress to a more active psychotic state. Because of impaired social skills and continuing distortion of environmental cues, he is unable to adapt to a new setting where he is unsure of the rules, expectations, and risks. He needs an orientation to this setting that is calibrated to his ability to absorb and process new information and find the familiar in the new.

In the case of Mr. K, his disease interfered with his ability to make a necessary transition because of the meaning he attributed to the unsuccessful orientation: that it posed a threat to him. While we have methods to assess the *presence* of a disease, we can appreciate the *meaning* of the disease largely through the use of empathy. The writer, Susanna Kaysen, in her account of a two-year inpatient treatment at McLean Hospital in the late 1960s, illustrated the gap between her own perception of what was happening to her and the observations and assumptions of her caregivers, as represented in their progress notes. The clinicians in this account are characterized as objectifying, at times callously so, and often just plain wrong (Kaysen, 2000).

Appreciation of the patient's experience must occur not just once, but continuously through an episode of care lest we lose touch with the person who is ill and who, though retaining the same diagnosis, may change considerably. Thus, a formulation evolves. We should recall when we speak of disease that we are not discussing an absolute, but a relative state: a state of health, fully appreciated only with reference to the patient's premorbid baseline. The empathic process seeks to capture the patient's perspective on such a relative state and integrate that perspective into the treatment plan as a means of establishing objectives that are consistent with the patient's own goals. As treatment proceeds, and the patient's state of health is modified by it, empathy becomes one instrument by which the personal dimension of progress may be measured and monitored. The following case example illustrates the type of misunderstanding that may occur in the absence of empathic monitoring, when only objective measures of progress are considered:

> In the early 1970s I was hired to participate in a Public Health grant which involved teaching the principles of psychological medicine to medical house officers on the wards of a large metropolitan general hospital. One day, while accompanying the resident on morning rounds, I observed the following interaction, which took place at the bedside of a 55-year-old woman who was recovering from an episode of cholecystitis. We will call her Alice S:
>
> "Good morning, Mrs. S," said Dr. R, "You're looking fine today!" "Oh, Doctor, I feel awful." "But, Mrs. S ... (looking at her chart): your temperature is normal, you've been eating, have been out of bed ... [feeling her calves, percussing her chest, listening to her heart], ... you show no signs of complications." "But I feel very bad, Doctor, worse than before." "I see [looking at the chart again] that your lab values are in the normal range, you are doing very well!" Dr. R then prepared to move on to the next patient, but I inter-rupted: "Who, I asked, is likely to win this argument?" Dr. R stopped and reflected on my question. "What argument?"
>
> We returned to Mrs. S's bed and asked her what she meant by "feeling awful," she clarified her perspective. A highly conscien-tious and devoted mother and wife, she had left her family to fend for themselves while she was hospitalized. When she felt too sick to have a choice, she had been able to manage her guilt at leaving her post, but now that she was in fact feeling in better health, she was suffering a different type of discomfort: What was she doing lying around in a bed, being attended by others, watching tv when there was work to be done at home? Either the doctors weren't telling her what was really wrong with her or she should be home cleaning the house! Either way, she felt awful. When I told her I agreed that someone as healthy as she now was belonged at home and Dr. R offered to return to discuss a discharge date, she bright-ened and told us to attend to Mrs. L ..., in the next bed, who had been up all night, coughing.

A discrepancy between the patient's biological and psychological well-being is commonly missed by practitioners. In this case, the patient's gall bladder was recovering at a more rapid rate than its owner. Dr. R, who viewed his patient's progress from his perspective rather than her own, might have concluded either that Mrs. S was not yet fully recovered or that she was anxious about leaving the hospital; both of these assumptions (which might have been expressed as formulations) would have been in error. For a health care professional such as Dr. R, who understands pathogenesis, pathophysiology, and the like, disease is a known entity. Health is likely to be understood as the residual state of affairs when disease is overcome. For the patient it is likely to be the other way around: health is knowable through a feeling of vitality and a sense of well-being. For this particular patient, health meant the energy to maintain her home and take care of her family, a restful night of sleep, a good appetite, and so forth; for Mrs. S, it was disease that was the abstract concept. It might be said that *for her, disease means the absence of health, while for her doctor health means the absence of disease.* In her attempt to interpret the fact that she was being kept in the hospital (a place for sick people), she assumed she must still be sick and therefore ought to feel "awful" to justify being there. Recovery, therefore, required being sent home. In the absence of a formulation, Mrs. S was not being treated, her gallbladder was. It should be noted that she had her own (erroneous) formulation.

Since our patients present biological, psychological, and social barriers to recovery, the focus of our interventions must be based on an accurate understanding of each, and the ways in which they intersect. This is a practical means of understanding the concept of formulation. The caregiver must consider both the objective data and the meaning of that data to the patient. When the meaning is not clear, or when the patient cannot articulate it, inconsistencies between behavior and predicted behavior may occur, calling for initiatives from the therapist to stretch awareness imaginatively: in other words, to empathize. The following case example illustrates this use of empathy:

> Sandra M was a 22-year-old nursing student who sought therapy after sustaining an assault in which she narrowly escaped rape. She entered treatment one week after this event, the proximal cause being an argument with her fiance in which he suggested to her that she had been careless and may have "invited" the assault. She was bitterly disappointed in him and very angry. He, in turn, appeared to be responding to her sudden emotional unavailability which, along with hyperarousal, mild derealization, incomplete memory of the precipitating event, nightmares of being attacked and avoidance of exposure to the neighborhood in which the event had occurred (which had prevented her returning to work) met criteria for the diagnosis of an acute stress disorder. Her therapist's initial objective was to establish a safe place (the relationship) where Ms. M might begin to consider what had happened to her

and confront her anxiety. Treatment included the use of a ben-
zodiazepine and a course of cognitive psychotherapy but, after
several sessions, symptoms persisted. Because treatment appeared
at an impasse, her psychotherapist began to feel frustrated and
wondered about secondary gain. At this point, he noted that his
patient appeared defensive in her sessions, as though she might
suspect that he was critical of her. Recalling that her request for
help had followed her fiance's "blaming," Dr. V asked her whether
anyone in her past had ever blamed her for something bad that had
happened to her. She reddened, hesitated, and then shared an early
experience in which she had told her mother about being molested
by her maternal grandfather and her mother had become angry and
slapped her, calling her a liar. Following this session, the patient
became less defensive and treatment proceeded, based on a new
formulation that included her lingering sense of shame, the barrier
to her recovery. When she was able to share this information with
her fiance, he could understand her behavior as symptomatic of an
illness and not a personal rejection of him, allowing him to more
easily offer his support. His validation contrasted with her mother's
earlier behavior and helped in her recovery from both the acute
and the older trauma.

The idea of focus is deceptively simple in theory but quite complex in
practice, where it must be derived from an understanding of the impasse that
brings the patient to clinical attention. Although the focus of treatment is
related to diagnosis, this relationship is indirect. It is important to understand
that diagnosis as currently used in psychiatry is essentially a characterization
of *what is wrong*. Built on a foundation of observable and historical information
about symptoms and behavior, diagnosis says little about health. Beyond its
attention to any impairments of thinking, it says little about the patient's point
of view. It neglects context, apart from attention to pathogenic influences such
as stressors, and pays no attention to the resources and strengths the patient
brings. Since diagnosis either presumes or neglects the matter of causation, it
does not provide clues to what *this patient* may require at *this time*. Diagnosis,
in fact, says nothing about treatment, and therefore does not shed light on the
capacity of the patient to relate to a helper or his/her expectations from such
a person. It is these variables that are encompassed by the term *formulation*,
the bedrock on which the focus of treatment is established.

If the patient brings a narrative account of illness to the therapeutic encounter, it is the job of the therapist to construct a response that takes that narrative
as its point of departure; thus, formulation consists in a kind of *counternarra-*

tive, by which the patient's problems can be reframed as a clinical hypothesis that provides a basis and a rationale for treatment. This counternarrative, which is shared with the prospective patient during the negotiation that establishes the objectives of psychotherapy, is inherently paradoxical in that it provides both validation for the patient's dilemma (the patient feels heard and understood) while suggesting a way out. Additionally, the treater asks something of the patient: a commitment to work toward change while acknowledging that there are barriers to the changes called for. Those barriers will be the focus.

FOCUS AND BREVITY

Although the idea of a focus in psychotherapy has been considered by many, it is usually associated with theorists who advocate brevity. This is unfortunate. While *all brief psychotherapy is focused*, the converse of this statement, that *all focused psychotherapy is brief*, is not true. It might be said, however, that the key to keeping an intervention as brief as possible lies in deciding on the appropriate focus: one that takes into account the change(s) necessary, the forces that can be drawn on to bring it (them) about and the barriers to its (their) accomplishment. Not only is focus the most important variable in guiding an intervention toward its desired outcome, but it also becomes a means of gauging the effectiveness of the strategies of intervention that have been selected. Both focus and the formulation on which it is based are dynamic elements that evolve during an episode of care.

One common mistake that is made by clinicians is to equate focus with diagnosis or, even more broadly, with symptoms. As the term is used in this book, a higher order of specificity is meant: not only should *a focus* be developed, but *the focus* should be found; in other words, *for any episode of treatment there exists a focus that is appropriate*. It is the job of the evaluator to determine, jointly with the patient, what that focus ought to be. The closer the focus is to the patient's own ideas about what must be accomplished, the more likely it is that an alliance will develop. Some overlap or even disagreement is common, a situation that carries the potential for competing agendas.

Earlier in this book, we have considered the matter of divergent agendas based on differing worldviews, the tension that exists between the art and science of treatment, and the variety of contextual factors that impose on the participants in a psychotherapeutic endeavor. All of these factors are relevant to the matter of determining an appropriate focus. When the therapist is uncertain about focus, or selects a focus that reflects a clinical bias, resistance can be anticipated. The most common example of this is when the therapist makes the diagnosis the focus; in such a situation, where the disorder and not the patient is being treated, an alliance is unlikely. The common term "compliance," which some therapists see as desirable, may be all that can be expected in such a situation. It is ironic that the term "noncompliance" (which is bad) is usually contrasted with "compliance" (which is good) rather than with "alliance."

A common consequence of poorly focused treatment is run-on therapy: treatment that has no clear endpoint. While no psychotherapist would describe his/her work as *unfocused*, other terms might be used that indicate a lack of specificity, for example, the work might be characterized as *exploratory*, or *growth-promoting*. While these are worthwhile and beneficial aims, they are ambiguous in nature, difficult to track, and almost impossible to measure.

Much of dynamic psychotherapy is based on the primacy of insight in resolving conflict. Therapy that is *analytic* seeks to create mastery through understanding, such as that presumably achieved through rendering the unconscious conscious. By contrast, psychotherapy designed to bring about necessary change may be categorized as *catalytic*, insofar as the objective is change, itself, and the role of the psychotherapist facilitative rather than informative. In the current era, where third-party payment has emerged as the dominant force in shaping treatment methodology, it is fair to say that most psychotherapy practiced under third-party auspices is catalytic in nature. If psychotherapy is inextricably bound up with necessary change, then certain questions must preoccupy psychotherapists. First, how do we and the patient know what change is necessary? Second, what is the role of psychotherapy in facilitating such change? And, third, where and how does such change take place? These questions direct our attention to the entry point of the patient into treatment and, in particular, to the much neglected matter of formulation.

FORMULATION AND CLINICAL IDEOLOGY

The idea of formulation has not been treated kindly by scientific psychiatry. In fact, it is difficult to find agreement on whether a formulation is important or not, what should go into one, how practitioners should be trained to formulate, and how a formulation should be used. Historically, the concept is associated with psychoanalysis and with dynamic psychiatry, though as it will be used here the term is equally consistent with cognitive or behavioral treatment, the various somatotherapies, group and family treatment—in fact, the full range of treatment options, since a formulation implies the *objectives* but not necessarily the *methods* of the proposed treatment. Considered broadly, a formulation is the means by which assorted evaluative data is integrated and rendered as a coherent hypothesis accounting for the patient's presentation at a particular point in time and suggesting what approach to treatment may be useful and appropriate. Before considering formulation as the outcome of a careful assessment process, we turn our attention to the most common obstacle: overinvestment of either the clinician or patient in an inflexible ideological position.

Most commonly, a formulation represents a tapestry woven by a believer (the psychotherapist) to provide a rationale for a particular form of intervention thought by the weaver to be correct. In other words, it is presumed rather than crafted. When method is reified, and precedes rather than follows formulation, patient selection becomes important, a luxury that does not exist in a population-based system of care. James Mann, a pioneer who explored the existential implications of time through using a 12-session contract (Mann, 1973), worked within a university setting, and therefore with a highly selective population where certain common developmental themes might be expected. In developing a focus to be addressed, Mann advocated finding a link between the patient's presenting problem and some chronically present, organizing belief about the self (a "chronic and enduring pain"). It was Mann's belief that the structure of the treatment (a time limit) created a link between the central issue and the existential issues associated with time: limited achievement, inevitable loss and disappointment, ambivalence. The formulation placed emphasis not only on the flawed image of the self, but on the patient's place in his or her history and, implicitly, the need to come to terms with life's limits without allowing ambivalence to distort self-image (Mann, 1981). For Mann, the formulation concerned a chronic and persistent idea about the self, extracted from the patient's reason for seeking help. The focus was on changing the self concept through accepting the limits created by the structure of the treatment. Neither the formulation nor the structure of treatment in this model derived from any particular patient; the best that could be said about a patient who failed to benefit was that s/he was not a good candidate for the method.

When formulation precedes the patient's presentation, there is a tendency to shape the patient to fit the theory: the Procrustean dilemma. The danger is in circular reasoning, where the patient's failure to conform to the model is interpreted as pathology that then confirms the validity of the model itself. This type of criticism has been leveled at psychoanalysis in general, and at Freudian theory in particular, but it can be applied as well to any inflexible system of categorization: in contemporary times, formal diagnosis is often used in this manner.

A clinical formulation that is too heavily invested with ideology creates a relationship between therapist and patient akin to that between a salesperson and a customer. In such situations, the formulation may be used to shape the patient's thinking toward a particular school of thought, technique, or strategy of intervention, and refusal to comply may be wrongly interpreted as pathology.

For example, traditional psychoanalysis and the brief therapies emanating from it assume conflict to be the cause of symptoms and practitioners are apt to select from the presenting complaints those elements that are consistent with such theories. Sifneos, in his practice of short-term anxiety-provoking psychotherapy, excluded patients whose problems did not fall into three categories: unresolved Oedipal difficulties, separation issues, and grief reactions (Sifneos, 1981); for patients who fell within the confines of his acceptance criteria, he brought a template that presumed one of these categories to be present. Alternative formulations were not considered. Malan, whose work evolved from psychoanalysis, also posited the centrality of conflict and, even when planning the treatment of patients with severe disorders, for whom more basic impairments are usually present, he assumed the same pathogenesis (Gustafson, 1981).

While there is some evidence that the belief of the therapist in an ideology and its accompanying methodology may contribute to the success of treatment, persistent adherence to a school of thought is inconsistent with a population-based approach to care. In the past, when patients had broad choice of therapists, when dyadic and insular treatment was the norm, and when psychotherapy was unmonitored, therapists and patients of like mind were free to find each other and work together in benign neglect of alternative approaches even when therapy was not productive. There is considerable nostalgia among psychotherapists for this disappearing state of affairs. A survey conducted by Consumer Reports ("Mental health," 1995) illustrated that patients related their satisfaction with psychotherapy to its duration, and also believed the therapy more helpful when it was more extended. Seligman (1996) has attributed this finding to patients' ability to choose a therapist and a type of therapy, and to the belief of both patient and therapist in the value of what they were doing together. This study, however, included only self-reports of progress. Much of run-on psychotherapy may be traced to such circumstances, especially when no objective measure of progress is involved. Under these circumstances, the assumption of the role of patient is a powerful shaper of behavior and attitude, and the trained patient's point of view is likely to configure to that of the therapist over time; in some instances, failure to accept the therapist's frame of reference may be construed as resistance to treatment. This inequity may lead to therapy dropouts or, in some instances, characterization of the patient's point of view as symptomatic; not uncommonly, a frustrated psychotherapist may render a personality disorder diagnosis following such a disagreement.

With the changes that are taking place in the health care system, insular psychotherapy relationships of extended duration are becoming the exception rather than the rule. In a system where the choice of therapist is limited, greater accommodation may be required of both therapist and patient. Similarity of cultural and ethnic background may enhance empathic resonance, while dissimilarity may make the work harder but may prove more useful in the long run in that dissimilarity discourages facile identification and forces patient and therapist to negotiate and develop a common frame of reference rather than assuming one. This may be beneficial, in that it inclines toward a less hierarchical relationship between patient and therapist. In a health care environment characterized by diverse resources drawn on selectively by an informed patient, contact with a psychotherapist may be but one element in the treatment plan, and various helpers may be involved, each bringing a different perspective, leaving the patient in charge of balancing their roles. Although this may backfire when collaborators do not, in fact, collaborate, with some patients having this degree of control over treatment is helpful.

THE SCIENCE OF FORMULATION

Of course, there is no such thing as a psychotherapist who does not bring certain templates to the clinical encounter. The challenge is to regard such templates as hypotheses, and to be prepared to surrender them. The attitude that favors this best is one of naivete: to approach each new patient as though in a foreign land, knowing only the rudiments of the language. Perhaps a good psychotherapist may be characterized as someone who combines ingenuousness with ingenuity.

The negotiation that leads to a formulation begins at the point of entry into treatment, which may precede the first appointment. Most commonly, an evaluator brings a template that serves to select and organize the data noted, leading to a clinical hypothesis that accounts for the presentation and implies what must be done in response. While complete impartiality is a myth, since everyone brings something preconceived to an encounter, at its best, the reasoning process is inductive and the evaluator is able to avoid the type of circular reasoning previously described. The initial encounter will ordinarily lead to a testable hypothesis, the testing to take place in the course of therapy, not once, but repeatedly. The process is not a linear one, but circular: data-gathering, leading to an inductively derived hypothesis, deductions from the hypothesis that suggest tests to confirm or disconfirm it, and a return to data-gathering when the hypothesis proves incomplete or incorrect. This sequence is consistent with the scientific method. Perry has stated that the clinical formulation appears at the junction of therapy, theory and science (1989).

A formulation is integrative; but what is it that should be integrated? Weerasekera (1993) has suggested a biopsychosocial grid that specifies the

Alfredo Castañeda, *When the Mirror Dreams with Another Image* (1988).

predisposing, precipitating, and perpetuating factors first described by Kline and Cameron (1978). These include both individual and systemic variables associated with the patient's presentation. Additionally, Weerasekera has included adaptive and protective factors, so that a measure of overall health status may be made. This tabular approach, while comprehensive and certainly eclectic, lacks organization and prioritization. Reminiscent of the anamnesis some of us were required to complete in our training years, it leaves the therapist wondering what to treat first and where to stop. Toews has wisely observed that formulation cannot be found in the boxes of a grid, but involves a process of synthesis and integration of data, which is to be found *between* the boxes (Toews, 1993). McDougall and Reade (1993) have examined the cognitive process that is involved in integrating data with presumed models of illness, to come up with an understanding of a given individual's state of illness and need for treatment, suggesting the need is to find a fit, but they fail to include attention to the patient's perspective as one of the important variables to include. We will speak to this latter point in great detail.

If tabular, descriptive approaches to formulation are burdened by an excess of data, those that are associated with a theoretical template may suffer from too limited a perspective. The work of David Malan, which I have alluded to above, is an example of applying an immutable formula to the care of patients who vary from each other in fundamental ways. For Malan, the formulation centered around identification of a current conflict and an underlying nuclear conflict prone to recurrence and curable through interpretation. The evaluative process was designed to elicit the expected clinical target. One of the pioneers of brief psychotherapy, Malan bridged psychoanalysis and the focal psycho-therapies, and attempted to treat complex disorders while holding on to the theories of classical psychoanalysis. As Gustafson pointed out, his actual treat-ment did not always coincide with his theories (Gustafson, 1981).

Michael Balint, who was also a psychoanalyst, took the brief treatment of patients with complex disorders in new directions. In the classic *Focal Psycho-therapy*, he and his two colleagues, Paul Ornstein and Enid Balint, described the 27-session treatment of a patient suffering from delusional jealousy (1972). The patient, referred by his general practitioner, had been troubled for many years by his wife's relationship with another man whom she had known prior to their marriage. His jealousy had erupted into episodes of illness on two occasions. The first followed his move into a new house he had built for his family and the death of his father-in-law (who had initially opposed his mar-riage) at about the same time; the second followed his and his brother's purchasing majority interest in the family business from their father. Balint's formulation was consistent with psychoanalytic theory: that his patient suffered from latent homosexual wishes, making it difficult for him to accept his triumph over his male rivals without guilt. The work of therapy, however, did not involve interpretation. Because of the severity of the patient's disorder and the risks that he could not manage to contain his behavior if a full-blown transference neurosis were to develop, Balint departed from the use of inter-pretation. He considered two aims, one more limited than the other: either to help the patient tolerate defeat of his rivals with less guilt or avoid the matter of defeat entirely by developing a close relationship that would entail a sym-bolic sharing of his wife with a loved man, the therapist. Balint did not posit a focal conflict; his focal aims involved use of the treatment relationship that anticipated interpersonal and existential models of psychotherapy that were to follow.

An important feature of Balint's treatment was his sensitivity to the responses of his patients. Based on his formulation, two possible focal aims were devel-oped. Specific strategies were considered but rejected while others were se-lected and then modified as needed, all in pursuit of the focal objective: helping the patient tolerate victory over his rivals. Treatment followed the patient. What could he and would he tolerate? To what extent was he prepared to give up his symptoms? These questions addressed more than motivation, a general term that may be varyingly defined. Balint was concerned with the patient's readiness for the necessary change. Although Balint and his coworkers did not refer to it by name, the treatment was replete with empathic processing. One category in the report underscores the monitoring function. In each session, Balint cited "interpretations thought of but not given." One is reminded of Ferenczi's definition of empathy as "tact." Although Balint and his coworkers did not discuss it, it is obvious that the formulation in this case evolved through the treatment episode, that is, the cautions exercised and the choices of strategy that were made reflect modifications not only of procedure, but of the formulation, based on empathic understanding.

The literature includes numerous models of formulation that lend themselves not only to the development of focal objectives, but to scientific research as well. Some of these have been manualized. The aim of such instruments is to standardize the observational and data-gathering process in order to minimize the role of inference; theoretically, clarity of focus will result. Three of the best-known formulation models are the Core Conflictual Relationship Theme (CCRT), the Plan Diagnosis (PD), and the Ideographic Conflict Formulation (ICF). Although developed in support of brief psychotherapy, all can be applied without reference to the duration of treatment. Perry and colleagues (1989) have characterized and compared them as follows: "The CCRT focuses on relationship patterns as the central feature of individual dynamics and transference in or out of the treatment situation. The Plan Diagnosis focuses on dynamic features related to transference, resistance and insight in therapy. The Idiographic Conflict Formulation focuses on stress and internal conflict, and the individual's adaptation to them in or out of treatment." Each paradigm relates to a body of theory and suggests optimal strategies of intervention. For each, a conflict between wishes and fears is involved. Each relies on the development of representative patterns of behavior in the transference, and each stems from a psychoanalytic conceptual belief system that relates symptoms to conflict.

The CCRT was developed by Luborsky and his colleagues at the University of Pennsylvania (Luborsky & Crits-Christoph, 1989; Luborsky, 1977). In the evaluation phase, particular attention is paid to recurrent interpersonal dilemmas that suggest conflict. A core relationship theme is one that involves wishes or intentions, expected responses from the other, and resultant adaptation of the patient to the other. Both conscious and unconscious conflicts are noted as the patient describes experiences with others and the most frequent patterns are noted. The evaluator searches for conflicts either between wishes or between a wish and a fear. Standardized lists and methods of observation have been developed. The underlying assumption is that conflict exists and leads to symptoms and that resolution of conflict is the desired outcome of psychotherapy. This method seeks to standardize data extracted from a patient narrative; while attention to the patient's dilemma is a feature, there is little attention paid to the therapist's empathic awareness of the patient's actual point of view.

The Plan Diagnosis method can be traced to the work of Weiss, Sampson, and Silberschatz (Weiss *et al.*, 1986). Based on the belief that pathogenic beliefs about the self and others originate in childhood traumas, this formulation posits an unconscious plan on the part of the patient to achieve mastery through either confirming or disconfirming key beliefs. What is most important for our purposes is the assumption that the patient comes to therapy with the propensity to test the therapist; sensitivity, therefore, to the patient's initiatives in the treatment context becomes essential to assessment of clinical need. The therapist seeks to identify what the patient is seeking to achieve: desired changes, goals; what types of irrational beliefs or fears obstruct achievement of these goals; and what types of testing the patient does. This method is highly tailored to the individual patient and strongly attuned to eliciting his/her point of view. As with the CCRT, it is interpersonal in nature, but relies predominantly on the dynamics of the treatment relationship, itself. There is also a cognitive dimension, in that schemas or persistent worldviews are involved and must be recognized. There is less reliance on historical data and more dependence on the sensitivity of the therapist to both verbal and nonverbal cues, and thus on empathic awareness.

The Ideographic Conflict Formulation Method originated in work with patients diagnosed with borderline personality disorder. The interview focuses on patterns of conflict as determined by history taking. Five questions are addressed: conscious and unconscious wishes, fears, symptoms and avoidant patterns evoked by fears, stressors that act as triggers, and best methods of adaptation. As with the other two, this method assumes conflict to be causative of symptoms and, by implication, encourages conflict resolution. While there is less emphasis on therapist–patient interaction, it is clear that observations made within the therapeutic context would be important validators of presumed areas of interpersonal difficulty.

While the three methods described are strongly shaped by psychodynamic theory, other clinical researchers have developed models more closely associated with cognitive science. Horowitz (1997) has developed a model that shares some features with CCRT, which he termed "configurational analysis." Beginning with symptoms and signs, this method also seeks to explain causation as well as the failure of the patient to overcome his/her difficulties. Based on cognitive and interpersonal theory, configurational analysis allows for integration of data from the biological and social domains as well as the psychological. The patient's state of mind, and the tendency to sequence from one state to another, are associated with defensive maneuvers designed to hold "dreaded states" at bay. These defenses limit the ability to process and resolve internal conflicts and may keep a person from achieving desired states. The therapist, drawing on data acquired through the narrative as well as the experience of being with the patient, develops a picture of the organizing ideas that shape the individual's views of self and others (schemas). An important feature of such schemas is the quality and nature of relationships that result from defensive activities and compromise healthy and adaptive behavior. Such "role relationships," reminiscent of those characterized in the CCRT, are by their nature maladaptive. Therapy involves the use of interpretation as well as trial and error, to counteract dysfunctional or avoidant interpersonal behavior. This approach to treatment may also take into account concurrent attention to biological or social factors that are associated with the mental states noted.

While Horowitz's approach is consistent with brief therapy, it also may be used as a way of understanding chronic patterns of behavior such as those associated with personality disorder. In that sense, it goes beyond CCRT but is consistent with ICF and PD. As with PD, attention to mental states and their association with roles requires considerable attention on the part of the therapist to the patient's shifting states of mind. Data necessary for this emanates not only from observation, but from the type of interpersonal activity we have characterized as the empathic process. Most important, Horowitz made it clear that formulation is dynamic, that it evolves through the treatment, and that a cyclic sequence involving inductive and deductive phases is involved. I will have more to say on this important qualification in the chapter that follows. Role relationships for Horowitz (1997) fall into four broad categories that correspond to four types of schemas: desired states, dreaded states, compromises that are adaptive, and compromises that are problematic. The individual, he theorized, shifts from state to state in accord with circumstance and in line with enduring transactional scripts: proclivities to shift into a given state of mind and behave in a predictable interpersonal fashion. The intervention is long term (presumably continuous as opposed to intermittent) and dyadic, with the objective of character change. For Horowitz, it is the complexity of behavior and inconsistencies in self-organization that must be addressed. In summarizing his method, he stated, "Personality is a plurality of possible states, possible selves, possible relationship patterns, and possible styles of defensive control of emotions" (Horowitz et al., 1995, p. 632).

Horowitz's Role Relationship Model (RRM) was an attempt to integrate psychodynamic and cognitive theories. In recognizing the impact of context on mental state, he opened the door to considering the patient's real life context, but because the treatment is dyadic, failed to do so. Because the objectives are diffuse, a focus would be difficult to define. He remained committed to the idea that conflict underlies psychiatric disorder, though raising the hope of integrating psychodynamic and cognitive science. Reiss, in considering the consistency of this model with other frames of reference, pointed to the literature linking character to temperament, and therefore biology, which is not easily reconciled with the RRM model. Additionally, the social origins of self-representations cannot be addressed by models that are based on two person relationships (Reiss, 1995). The idea that schemata may be associated with *particular* relationships and that the assessor must cast a broader net in order to appreciate such uniqueness has been pointed out as well by Emde (1995). These problems are common to the models of formulation we have considered to this point. They neglect the context in which problems are experienced and presume patterns will show up in the transference; as clinical instruments, they are cumbersome and labor intensive, suffering from some of the problems previously described with grids. All of these models seek to reduce the role of inference, but fail to do so; indeed, where transference is a major method of learning about the patient, inferential thinking cannot be eliminated. All inferential thinking involves a leap, of faith or otherwise, from what is to what may be—from the world of observation to the inner world of meaning of the other person.

The strength of the models considered is, first, that they balance diagnosis with an explanatory hypothesis that establishes the groundwork for a treatment plan; second, that they address the interpersonal domain, the context within which illness occurs; third, that they offer an intelligible frame of reference derived from the patient's narrative that can be used to predict future behavior both in and out of treatment; and fourth, that they underscore the importance of transference as a source of important data. The last of these, in particular, speaks to the importance of therapist sensitivity to the nuances of interpersonal behavior, and especially to those inconsistencies of response in the treatment situation that are often the key to understanding the patient's dilemmas. Each attempts to create a three-dimensional picture of the person who is the patient, and who suffers from the disorder that has been diagnosed: to enter into his/her world, grasp his/her perspective, and develop a treatment plan that is consistent with his/her own personal vision of a better self. Attempts to systematize, standardize, and document the clinical activities common to experienced psychotherapists are valuable. Models such as those considered stand midway between diagnosis and treatment and at least allow for, if not always indicate, the development of a focus. They have much to teach us.

CONCLUSIONS

In the early chapters, we reviewed the history of empathy as a clinical variable in an effort to understand its nature, its role in the healing process, and the contextual and personal elements that impact on the protagonists in a dyadic clinical encounter and either facilitate or impede empathic communication. We have examined the contributions of contemporary science to our topic, by reviewing the evidence that empathic capacities originate within identifiable portions of the brain and subserve important, even vital, functions as human beings continue to evolve and seek to maintain their place as successful life forms. Our journey began therefore in the clinical consulting room, detoured through ancient Greece, wended its way through the perilous straits bordered by dualistic and reductionistic thinking to emerge in the sunlight of nonlinear science. But scientific validation left us in a precarious situation, since the world of the psychoanalysts and experiential psychotherapists who discovered and advanced the concept of empathy is not so readily to be found anymore. Where, then will the empathic healer find a new home?

Unfortunately, this question is considered by some among us to be a rhetorical one, stemming from the confusion of *endangered* with *extinct*. It has become common for mental health professionals to succumb to the temptation to lament the changes in the clinical environment as "counter-evolutionary"; many wax nostalgic for the better days in which empathic healers might ply their trade in the peace and sanctity of an insular dyad, treating until the patient was healed or ran out of funds. Had we accepted this gloomy perspective, we might have brought this book to a close much earlier, and hoped for the best: perhaps the arrival of an anti-managed-care messiah. But this would be of little help to the practitioners who work in the real world: one in which scrutiny is a daily reality, brief intervention the norm, and income contingent on outcome. This and the following chapters represent an attempt to provide some guidance to the practitioner who agrees with the characterization of clinical empathy presented in the early chapters but wonders about its relevance in the current and coming environment of practice. To the question "whatever happened to empathy?" we reply: it is alive and well, but not as easily recognized.

Clinical empathy, it is proposed, is not only compatible with the environment in which we practice, but it is an essential component of the treatment relationship, to be drawn on in support of such aims as efficiency, clinical effectiveness, and improved outcome through targeted psychotherapy. In this chapter, we have examined the variables that are associated with population-based care, where the practitioner is charged with the task of offering a little service to a large number of people, and therefore must maximize the impact of a clinical encounter. I have proposed that the key elements in practicing psychotherapy at the present time are two: focus and the formulation that precedes it. We have considered how empathy operates to facilitate the development of a formulation and the establishment and maintenance of a clinical focus. It remains to examine, at a higher power of magnification, how the psychotherapist processes and integrates the data brought by the patient so that the unique is not lost in the general, the person in the illness, the illness in the disease. Each patient brings a narrative that must be understood in terms that create a rational basis for an intervention, even while the objective hallmarks of disease are noted, appreciated and addressed. To paraphrase Rachel Remen (1996), we are all stories seeking to be heard, acknowledged, and understood. In the following chapter, we will look more closely at how a therapist proceeds to turn a narrative into a treatment and the important role that empathy plays in the process.

REFERENCES

Balint, M., Ornstein, P., & Balint, E. (1957). *The doctor, his patient and the illness*. New York: International Universities Press.

Balint, M., Ornstein, P., & Balint, E. (1972). *Focal psychotherapy: An example of applied psychoanalysis*. London: Tavistock Publications.

Basch, M. F. (1983). Empathic understanding: A review of the concept and some theoretical considerations. *Journal of the American Psychoanalytic Association, 31*, 101–126.

Bennett, M. J. (1993a). View from the bridge: Reflections of a recovering staff model HMO psychiatrist. *Psychiatric Quarterly, 64*(1), 45–75.

Bennett, M. J. (1993b). The importance in teaching the principles of managed care. *Behavioral Healthcare Tomorrow, 2*, 28–32.

Bennett, M. J. (1996). Is psychotherapy ever medically necessary? *Psychiatric Services, 47*(9), 966–970.

Burns, D. D., & Nolen-Hoeksema, S. (1992). Therapeutic empathy and recovery from depression in cognitive–behavioral therapy: A structural equation model. *Journal of Consulting and Clinical Psychology, 60*(3), 441–449.

Castonguay, L. G., Goldfried, M. R., Wiser, S., Raue, P. J., & Hayes, A. M. (1996). Predicting the effect of cognitive therapy for depression: A study of unique and common factors. *Journal of Consulting and Clinical Psychology, 64*(3), 497–504.

Mental health: Does therapy help? (1995, November). *Consumer Reports*, pp. 734–739.

Emde, R. N. (1995). Diagnosis, assessment and individual complexity. *Archives of General Psychiatry, 52*, 637–638.

Frank, G. (1974). *Persuasion and healing*. New York: Shocken Books.

Glenmullen, J. (2000). *Prozac backlash: Overcoming the dangers of Prozac, Zoloft, Paxil, and other antidepressants with safe, effective alternatives*. New York: Simon & Schuster.

Gustafson, J. P. (1981). The complex secret of brief psychotherapy in the works of Malan and Balint. In S. H. Budman (Ed.), *Forms of brief therapy* (pp. 83–128). New York: Guilford Press.

Herman, J. L. (1992). *Trauma and recovery*. New York: Basic Books.

Horowitz, M. J. (1997). Configurational analysis for case formulation. *Psychiatry, 60*, 111–119.

Horowitz, M. J., Eells, T., Singer, J., & Salovey, P. (1995). Role-relationship models for case formulation. *Archives of General Psychiatry, 52*, 625–632.

Howard, K. I., & Orlinski, P. E. (1986a). Process and outcome. In S. L. Garfield & A. E. Bergin (Eds.), *Handbook of psychotherapy and behavioral change* (3rd ed.) (pp. 311–381). New York: Wiley.

Howard, K. I., Kopta, S. M., Krause, M. S., & Orlinski, P. E. (1986b). The dose–effect relationship in psychotherapy. *American Psychologist, 41*, 159–164.

Kaysen, S. (2000). *Girl, interrupted*. Thorndike, ME: Thorndike Press.

Kleinman, A. (1980). *Patients and healers in the context of culture*. Berkeley: University of California Press.

Kline, S., & Cameron, P. M. (1978). Formulation, I. *Canadian Psychiatric Association Journal, 23*(1), 39–42.

Krupnick, J. L., Sotsky, S. M., Simmens, S., Moyer, J., Elkin, I., Watkins, J., & Pilkonis, P. A. (1996). The role of the therapeutic alliance in psychotherapy and pharmacotherapy outcome: Findings in the National Institute of Mental Health Treatment of Depression Collaborative Research Program. *Journal of Consulting and Clinical Psychology, 64*(3), 532–539.

Liberman, R. P. (1988). *Psychiatric rehabilitation of chronic mental patients*. Washington, DC: APA Press.

Linehan, M. M. (1993). *Cognitive–behavioral therapy of borderline personality disorder*. New York: Guilford Press.

Luborsky, L. (1977). Measuring a pervasive psychic structure in psychotherapy: The core conflictual relationship theme. In N. Freedman & S. S. Grand (Eds.), *Communicative structures and psychic structures*. New York: Plenum Press.

Luborsky, L., & Crits-Christoph, P. (1989). A relationship pattern measure: The core conflictual relationship theme. *Psychiatry, 52*, 250–259.

Mann, J. (1973). *Time-limited psychotherapy*. Cambridge: Harvard University Press.

Mann, J. (1981). The core of time-limited psychotherapy: Time and the central issue. In S. H. Budman (Ed.), *Forms of brief therapy* (pp. 25–43). New York: Guilford Press.

McDougall, G. M., & Reade, B. (1993). Teaching biopsychosocial integration and formulation. *Canadian Journal of Psychiatry, 38*, 359–362.

Michels, R. (2000). *Thinking while listening*. Lecture no. 13, delivered at the Annual Meeting of the American Psychiatric Association, 16 May.

Perry, J. C. (1989). Scientific progress in psychodynamic formulation. *Psychiatry, 52*, 245–249.

Perry, J. C., Luborsky, L. Silberschatz, G., & Popp, C. (1989). An examination of three methods of psychodynamic formulation based on the same videotaped interview. *Psychiatry, 52*, 302–323.

Remen, R. (1996). *Kitchen table wisdom*. New York: Riverhead Books.

Reiss, D. (1995). Personality theory: Clinical practice, social development, and the biology of individual differences. *Archives of General Psychiatry, 52*, 633–635.

Roback, H. B., Barton, D., Castelnuovo-Tedesco, P., Gay, V., Havens., L., & Nash, J. (1999). A symposium on psychotherapy in the age of managed care. *American Journal of Psychiatry, 53*(1), 1–16.

Santos, A. B. (1997). ACT now! Assertive community treatment. *Administration and Policy in Mental Health, 25*(2), 101–104.

Seligman, M. E. P. (1996). Science as an ally of practice. *American Psychologist, 51*(10), 1072–1079.

Sifneos, P. E. (1981). Short-term anxiety-provoking psychotherapy: Its history, technique, outcome, and instruction. In S. H. Budman (Ed.), *Forms of brief therapy* (pp. 45–81). New York: Guilford Press.

Test, M. A., & Stein, L. I. (1976). Practical guidelines for the community treatment of markedly impaired patients. *Community Mental Health Journal, 12*(1), 72–82.

Toews, J. A. (1993). Case formulation in psychiatry: Revitalizing an ailing art. *Canadian Journal of Psychiatry, 38*, p. 344.

Weerasekera, B. A. (1993). Formulation: A multiperspective model. *Canadian Journal of Psychiatry*, *38*, 351–358.

Weiss, J., Sampson, H., and the Mount Zion Psychotherapy Group (Eds.) (1986). *The psychoanalytic process: Theory, clinical observation, and empirical research.* New York: Guilford Press.

CHAPTER 9

Focal Psychotherapy

He listens with Indian patience, wary, serene,
Amused, giving everything new its old name.
History is a picture changing from familiar scene
To scene, to one who listens beyond the frame.
He hears what the archeologists listen for,
That part of the story after the story's end,
The more that children ask when they ask for more.

John Holmes

S elective listening is the core requisite for practicing the art of psychotherapy. The science of psychotherapy requires something more: a systematic
way of transforming the subjective experience of suffering into objectives
that may be achieved through treatment. It has been proposed that the focus
of psychotherapy is the means by which this may be achieved. In this chapter,
we will consider how this may be accomplished within the framework of a
system of mental health care that allocates limited services to the many who
require them.

The term *focal psychotherapy* has been used to describe different models of
treatment. For example, Bennett and Cummings and Sayama have used it to

characterize a pattern of discontinuous, eclectic interventions keyed to a patient's place in the life cycle (Bennett, 1997; Cummings & Sayama, 1995). In the Balint version (Balint *et al.*, 1972), an enduring impairment was targeted through the strategic use of transference supported by minimal interpretation: an object-relations model. In this book, the term refers to treatment, usually but not always brief, that is designed to mitigate barriers to necessary change. It is not associated with any particular school of psychotherapy, since the question of methodology is a secondary concern. Methodology is a strategic matter that depends on the answer to four questions:

1. Why is the patient seeking help *now*? ("why now?")

2. What state of health does s/he bring to the task? ("what now?")

3. What is the impasse that produces the pain leading to a request for help? ("what impasse?")

4. What help is required *now*? ("what next?")

Certain assumptions guide our approach to answering these questions. The first of these is that it is the legitimate task of a health care professional to treat rather than to heal. Although this somewhat overstates the case, since the boundary between these two aims is blurred, the purpose of making such a distinction is to free the psychotherapist from the unrealistic expectation that s/he will accompany the patient on the long journey from illness to health. That our clinical ancestors actually did or could do this is an exaggeration. Healing, the restoration or achievement of a state of greater health, may be promoted by effective treatment, but something more than treatment is generally required as well. The diverse factors that promote healing operate, for the most part, outside the formal health care system. They can be found within the context of the sufferer's life. The type of social resources that I have termed *patholytic*, those capable of counteracting the effects of an illness, include psychotherapists but also mentoring relationships, teachers, love partners, and self-help programs, to mention but a few. It is one of the functions of a treater to support the development of patholytic influences. While the treater may be considered one such influence, s/he is never the sole one and usually is not the most important or influential one.

A second and related assumption has to do with the nature of treatment, itself. Treatment consists in those clinical activities that are designed to mitigate the barriers to healing. The objective of treatment is recovery from illness and return of the patient to his or her developmental trajectory. If the way has been properly paved, healing will proceed. Healing, in this sense, is closely related to continuing development, which is presumed to continue through the life cycle. The treater, therefore, is concerned with barriers: barriers to necessary change (the focus of an intervention), to recovery from illness, and to healing (continuing development).

The third assumption is that an understanding of the patient's psychodynamics is essential to any psychotherapeutic mode. A formulation that incorporates such understanding is the touchstone for all forms of psychotherapy and therefore should precede the choice of treatment method. This assumption reverses the common polarity where method is presumed and the patient examined for goodness of fit to it. In a population-based system of care, where all members have access to services according to need, the clinician must configure to the patient's preferred method of learning and therefore must understand the need before selecting the method. Although the formulation will be considered mainly from a psychodynamic perspective, the treatment methods may vary. Unlike the systems for developing a formulation that were described in chapter seven, the case examples that follow will not presume a psychodynamic treatment model, only a psychodynamically informed treater.

The fourth assumption is that the empathic process is central to the development and maintenance of a psychotherapeutic focus. Both at the point of entry and through an episode of care, sensitive attention to the patient's perspective is essential. Psychotherapy is by its nature an educative process, capable in some instances of amending beliefs and behavioral patterns of longstanding duration. This will not take place, however, without careful attention to the patient's various states of mind as these relate to the illness treated. The channels of communication must include the nonverbal as well as the verbal, whatever the treatment strategy. Validation, attunement and shared meaning are central to the task.

Finally, since treatment precedes and anticipates continued healing that will occur in the ordinary context of the patient's life, collaboration with various concerned others is essential from the outset. This includes a role for family, other treaters, and those patholytic resources that can be identified and employed by the patient. When significant others are part of the problem, more active involvement in the process of treatment may be required. The overall aim is to mitigate social, psychological, and biological barriers to recovery and to the healing anticipated following recovery.

THE PROCESS OF ASSESSMENT

Responsibility for the care of a population mandates standardized methods of allocating resources, with the most needy receiving the most service. For the individual patient, clinical need may be assessed and met only through a multistage process that begins with the request for help and ends with a discharge plan. The person seeking help emerges from and will return to a context, so adequate treatment planning must take this context into account, both insofar as it relates to the presenting illness and as a presumptive locus for healing. The practitioner requires a systematic method for proceeding from a patient's request for service through an intervention geared toward such a healing context. The key to accomplishing this is in the evaluative and treatment planning process. The following sequence is one type of infrastructure that may be used to guide this task.

Because allocation decisions are always based on the broad concept of clinical risk, the assessment process must begin with an evaluation of risk status. Both at the point of entry and periodically through an intervention, objective gauging of risk will allow the appropriate steps to be taken to provide containment and/or safety planning when indicated. Although standardized approaches to risk assessment have been developed and should be used (Bennett & Foos, 1996; Risk Management Foundation of Harvard Medical Institutions, 1996), there is a role for empathic understanding as well. Buie has pointed out the danger of relying too heavily on empathy to determine when a patient may be at risk of self-harm (Buie, 1981), suggesting a more comprehensive and structured approach. I agree strongly with this advice; however, as a complement to an algorithm for identifying and monitoring risk factors, the ability to appreciate the patient's perspective and shifting states of mind remains crucial. After the initial decisions about patient safety and possible containment have been made, attention should be directed toward four questions: "why now?" "what now?" "what is the present impasse?" and "what should be done next?"

WHY NOW?

This is the most important question an evaluator in search of a focus can ask. The timing of a presentation often holds the key to understanding what the patient seeks and what expectations are brought into the treatment situation. The proximal cause of a decision to ask for help—which is the answer to the question "why did you seek help at this particular time?"—must be differentiated from the precipitant: the event or events that the patient believes initiated (and perhaps caused) the illness. While the latter may have contributed to the prospective patient's difficulties, the most common response to a precipitating event or stressor is adaptation: defenses are mobilized, efforts made to overcome or manage the impact and bring about homeostasis. Like the body, the mind has means to accomplish this. For most people, a single event is unlikely to overwhelm adaptive capacities, while a sequence of stressors may very well prove too much to handle. Commonly it is a failure of adaptation, rather than the stressor that called for adaptation, that occasions the request for help. Adaptive responses may prove inadequate to the task for various reasons, leading to a painful sense of impasse and, by implication, the need to change something. The immediate motive for seeking help is likely to be a subjective experience of pain that exceeds the individual's tolerance and undermines the tendency to handle matters in whatever the customary manner may be.

Although perhaps traceable to an event, the proximal cause of a request for professional help is not to be found in events, themselves, but rather in their meaning. Empathy is an important tool in extracting meaning from events since narrative alone often fails to provide it. This failure of narrative is often the case since narrative is itself a form of adaptation: a story (or, perhaps more properly, a myth) that an individual creates to make sense of personal experience. Identification of a precipitant begins, rather than ends, the search for motive. The question "what brings you?" is another way of asking "what broke?" or "what didn't work?" The relationship between a precipitant and the proximal cause of a request for professional help is illustrated in Table 9.1.

TABLE 9.1   The Relationship Between a Precipitant and a Proximal Cause

Precipitants	Proximal causes
I have been depressed since the death of my mother one month ago.	I had suicidal thoughts today and feel I am losing control ...
	I had to leave my job today because I broke down in tears at my desk. I fear I may lose my job.
I have a drinking problem. Two days ago, I had a bad performance review and began to drink. I have been drinking steadily since.	I hit my wife last night; I feel I am turning into my abusive father ...
	For the first time in my life, I "blacked out" last night. I am afraid I am losing my mind.

In addition to providing clues about limitations in the patient's adaptive resources and information about his/her threshold for symptom development, the "why now?" also indicates a great deal about the expectations that the patient brings. Cummings and Sayama (1995) have referred to unspoken wishes that may undermine therapeutic progress if not recognized and dealt with as the "implicit contract," by which they mean those hopes that run counter to stated therapeutic goals, for example, the patient who presents for detoxification from heroin in order to reduce the cost of sustained drug usage. Cummings and Sayama have accurately identified such implicit hopes as the anlage of treatment resistance. Failure to identify the unspoken hopes or expectations a person seeking therapy brings may unwittingly fuel the patient's hopes that the therapist will collude with them.

Sometimes the therapist is challenged to know more about the patient than strict attention to the narrative conveys. As the Plan Diagnosis Model of formulation (Weiss *et al.*, 1986) suggests, patients arrive with a plan that is not explicitly announced (and may not be fully within their awareness). This plan may be expressed in the form of a test for the therapist. Failure to pass the test may lead to the patient's flight. In the following case example, the therapist escaped the fate of two previous consultants by passing such a test.

Dorothy R was a 34-year-old unmarried actress who presented on the recommendation of her internist, whom she had consulted because she had experienced a panic attack while at home alone a week earlier. She had sought a medical evaluation fearing that she had a brain tumor. During the evaluation, it was learned that Ms. R and her cohabitant had been abusing cocaine for some time, and her attack had caused her to worry about brain damage from the drug. Her symptoms had occurred on a night when her boyfriend had failed to come home from work at the usual hour, causing her to fear that he had been in an accident and was dead. She associated from this memory to a series of earlier losses in her life: mother had suicided after father had died in a plane crash when the patient was in her early teens. A sibling had died of meningitis and another had been jailed during the past five years. As the interview progressed, the patient became increasingly sad. She spoke of her losses and her sense that she was "cursed." As the interview was coming to a close, she asked whether the interviewer thought she should give up cocaine.

The interviewer, who saw Ms. R as suffering from a dysthymic disorder, was concerned about the cocaine but, under the circumstances, hesitated to take her at her word; he did not yet know what value she placed on the drug, and therefore it was not clear what she was volunteering to give up. He responded to her question by stating, "Since I don't know you very well but see how much pain you are in, I hesitate to ask you to give up something more in your life without offering you something first. I think we should set up a second appointment. You are correct in seeing cocaine as dangerous to you, and it may be causing some of your symptoms. If you can avoid using it until we meet again, we can start with the question you just asked at our next meeting." Ms. R proceeded to tell the interviewer that she had seen two previous therapists, both of whom had refused to see her again if she didn't stop the cocaine, and she had failed to go back to either. She made and kept her follow-up appointment and informed him that she had not used cocaine in the interim.

In this case, the patient needed to know that the therapist understood her sensitivity to loss before she was willing to consider a commitment to treatment. Although there was data about loss, the meaning of Ms. R's question about giving up cocaine was not explicit and had to be hypothesized based on an empathic leap. The "why now?" of her presentation, it was believed, was not the panic attack, but the lingering doubt about damage to her brain. She was frightened of yet another serious loss. The therapist perceived this empathically, but did not comment on it since there was no immediate need to do so. He chose to administer his own test in the form of a challenge: could she abstain for a week? Did she, in fact, see cocaine as dangerous to her? Her response to his challenge was positive and her abstention confirmed his impression that the drug frightened her as much as it did him for her. In the treatment that followed, resources for helping Ms. R with her substance use were mobilized when she was ready for them.

Sometimes the "why now?" provides valuable clues to the patient's needs and expectations. In the following case example, a better understanding of the timing of the presentation might have prevented the adverse outcome.

Daniel M suffered from a bipolar disorder that had been under reasonably good control for the past two years with the use of lithium. He abruptly stopped his medication after an argument with his son, who referred to him as "crazy," and began to develop depressive symptoms several days later. Because he had been known to be suicidal in the past, and acknowledged ideation (without plan or intent), he was hospitalized and his medication restarted. He improved dramatically over the next several days, and initial concerns about lethality diminished so that precautions were discontinued. Mr. M left the ward and hospital grounds, went to a nearby bridge and jumped into the river, committing suicide.

It was later learned that Mr. M had been resistant to coming to the hospital until the morning of the admission, at which time his son had confessed that he had attempted suicide some months earlier and blamed him for "poisoning me with your lousy genes." It was in a fit of guilt that Mr. M's own suicidal thoughts had begun and he had agreed to seek help. Because this information was not known, the formulation was inevitably incomplete; consequently, the focus of treatment failed to include the patient's guilt about his disease. In this case, his disorder rather than Mr. M was treated.

Although careful history-taking will often elicit a "why now?" this is not always the case. Sometimes it does not become clear for some time why a patient has sought treatment; often the patient does not know. Consultation with significant others may be helpful, as in the preceding case example. Since the narrative may not reveal it, attention to what is *not being said* may be important. The thinking process of the therapist and his/her ability to listen to both internal and external signals will sometimes suggest the meanings that underlie narrative gaps. An empathic leap may then become possible.

WHAT NOW?

If the proximal cause of the patient's request for help is the answer to the question "what brings the patient?" the second question—"what now?"—asks what the patient brings. This question, which might be termed a "biopsychosocial history," is a type of inventory. The point to be made here is that we are not seeking a history of the illness, per se, but the illness against the backdrop of the patient's overall state of health. Illness may be understood as a relative state of health. Guidelines about history-taking (American Psychiatric Association, 1995) stress the importance of a biological, psychological, and social assessment, such as that envisioned by Engel and earlier by Meyer. Theoretically, such an assessment should be three dimensional, a portrait of the patient as a person, capturing those features relevant to the presenting need, strengths as well as impairments. Contemporary practice, unfortunately, places almost exclusive emphasis on pathology. By excluding what is right with the patient and elaborating only what is wrong, two problems result. First, the patient's demoralization is likely to be increased, at least temporarily. Second, and more important, s/he is encouraged to think of the treatment as reparative rather than facilitative. Exaggerated and unrealistic expectations may follow from a unidimensional characterization of clinical need. A patient who is experiencing a painful state of mind is not likely to perceive and report factual data objectively—for example, it is not uncommon for a depressed person to report that s/he has always been depressed. It may be helpful to remind the patient that s/he is more than his or her illness and that not all health has been lost.

Klee, *Outbreak of Fear* (1939).

As part of the evaluative process, it is useful to establish a picture of the limitations and impairments the patient brings. Diagnosis alone does not necessarily capture impairments that may be important to the patient; for example, in the case of Mrs. S, the hospitalized patient recovering from cholecystitis, the fact that she was unable to perform household chores to the degree required to sustain a sense of self-worth. In their *Casebook for Managing Managed Care*, Bjork and colleagues (2000) have made impairment the central organizing concept of the treatment planning process. An impairment profile that parallels but is not dependent on diagnosis provides a framework for treatment planning, monitoring, and reporting to a third party. The advantages of such a profile are that it broadly assesses function and creates an objective and documentable basis for interventions as well as a baseline against which progress may be gauged. It also implies what must be treated and the order in which treatment should be approached and includes data that suggest what resources should be mobilized in tailoring the treatment to the patient. The limitation of this approach is that it says little about the patient's overall state of health and therefore remains, similar to the DSM system, one-sided. Similar to Axes III and IV of the DSM, which have never realized their potential to position the syndrome in the patient's life context, an impairment profile presents a univalent picture of a person's troubles and does not say enough about the person who is troubled. In the course of actual treatment we are forced, sometimes to our dismay, to learn this important information only after we seek to draw on it and find it lacking.

An alternative way of conducting a biopsychosocial assessment is to conduct an inventory of both resources and limiting factors. What are the strengths? What can be drawn on to support recovery? What are the patholytic elements in the patient's life structure? A three-dimensional portrait, while it must include the biological, psychological, and social variables that contribute to a state of illness, should not neglect those features that indicate health. When an illness is regarded in a relative rather than an absolute sense, as an altered state of health rather than the absence of health, recovery, rehabilitation, and healing may take place against a backdrop of intact functions, resources, and healing potential. As an example, a patient who suffers from a schizophrenic disorder but who lives within an intact family and has financial resources to draw on, and who has access to a supportive recovery environment, is in a far different situation from one who carries the same diagnosis but lacks such assets. Similarly, a patient with chronic depression who has a supportive employer, education, and social skills has more to draw on than someone lacking such advantages. Further, some assessment must be made of the patient's attitude toward recovery, the capacity for treatment alliance, and the readiness for necessary change(s). Although these parameters are sometimes subsumed under the general heading of "motivation," the term is too vague. Every patient is "motivated"; the question is, "for what?"

It cannot be too strongly stressed that the biopsychosocial assessment itself must take as its point of departure the patient's reason for being there at the time. Failing this, we are buried by data and have little idea what to do about it. Was the patient abused as a child? Did the patient suffer early losses? Was upbringing defective in some manner? These questions are relevant only insofar as the past is present, that is, they are relevant if they constitute barriers to recovery. The distinction between *barriers to recovery* and *barriers to healing* is an important one. While barriers to healing include barriers to recovery, recovery from an illness may be only the first step in healing. Recovery, however, may be construed as the gatepost of the formal health care system, and therefore the principal immediate destination of the treater. Both biomedical and psychosocial need can be defined with reference to these parameters.

The concept of medical necessity is most closely linked to the biological assessment and to formal diagnosis, suggesting a limited (at times, too limited) role for the formal health care system. Biomedical need overlaps with psychosocial necessity: a softer concept, more prone to distortion or exaggeration. Although there is evidence that psychotherapy may be another route into the brain and therefore another means of meeting biomedical need, at this point in history it is primarily psychosocial rather than biomedical need that is the domain of the psychotherapist. A precise definition of psychosocial need is therefore called for in order to mitigate widespread concerns about the vagueness of psychotherapeutic objectives. When psychotherapy is regarded as facilitative rather than curative, it may be drawn on selectively alone or in support of other treatment strategies to promote recovery and prepare the patient for discharge into a healing context. Like biomedical need, psychosocial need can be defined primarily in terms of the barriers that impede this passage. These barriers constitute the third question to be framed: what is the impasse that must be overcome?

What Impasse Must Be Overcome?

The third question depends on the treater's ability to integrate the data acquired from the first two, creating a working formulation. The term "working" is important. Horowitz has advised, with regard to the clinical application of configurational analysis, that it is naive to assume that a single session or even a few sessions will always allow an accurate and complete understanding of clinical need (Horowitz et al., 1995). When we include such factors as the patient's readiness for change, the adequacy of the recovery environment, and overall measures of treatability, the matter is even more complicated. Treatability can never be fully defined before treatment is attempted. The best we can hope for at the point of entry is a provisional formulation, to be shaped and modified through the episode of care as new information, and especially as the treatment experience, indicate. But this complexity is not a reason to avoid constructing a test model. The utility of the formulation will be judged in vivo. Before we can decide what to do, how much to do, and who should do it, we must create an hypothesis that we and the patient can agree on as the basis for the work to be done. That hypothesis springs from the evaluator's ability to integrate the patient's reason for being there with an understanding of the context from which it springs. In the following case, the formulation suggested an impasse that was quite different from the patient's presenting complaint.

Carl N was a 46-year-old recovering alcoholic who was gay and had a long history of depression. He was brought to the hospital by his longtime lover after making a serious suicide attempt while intoxicated, which immediately followed loss of his job as a salesperson for a large corporation: a result of downsizing. The only child of an abusive, alcoholic father and a long-suffering, chronically depressed mother, Mr. N had a strong genetic predisposition to both conditions. His treatment over the years had included multiple psychiatric hospitalizations, detoxifications, periodic suicidal attempts, alternating with sustained periods of sobriety. He had been with his partner, who had been his original AA sponsor, for 10 years, and their relationship was a strong and committed one; he had held his job for 15 years and was known to be a reliable employee when sober. His employers had frequently supported him through difficult times. His medical health was good but for mild hypertension control-led by diet. He was on no medications, though he had used antidepressants at times in the past. When seen at intake, Mr. N was sober and quite depressed, meeting criteria for major depressive disorder, but denied being suicidal. He requested an admission so that he might have help dealing with the impact of his sudden unemployment.

Search for the "why now?" revealed the following. After losing his job one week earlier, Mr. N had begun to attend AA regularly and had recontacted his sponsor, fearing a relapse of his drinking. At a meeting the night before his suicide attempt, he had gotten into an argument with an older man who was dominating the group and had come close to hitting this person before a third man intervened. He was still agitated when he returned home, but did not know why. In the morning, he awoke in great despair and began to drink; shortly thereafter, he took a large overdose of his lover's imipramine but then asked him for help. The interviewer pressed Mr. N to describe his reaction to the argument; he initially resisted, claiming it had nothing to do with his depression. With persistence, the evaluator learned that during the argument the night before Mr. N had had a sudden vision of his father's face when he was drunk and enraged, and recalled thinking that he was turning into "the old man." With this acknowledgment, he began to weep and said that he loathed himself.

❖   ❖   ❖

The formulation in this case was as follows: Mr. N's suicide attempt was provoked by a negative identification with his abusive father, which had un-dermined his previously adaptive response to his job loss. The argument was reminiscent of those he had had as a child, when he had taken on the role of mediating between his mother and her dominating and threatening husband, and his impulsive "protection" of the group the night before had underscored his continuing unresolved "argument" with his father. The fact that Mr. N could not relinquish the role of protector even though it evoked the very behavior he detested constituted his impasse. His serious problems with depression and alcohol abuse had not kept him from sustaining a job and a love relationship, and both his capacity to work and his lover were important sources of strength and support, as was his participation in AA. The focus of psychotherapy, in support of his continued recovery, was on helping him to let go of his learned childhood role, and various models of psychotherapy might be considered. For Mr. N, this piece of the past that remained present led to an impasse that was the immediate barrier to his recovery. The continuing role of a psychotherapist in helping him find new work, sustain his recovery from depression and alcohol abuse, and modify his propensity toward recurrent episodes of illness remained to be determined. These could be construed as barriers to his continuing process of healing.

The idea of an impasse is central to defining psychosocial need. Sometimes the impasse requires interventions directed at someone other than the patient. If healing can be supported by patholytic influences, it may also be undermined by pathostatic ones—those that reinforce or perpetuate the patient's maladaptive behaviors. Impasses may also stem from a lack of a necessary resource, in which case manipulation of the environment may prove more important than treating the patient directly. As already indicated, an important task of the focal psychotherapist is to optimize the patient's healing milieu. This may require the mobilization of resources that overlap with the formal health care system, such as the day program and club used by Mr. K, shelters for the victim of domestic abuse, or residential placement. These resources may be transitional or, in some cases, used periodically. In the following case example, pathostatic factors were at play in the patient's environment and until the psychotherapist perceived this fact, treatment stalled.

Barbara Q was a 34-year-old woman who had suffered multiple episodes of major depression over a ten-year period, twice having attempted suicide. She presented with a recurrence that followed eviction from her rental apartment, after the building in which she lived had been sold to a developer. Closer questioning revealed that Ms. Q had not been using her antidepressant medication, sertraline, on which she had been successfully maintained for the past two years, for at least two weeks. Her symptoms, which included initial and terminal insomnia, loss of appetite and possible weight loss, poor concentration and anhedonia in addition to a profoundly depressed mood, had progressed to the point where she was considering "taking all my pills" in a suicide attempt. She was seen by her therapist on an emergency basis because she had found herself unable to look for a new place to live and was overwhelmed by the thought that she would soon be homeless. Unemployed and on welfare, Ms. Q had been divorced from her second husband for the past three years. Because of her symptoms, she was finding it more difficult over the past month to take care of her 7-year-old daughter. She was brought to the office by her brother, who lived out of town but who had been summoned by her ex-husband.

Ms. Q had been tried on numerous medications over the years, sertraline being the most recent and most successful; her two-year remission was her longest. Although she had periodically missed doses, this was the first time she had stopped the drug. Her psychotherapy had been largely supportive, centering around management of her chronic depression, which remitted only partially between episodes. The patient was college-educated but had not held a job since her first episode of depression; she was devoted to her daughter and had become active in her school, but was otherwise socially isolated. She had few friends and had broken off contact with most of her family because "they are bad for my health," remaining close only with the older brother who had brought her to the office and his wife. Efforts to explore Ms. Q's isolation and encourage job rehabilitation during her extended period of remission had failed, and referral to a psychotherapist for a course of cognitive treatment to complement her use of medication had been refused. She and her psychiatrist had settled into a pattern of monthly 30-minute meetings in which they spoke primarily about her symptoms of depression.

When seen for evaluation, the patient looked anxious as well as sad. She appeared to have lost hope. Efforts to determine why she had stopped her medication were greeted only with a shrug. Although her recurrence appeared precipitated by her eviction, the proximal cause appeared to be her awareness, that morning, that she was not able to mobilize her efforts to find a place to live, leading to the upsurge of suicidal ideation. Her ex-husband had noted her condition only because he had come to the house that day for his weekly visit with their daughter. Because of the risk of suicide and the impasse around use of medication, her psychiatrist recommended a hospitalization, which she readily accepted.

Dr. V was frustrated with his patient and had been so for some time. He sensed her pain but was puzzled at her passivity and self-sabotage. He wondered at her resistance to accepting help; it appeared to him that Ms. Q was "her own worst enemy." He began to wonder if she were competent to be a mother of a young child. It suddenly occurred to him that his patient must be asking the same question, which would be devastating to her remaining sense of self-worth. It was at this point that Dr. V realized that Ms. Q had not yet said anything about who would take care of her daughter while she was in the hospital. He began to wonder whether he was hearing the entire story. Rather than question his patient directly, he elected to approach her empathically by stating: "You may be ill, but you are still a mother and I know how important that is to you. How will you plan for Gloria's care while you are in the hospital?" Ms. Q averted her gaze and refused to answer, and it was Dr. V's impression that she looked ashamed. Rather than ask her again, he invited her brother into the office and informed him that he was concerned about Gloria and knew that Ms. Q must be as well. Her brother looked at Ms. Q, who remained silent, and then asked Dr. V if she had not told him that her ex-husband had initiated a custody suit two weeks earlier.

This information clarified the impasse: Ms. Q had stopped her medication and regressed in response to the threat of losing her daughter, reflecting both her fear and her wish. By regressing, she was in fact validating her ex-husband's position, with which she had begun to agree: she was not a competent parent. The issue in therapy, her repeated refusal of help, was manifest as well in her life outside the office, where she badly needed help in caring for her daughter but had resisted obtaining it. With clarification of this issue, Ms. Q was able to plan for her brother and sister-in-law's help both during and following her brief hospitalization. In addition to restarting her medication, the focus during her inpatient treatment was on her refusal to accept help. By capitalizing on her newly established wish to fight for her daughter, her treaters were able to resurrect a wish to fight for herself as well. As is often the case with an impasse, Ms. Q's crisis was also an opportunity. Her discharge plan included medication maintenance, a course of interpersonal psychotherapy to address her hyperindependence and vocational rehabilitation to strengthen her case as a fit parent.

WHAT NEXT?

The assessment process culminates in treatment recommendations that follow from the formulation. The general aim is to resolve the identified impasse through bringing about some form of necessary change. A series of decisions must follow: about the level or site of care, the optimal choice of caregiver(s), the specific strategies of intervention to be employed, and the manner in which treatment will be monitored and outcome assessed. The working formulation remains a hypothesis subject to refinement and/or correction. While there may be objective means to monitor therapy, the ability of the psychotherapist to monitor the patient's state of mind provides valuable clues to what is working in the treatment and what is not. Impasses within psychotherapy are common, and it is often the psychotherapist's attunement to his or her patient's mental state that highlights resistance. Often, as in the following case, such resistance stems from incongruence between the stated goals of treatment and other, inarticulated aims the patient may have.

Agatha L was 34 when she came for help following an assault by her latest boyfriend, one of many who had abused her over the years. Although she had sustained two rib fractures, she had put off seeking medical help for two days. She presented at the emergency room only after considering asphyxiating herself and actually starting to do so in her sister's garage before being interrupted by her sister and brought to the ER. She was admitted to the hospital after revealing persisting suicidal ruminations.

Ms. L's diagnosis was adjustment disorder with depressed mood, which was revised to major depression after the second hospital day, when her suicidal thoughts persisted and she complained of poor sleep and appetite, difficulty concentrating, and indecisiveness. Her disorder was attributed to the assault, and no further effort was made to determine the proximal cause of her presentation. She had never been in treatment before and denied previous episodes of depression. She refused to engage with other patients, kept to herself, was observed to be frequently tearful and distracted, and she made frequent requests for pain medication. On the third day, antidepressants were started. At her request, a meeting was scheduled with her boyfriend in order to break off the relationship. When he failed to show up, her depressed mood increased. She repeatedly refused to see her sister, but would not state her reasons.

Ms. L's history included a turbulent relationship with her mother, who had blamed her for her father's desertion after Ms. L, the second child, was born. Mother had repeatedly referred to her as "worthless." Although she had done well in school, she had dropped out of college after the first year and had married briefly, divorcing her husband, an abusive alcoholic, a year later. She had worked only intermittently, at menial jobs. Ms. L's sister had protected her during her early years from Mother's episodes of rage and had provided support and financial assistance when necessary, though disapproving of her promiscuous lifestyle. Ms. L described her as "a self-righteous prig." There had been no contact with her father for many years and she did not know if he was alive.

In her sessions with Ms. J, her therapist, a woman of about the same age, Ms. L was taciturn and angry. She complained about all aspects of her care, alienating other patients and testing the patience of staff, who saw her as "infantile." Axis II diagnoses were considered. On the fourth hospital day, the managed care reviewer pressed for a step-down by day 7. Ms. L's therapist considered the treatment impasse and decided to invite the sister to join them without informing her patient, though she offered Ms. L the opportunity to withdraw from the meeting if she preferred to do so. The patient elected to stay, and the joint session proved a turning point. When asked by her supervisor why she had thought to deal with the patient's resistance in this manner, Ms. J replied that her patient's behavior with the staff and with her had suggested that she was ashamed, and she had wondered about the description of the sister as "self-righteous" as possibly linked to such a sense of shame. Ms. L's response to being asked whether she felt ashamed had validated the empathically derived hypothesis: she had become more silent, averted her gaze, but had not disagreed. The patient later revealed that the therapist's initiative in overruling her refusal to have her sister visit had been perceived as an act of understanding and caring.

In the joint session, Ms. L's "why now?" emerged. She had sought sanctuary at her sister's home but had been refused for the first time. Her rumination about suiciding in her sister's garage was a sign of her anger and disappointment. Her sister had experienced the same sense of frustration that the therapist and staff had been feeling, which was a measure of Ms. L's own feelings of disempowerment and fatalism: she felt doomed to validate her mother's opinion of her as "no good" and to perpetuate her drama until it came to a natural end, possibly through her death. This accounted for her provocative behavior in the hospital. The joint session was the beginning of the patient's recovery. The barrier to her recovery was her continuing identification with her mother's point of view; she needed to "unlearn" the belief that she was "worthless." This would take time. Her immediate need, the focus of treatment, was on negotiating a relationship with her sister that supported a healthier view of herself but did not enable maladaptive behavior. Her sister, who had withdrawn from her, required help in staying involved without allowing herself to be manipulated. Ms. L was placed in contact with a local self-help program for abuse victims, where she began group work to modify her pattern of selecting hurtful men. She became progressively more active through this program and some months later began to volunteer at a shelter. She was able to discontinue her individual psychotherapy and continue her healing process outside the formal health care system.

CONCLUSIONS: EMPATHY AND FOCAL PSYCHOTHERAPY

The key to performing focal psychotherapy is in entering the patient's world, finding meaning in disease, and bridging the objective and subjective dimensions of the presenting dilemma. This is not a one-time phenomenon, but a recurrent one through an episode of care. As we have seen, empathy may be crucial in establishing a helping relationship, identifying the "why now?" and constructing a formulation from which the focus may be derived. The course of a focal intervention may be understood as rehearsal for necessary change, with the locus of change moving progressively from the office to the context of the patient's life. When feasible, certain portions of that context may be part of the treatment from the beginning, for example, in couples or family treatment. Resistance is often based on unacknowledged wishes or fears, as was the case with Ms. L, and the key to understanding the patient's impasse may lie in experiencing it in the course of doing the work of therapy. Empathic attunement facilitates such perception.

Psychotherapy is distinguished from other forms of participation in the life of another by its dual nature: the treater is both participant and observer. The therapist continues to think as a separate person, retains an objective posture, notes discrepancies and questions them; s/he validates while encouraging and expecting necessary change. Empathic capacities alert the psychotherapist to the ever-present risk of repeating prototypical interactions with the patient rather than interrupting the pathostatic cycle and thereby contributing to their modification. While it is essential that the therapist participate in the patient's drama *to a point*, the role of observer is never abandoned. The psychotherapist does more than feel, more than experience the patient's world; his or her job is to do so correctively. Formulation is the cognitive process that guides the sequence: always hypothetical, always subject to revision, always seeking new data.

As has been stated earlier in this book, it is often the sense of impasse in treatment that calls for the empathic leap, which in turn leads to a better understanding and reformulation. Formulation follows the acquisition of data but also suggests where the searchlight should be directed: which type of new data is important. The process is cyclical: inductive thinking that leads to the development of hypotheses (formulation, focus); deduction from these hypotheses to indicate the tests that will confirm or disconfirm them (strategies of treatment); new questions raised by the results of testing (partial success or resistance to necessary change); followed by a search for new data that will allow revised hypotheses (reformulation, new foci). Since life goes on, with or without successful psychotherapy, the patient and therapist change in one way or another from session to session: the treater is always shooting at a moving target. Evaluation occurs not once, but continuously.

Far from being inconsistent with the requirements of contemporary managed systems of care, where the needs of a population must be met within an established budget, where psychotherapists are held accountable for their work and where the effectiveness of treatment is monitored and assessed, empathic understanding is vital to success. The psychotherapist's understanding of the patient's state of mind allows for the development of strategies of intervention that are tailored to the unique individual with the disease: a specific patient at a specific time in his/her history, a history that continues to unfold even as the work proceeds. Without empathy, the therapist fails to span the gap between what is being said and what is implied but unspoken, between what is objectively observed and what the patient is subjectively experiencing. In Norretranders' (1998) words, the therapist responds to the *information* but not the *exformation*. The disease cannot be treated directly, only through treatment of the person who suffers from it.

The case examples illustrate how a formulation may be developed by using an infrastructure that places the presenting problem in the dimension of time: a specific point in a patient's life, a current iteration of themes that may be recurrent or present chronically, and are now active. By capitalizing on the specific motive that drives the patient to seek help then, as opposed to earlier or later, it is proposed that the treater may work in the most expeditious manner to facilitate a necessary change. Change, it is proposed, creates ripple effects that carry great potential for lasting gains, beyond the consulting room door. The discharge plan, commonly associated with inpatient treatment, is equally important in outpatient care, where the optimal destination is an environment capable of continuing the healing process which has begun. We turn now to that next phase of healing.

Thus far we have considered empathy primarily as it operates within the clinical setting, while suggesting that it is ubiquitous. In the concluding chapter, we will consider how healing outside and beyond the formal health care setting may take place. Special types of relationships that may be found outside the formal health care setting expand the impact of formal treatment and are the *aftercare* that make focal interventions effective. In considering the impact of healing resources, we will pay attention as well to the remarkable changes that are taking place in communication, information sharing, and newer technologies: changes that promise new adjuncts to expand therapeutic possibilities at the border of the formal and informal care systems.

If the core of formal health care is clinically empathic treatment, provisions must be made to preserve the attitudes and behaviors that allow for it. Although this is not a book on training health care professionals, part of its purpose is to reconcile the realities of the practice environment with the ideals of empathic healing. We cannot complete the task without some attention to the matter of preservation of this endangered species. Initiatives currently taking place in the general medical setting indicate a rebirth of interest in the doctor–patient relationship. As we bring the book to a close, we will consider these and the promise they hold for preserving the basic tools of our craft, even as that craft itself becomes reshaped in conformance with the demands and opportunities of the new century.

REFERENCES

American Psychiatric Association, Work Group on Psychiatric Evaluation of Adults (1995). Practice guidelines for psychiatric evaluation of adults. *American Journal of Psychiatry, 152*(11), 65–80.

Balint, M., Ornstein, P., & Balint, E. (1972). *Focal psychotherapy: An example of applied psychoanalysis.* London: Tavistock Publications.

Bennett, M. J. (1997). Focal psychotherapy. In L. I. Sederer & A. J. Rothschild (Eds.), *Acute care psychiatry: diagnosis and treatment* (pp. 355–373). Baltimore: Williams and Wilkins.

Bennett, M. J., & Foos, J. (1996). *Best practices for assessing and managing the suicidal patient.* St. Louis: Merit Behavioral Care Corporation.

Bjork, J., Brown, J., & Goodman, M. (2000). *Casebook for managing managed care.* Washington, DC: APA Press.

Buie, D. (1981). Empathy: Its nature and limitations. *Journal of the American Psychoanalytic Association, 29,* 281–307.

Cummings, N., & Sayama, M. (1995). *Focused psychotherapy.* New York: Bruner/Mazel.

Horowitz, M. J., Eells, T., Singer, J., & Salovey, P. (1995). Role–relationship model configurations: A summation. *Archives of General Psychiatry, 52,* 654–656.

Norretranders, T. (1998). *The user illusion.* New York: Penguin Putnam.

Risk Management Foundation of Harvard Medical Institutions (1996). *Guidelines for identification, assessment and treatment planning for suicidality.* Cambridge: Author.

Weiss, J., Sampson, H., and the Mount Zion Psychotherapy Group (Eds.) (1986). *The psychoanalytic process: Theory, clinical observation, and empirical research.* New York: Guilford Press.

CHAPTER 10

Empathy Redux

My true love hath my heart and I have his,
By just exchange one for another given:
I hold his dear, and mine he cannot miss,
There never was a better bargain driven:
My true love hath my heart and I have his.

Sir Philip Sidney

How bright, how well-dressed is spring!
Look into my eyes, as you used to do,
And tell me: why are you so sad,
why have you become so caring?
But you are silent, as weak as a flower ...
Hush now! I need no confession ...
I recognize this tenderness of farewell ...
I am alone again.

Taras Shevchenko

*D*espite the advances in technology, the biological revolution has thus far failed to realize its promise. In our search to understand and treat the various disorders that afflict the mind, we are finding that the matter remains complex: there is no magic bullet. Though undoubtedly related to brain function, mental illness and its variants are also inseparable from the existential realities that stem from our basic humanity: the reality of our limited time on earth, the limitations in our adaptive capacities, our need for each other, and the burden of self-awareness. We can grow to understand mental disorder at a neurochemical, molecular, or even an atomic level, but its treatment will continue to call for something inherently human as well: the power of relationship to optimize health and, when necessary, promote healing. Because psychotherapy remains an interhuman experience, it will continue to be important to those who seek treatment and to those who seek to provide it. At its artistic and scientific core is the facilitating phenomenon of empathy.

In this chapter, we will consider the healing environment as it exists outside the formal health care setting. What are its essential elements and how may they be drawn on to expand our capacities as treaters? More specifically, how should the special places that treaters inhabit, places that have, in Jerome Frank's words, "the aura of scientific healing" (Frank, 1974, p. 326), be linked to the world beyond the gateposts of formal health care, which our patients inhabit? What do we mean when we speak of "community" as a site and resource for healing, and how do relationships contribute to health? We will consider, at both a psychological and biological level, how empathic interactions relate to the promotion or restoration of health and what the implications are for treaters. The advances in science are often regarded as barriers to empathy. How may they be used to promote or enhance it, both within and outside the clinical setting? Finally, what trends can be found within the professional community that suggest growing concern about the endangered status of personalized health care, and which initiatives hold the greatest promise for preserving the humanistic core of health care while incorporating the dazzling scientific advances that are taking place?

Our patients, who complement or in some instances replace formal health care with health-promoting activities that range from herbal therapies to self-help programs to the laying on of healing hands, are conveying a message that we are only beginning to hear (Neims, 1999; Unützer et al., 2000). Are they not telling us, as they "vote with their feet," that the void created by professional medicine must be filled from outside rather than from within? The growing legitimacy of the informal health care system is signaled by the change in terminology from "alternative" to "complementary" medicine: a shift that seems to promise collaboration rather than competition, overlap rather than alternative. Those who purport to be healers reside increasingly outside formal health care settings (or, more recently, invited in as carefully monitored guests); while it remains important to differentiate between those healing strategies for which evidence of effectiveness exists and those for which it is more dubious, there is little doubt that scientific medicine and humanistic healing must learn to coexist. How will this take place with regard to mental health practice, as psychiatry joins the rest of medicine in its quest for a defining technology? Alternative medicine, however, is only a small part of the story. The healing environment is not limited to practitioners of any stripe; it is much more prosaic.

FEATURES OF THE HEALING ENVIRONMENT

There is considerable evidence that the interpersonal environment contributes to healing of both somatic and mental disorders. Psychiatry has capitalized on this phenomenon by creating, in the dyadic relationship, a milieu capable of promoting healing; however, with the financial limitations imposed on health care practitioners in general and on psychotherapists in particular, many payers now believe that the creation of such a milieu and the time and cost associated with it are no longer an affordable alternative. The concept of medical necessity, which reduces formal mental health care to the restoration of function and the achievement of (often only partial) recovery from episodes of illness leaves patients and practitioners alike with a frustrating sense of incompleteness. Those who treat patients with mental disorder come to understand its complexity, cost in human suffering, and the time required to master its impact. It is interesting to note, in this regard, that the passage of time may be more important than the actual duration of treatment, that is, healing takes place over time, but that time need not necessarily be spent in the office of a therapist (Budman & Gurman, 1988; Johnson & Gelso, 1980; Alexander & French, 1946/1974). An important function of the treater, therefore, is to prepare the patient to exploit opportunities for healing in his/her own environment and, when necessary, to aid in creating such opportunities. This requires familiarity with what is "out there" as well as a discerning eye for the individual patient's need.

What are the elements of a healing environment? In an interview with Bill Moyers, Ron Anderson, CEO of Parkland Hospital in Dallas, made the following statement: "When you think of a disease, you can think of the hospital. But when you think of an illness, you've got to think of home and family and community" (Moyers, 1993, p. 37). The idea of community as a resource presumes, of course, that the individual who is recovering from illness finds support and affirmation rather than indifference or worse. The term *community* is itself problematic and defies easy definition. The American Heritage Dictionary (1969, p. 270) provides the following four:

1. A group of people living in the same locality and under the same government.

2. A social group or class having common interests.

3. Similarity or identity: a *community of interests*.

4. Society as a whole: the public.

For the purpose of this discussion, the second and third of these, which make shared interest the defining characteristic, are most salient. But how is such interest to be defined, and by whom? The satirist Kurt Vonnegut pondered this question. In *Cat's Cradle* (1963/1998), Vonnegut suggested that "humanity is organized into teams that do God's Will without ever discovering what they are doing" (p. 2). This means that we are linked to each other but in mysterious ways. He labeled God's team a *karass* and contrasted it with a "seeming team," a false *karass*, which is "meaningless in terms of the way God get things done." He gave the following examples of false karasses: "The Communist Party, the Daughters of the American Revolution, the General Electric Company, the International Order of Odd Fellows, and any nation, anytime, anywhere" (pp. 91–92). Although this somewhat overstates the problem, with characteristic irony, Vonnegut was saying that a community cannot be constructed arbitrarily, since it is defined more by its function than by its structure. In this era of global villages and internet chatrooms, neither is a community defined geographically. How, then, can it be characterized?

Nathanson, in his blueprint for a community that might be characterized as healing, suggests that the defining feature is that it modulates affect in its members, that is, that it has the means to support affective expression while maximizing positive and minimizing negative affective states (Nathanson, 1995). This characterization is derived from the work of Sylvan Tomkins (1962, 1963) and is similar to ideas expressed late in his career by Carl Rogers, who also considered how empathy might operate at a public level (Teich, 1992). Nadelson (1993), in characterizing the health care system as unempathic to the perspectives and needs of women and minorities, also noted the reciprocity between the well-being of the individual and the integrity of the larger group. O'Hara (1997) offered a broad vision of community by contrasting Western and Eastern cultures and their associated psychological perspectives. She termed Western culture "egocentric" because of its emphasis on the self and on boundaries between self and other, which favor objectivity and rigid distinctions between health and illness. In contrast, "sociocentric" cultures place greater importance on subjectivity and sensitivity to the needs and well-being of others, and belonging is highly valued. It is tempting to relate the anomie associated with many forms of mental disorder to what O'Hara calls "the rupture between self and context"; if this is so, then one benefit of a healing community may be that it confers such a sense of belonging.

Although the polarization suggested by O'Hara is of heuristic value, it appears anachronistic. With the breakdown in geographical borders, cultural purity is hard to find. To paraphrase, "East may be East and West, West, but ever the twain do meet." Many of the features of sociocentric cultures are readily available in the West as well as the East, and these features are heavily represented in nontraditional healing milieus.

Sociocentric cultures can be found at the micro as well as the macro level. For example, a self-help program such as the National Depressive and Manic–Depressive Association constitutes a subculture that has many of the features noted above; the same can be said of Alcoholics Anonymous (AA) and Narcotics Anonymous (NA), as well as myriad other resources that have sprung up nationally and internationally to meet a need for support, dialogue, and guidance springing from common experience and shared sources of pain. The potential for empathy is strong. Still other resources may be health-promoting as a byproduct of their other functions. A patient of mine, a young man who had tragically lost his wife to cancer after a brief marriage, and who had become depressed two years later when he had moved from the home which they had shared, foundered in his attempts to find support because others expected him (as they usually do) to have "gotten over it." He had wandered into a small synagogue several blocks from his new home and, to his amazement, discovered a tightly knit group of people who welcomed him warmly. An artist who had always found traditional religion alien to his personal spirituality, he encountered others of like mind; in fact, the ethos was reminiscent of the climate of tolerance, interest, and respect he had enjoyed in his marital relationship: validation that had compensated for many years of experiencing the opposite in a failed previous marriage. He felt he had found "a home." His depression, which had responded only partially to medication and psychotherapy, improved considerably. He decided to join the synagogue. The Yiddish word for family, "mishpocheh," comes to mind. As with most Yiddish words, there is no exact English translation. The humorist, Leo Rosten, suggested that "clan" may be closest, since members of the extended family, including ancestors (back 6000 years or so) may be included. Rosten suggested that the sense of shared heritage, common values, and obligations constitute the essence of this term (Rosten, 1970, p. 250).

In considering community as shared experience, and underscoring the role that empathy plays in creating linkage, a personal experience comes to mind. My family and I attended the performance of a string quartet given at noontime at a local university. Just before the concert began, we noted with some unease that a group of obviously retarded young men and women were led into the

Gustav Vigeland, *The Column*, sculpture, Frogner Park, Oslo.

room and noisily took their places in the audience. Though ashamed of our initial response, we noted that others around us also appeared ill-at-ease, initially glancing in the group's direction and then studiously avoiding eye contact. Both our unease, which we attributed to the prospect for disruptive behavior, and our shame diminished as the concert proceeded uninterrupted until, during one particularly lengthy adagio, one of the young men suddenly blurted out, "I'm hungry." There was a moment of hushed silence, broken only by one of the group's attendants who said, "Good behavior, please. John, we'll eat soon." John was not cajoled; he went on to say, "But I want to eat now!" The audience, as one, erupted in laughter. It was not one of your quiet, stifled laughs, but unconstrained and hearty: the shared laughter of hungry but well behaved men and women who had surrendered but not completely forgotten their lunch hour. The laughter was unabashed, spontaneous, and joyful. The performers, who laughed as well, played on without further incident. Empathy can be a group phenomenon and community can arise spontaneously.

MARRIAGE AND THE HEALING ENVIRONMENT

There is considerable evidence that the most common form of healing dyad, a successful marriage, is good for health. We have long known that its opposite is bad for health. Drawing on a series of studies of normal families conducted by the Timberlawn Research Foundation, psychiatrist Jerry Lewis (1998) has suggested that some marriages, which he termed "competent," create a milieu in which old wounds and traumas may be healed. Competent marriages are characterized by a balance of closeness and autonomy, sharing of power, tolerance for differences and for the expression of affect, and mechanisms for resolving problems and conflicts. Empathy, according to Lewis, is likely to be found in such marriages. The compulsion to repeat, first noted by Freud, implies the wish to master and overcome.

While for many of our patients the choice of a love partner appears to replicate rather than correct past damage, the recognition of such a pattern may be transformational. When the focal objective in treatment involves transitioning from a destructive context to one that supports new learning, the patient may be freed up to make better choices. The psychotherapist, through facilitating necessary transitions, serves to prepare the patient for healing relationships. Ultimately, it is life that heals the patient; the job of the treater is to pave the way.

For many patients, core historical themes are repeated in behavioral patterns that evoke familiar but painful responses, a phenomenon considered in chapter seven. The identification of such repetitive patterns may help therapists to understand the sources of the patient's suffering. Luborsky's (1977) theories about core conflictual relationship themes speaks to this issue. Such patterns may also be discerned through experience in the transference, as the Plan Diagnosis (Weiss *et al.*, 1986) scheme of formulation indicates. The identification of such themes indicates not only pathology; there is also an implicit striving toward health: toward overcoming and mastery, toward better endings. Sometimes such better endings occur as the result of good fortune, and sometimes as the result of therapy—for example, a patient may modify a key relationship or end a destructive one. Although for some patients the relation-ship with the therapist may serve as a model in certain respects, its major function is to encourage and facilitate changes in behavior, increasing the likelihood that healthier choices may be made.

As we have previously considered, psychotherapists who are too preoccu-pied with reversing pathogenic events that took place in the past may miss the opportunity to help a patient reshape the present. This can be done in two ways: by mitigating the influence of those environmental factors that perpetu-ate pathology and by strengthening the healing potential of others that are beneficial. Braverman (1995) has suggested that the work of therapy may be facilitated (and perhaps shortened?) through interventions not only with part-ners, but with parents as well, which he referred to as "intergenerational work." Here, too, the aim is to change the dynamics of the environment. Patients with borderline personality disorders, many of whom have trauma histories, are believed by some psychotherapists to require prolonged healing relationships. There is no general agreement, however, on how far therapists should go in *constituting* rather than *mobilizing* such relationships. Some have suggested that supportive and validating marriages may exert a favorable impact on the course of such disorders (Links & Heslegrave, 2000; Paris & Braverman, 1995), while Johnson and Williams-Keeler, at the University of Ottawa (1998), have re-ported on the ability of a focused form of marital therapy, designed to create a secure attachment, to reduce the symptoms of posttraumatic stress disorder.

Lewis (1998), in summarizing the literature on the benefits of healing marriages, noted that the term "corrective emotional experience," which has been attributed to successful psychotherapy, applies as well to certain mar-riages. Sometimes, however, the impact of marriage is the opposite: it worsens rather than heals wounds. When this is the case, treatment of the individual alone is likely to fail. Attention to the marriage or family dynamics is essential. The schizophrenic patient who lives in an environment characterized by in-tense emotion may do poorly, and treatment of the family has been shown to prolong remission. The same finding applies to patients with unipolar depres-sion (Hooley et al., 1986) and bipolar disorder (Miklowitz et al., 1988).

If bad marriages perpetuate disease (and contribute to illness) and good marriages heal, the question that needs to be asked is: what is the difference? Lewis (1998) identified the key ingredient as empathic communication. Within the shelter of a trusting relationship, one which creates what Havens (1989) has referred to as "a safe place," work that is unfinished may be addressed. Marital partners, by virtue of the amount of time spent together, and the joint responsibilities and challenges they face in ordinary day-to-day living, have the opportunity to reveal themselves to each other (or, more properly, cannot avoid doing so). The response to such vulnerability, if empathic, can be affirming for all the reasons considered in earlier chapters; failures in empathy can lead to anger, disappointment, and a breakdown in communication, but also to repair and new learning. As we have seen, the environment continues to shape neural and genetic events; the treater who is able to exploit this potential may unleash powerful healing forces.

THE INTERPERSONAL ENVIRONMENT AND THE IMMUNE SYSTEM

The discovery of neural connections within the immune system has established a somatic basis for the well-recognized relationship between emotional and physical health. As we come to understand the ways in which the nervous and immune systems interact, the impact of stressors and the mitigating effects of positive social influences become clearer. Stress-induced abnormalities in the secretion of corticotrophin-releasing factor (CRF) have been linked to the increase in hypothalamo–pituitary–adrenal (HPA) axis activity found in depression, the most common psychiatric disorder (Nemeroff et al., 1984; Banki et al., 1987). The relationship between stress and illness, both somatic and mental, appears to be mediated through this complex network, which constitutes a core component of the immune system.

Neurotransmission is primarily a chemical event. At a molecular level, the immune response to injury and infection is mediated through cytokines, proteins which serve as messengers within the brain and elsewhere, and which modulate body responses to reestablish homeostasis (Kronfol & Remick, 2000). Through feedback loops, immune activity is regulated and cytokine production kept in balance with HPA activity. Because of these connections, immune function at a cellular level reflects the impact of external and internal events, some of which are emotional and psychosocially induced. The immune system plays an important role in adaptation, affecting behavior through its effects on the internal milieu. One example of such adaptation is the role of cytokines in bringing about some of the phenomena associated with infection, behaviors known collectively as "sickness behavior," such as increased sleep, decreased appetite, and decreased sexual drive (Kronfol & Remick, 2000). It is interesting to note in this regard that severely depressed individuals, such as those suffering from melancholia, also manifest similar behaviors: the so-called "vegetative symptoms."

In addition to cytokines, the immune and nervous systems are also linked through the activity of the endogenous opioids: endorphins and enkephalins. These peptides have been found in animal research to interact in various ways with cytokines, and may serve to regulate their production (Carr, 1991; Bertolucci *et al.*, 1996). As with the cytokines, the endogenous opioids may prove to be useful in the treatment of cancer and other somatic disorders (Zhong *et al.*, 1996), and may also find a role in the treatment of psychiatric disorders. Endogenous opioids are affected by various environmental factors, including exercise (Sforzo, 1989; Hennig *et al.*, 1994) and stress. They shape mood and behavior through their impact on the neurotransmitters involved in psychiatric disorders. Abnormalities in immunity that appear related to opioid peptide activity have been observed in depression and anxiety (Castilla-Cortazar *et al.*, 1998; Darko *et al.*, 1992), suggesting that the higher rates of morbidity and mortality associated with many major mental disorders are brought about by dysregulation of the immune system.

Neuroimmunology, the investigative subspecialty that bridges neuroscience and immunology, has begun to provide us with intriguing information about how we maintain health as well as how we become ill; psychoneuroimmunology adds yet another dimension: the contributions of mind. The importance of relationships, certain types of relationships in particular, in modulating the impact of stressors and reducing vulnerability to some types of illness is a significant and repeated finding. A great deal of attention has been paid, for example, to the impact of psychotherapy and the healing value of positive relationships on the course of cancer. Over some years, psychiatrist David Spiegel has been a strong advocate of group psychotherapy for women suffering from breast cancer. In a series of articles describing his research, Spiegel has presented data demonstrating the beneficial effects of such groups on mental health and also has presented evidence of prolonged survival (Spiegel *et al.*, 1989, 1999; Spiegel, 1990, 1994, 1995; Blake-Mortimer *et al.*, 1999). Spiegel has attributed the favorable impact of group treatment on the progression of cancer to the social support offered in his groups, a finding supported by data that indicate that daily contact with others, strong marriages, and the availability of a confidante promote healing. Along with others who have studied the impact of psychosocial intervention on cancer progression, he attributes the favorable impact to enhanced immune function (Spiegel *et al.*, 1998; van der Pompe *et al.*, 1996).

While it is clear that mental disorder—for example, depression—is improved in cancer patients, actual prolongation of life through such means remains unproven. What is clear is that the group context is a powerful method of creating support that assists patients in dealing with their illnesses and with the prospect of their death. Cancer support groups have become a standard part of many hospital programs in recent years, partly in response to such findings. As Rachel Remen's distinction between healing and cure suggests

(Moyers, p. 344), cancer support programs target the former even when they may be unable to effect the latter.

One of the main contributors to the psychoneuroimmunology literature was Norman Cousins, editor of the *Saturday Review*, who attributed his recovery from ankylosing spondylitis to his use of humor as a healing vehicle. Having received a grim prognosis, he balanced chemotherapy with Marx Brothers films and found he could mitigate his pain as well as improve his mood. Such strategies may help to reverse a compromised immune system. A large body of literature links stress with a decrease in immunity. In a review of the literature, Herbert and Cohen (1993) cite such factors as the duration of the stress and its nature, with interpersonal stress being particularly damaging. Brosschot and colleagues at the University of Amsterdam (1998) demonstrated reduced T helper cells in situations where the stressor was experienced as uncontrollable. This finding is consistent with the beneficial effects of group psychotherapy even when patients are terminally ill, since a reduction in felt helplessness may lead to increased feelings of control.

If stress adversely affects immune function, and if the impairment of immune function is one important variable in both somatic and mental disorders, then treatment of patients should include attempts to mitigate and possibly reverse such effects. There is now considerable evidence that interpersonal relationships do exercise a protective function and may be helpful in promoting recovery. Kennedy, Kiecolt-Glaser, and Glaser at Ohio State University have reported on experiments that demonstrate both cellular and humoral immunity are adversely affected by social stressors, and interpersonal resources such as a good marriage afford protection (Kennedy *et al.*, 1988; Kiecolt-Glaser, 1999). Their studies indicated that interventions that promote relaxation or include self-disclosure were also protective. Loneliness, absence of closeness, and marital stress all adversely affected immune function while the opposite promoted health. Kiecolt-Glaser (1999) further stated that it was not intact marriage alone, but a satisfying marital relationship that offered the greatest protection against the effects of stress on immune function. These same researchers have reported on studies involving caregivers of demented spouses (Kennedy *et al.*, 1988), which demonstrated an increased rate of both physical and mental disorder, as well as a lower level of responsiveness to administered cytokines: a measure of immune system dysfunction. Once again, the degree of impairment was related to the quality of social support present. Such effects tended to linger even after the caregiving role terminated. Depression is common in this group of individuals, and, like immune dysfunction and ill-health in general, tends to linger. Kiecolt-Glaser (1998) pointed to the importance of this observation since this (growing) subset of the population may also have poorer social supports and therefore lack mitigating influences. Despite what we know about optimal environments, sometimes they simply do not exist for a given patient. Group homes, day programs, clubhouses, and other such structured alternatives may prove crucial in such situations.

HEALING IN A TECHNOLOGICAL ERA

Psychiatry, until very recently, could not boast of procedures and lacked a technological dimension. That situation is changing rapidly. In considering the benefits of a targeted intervention that is designed to mitigate barriers to healing, followed by a process that takes place within an environment that supports it, I have repeatedly emphasized the importance of empathy. Empathy, in turn, has been characterized as an interpersonal phenomenon that relies heavily on thoughtful listening by an interested, sympathetic human being. How can this be reconciled with our growing reliance on machines? Make a telephone call, and you get a machine. Letters are written from one machine to another. Diagnostic procedures and some treatment procedures are conducted partly, or in some instances, completely, by machinery. Medical physicians make their hospital rounds holding palm-tops that contain algorithms for treating a variety of disorders or for determining drug–drug interactions, to mention only two of many possible functions. Health care providers communicate with their patients by electronic mail and some have developed their own websites, with the blessing of professional organizations, to assist them in managing their practices. Telemedicine, an innovation used primarily to provide expert services where there was a dearth of qualified practitioners, now is available through ordinary desktop computers and soon will be widely available through portable equipment. Virtual reality is on the not-too-distant horizon. What is the fate of empathy?

There are two features of the technological revolution underway that deserve our attention in this book. First, the playing field has been leveled. Our patients have access, for the first time in the history of medicine, to the same information that their treaters do. Data are available about disease, treatment options, comparative outcomes, the risks and benefits of procedures, and provider and system performance. Although there is variability in the quality of information available on the internet, there is no problem in finding any information being sought if the seeker is persistent. A second consideration is that caregivers are pressed to take care of more patients within shorter periods of time, which makes reliance on technological extenders more appealing. Mental health practitioners, like their medical colleagues, can be expected to turn increasingly to technology to facilitate and improve care, to standardize procedures and to monitor process toward a desired outcome. An example is the increasing interest in developing personal websites to support clinical practice. Outcome assessment is likely to become a standard aspect of practice, most likely through the use of evaluative instruments that are self-administered. The maintenance of an I–Thou perspective will be challenged by such trends, which are likely to lead to clearer distinctions between activities of treatment and the process of healing.

It is not unusual for patients to acquire more up-to-date information about their conditions than is known by their treaters. Elvin Semrad, a psychoanalyst with remarkable empathic abilities, was fond of relating an anecdote involving a highly intelligent, narcissistic man who paraded his intellect before his analyst as a means of defending against the insult of his depression. Semrad commented, "All right, you're smarter than I am, but it's my job to help you" (Semrad, 1963–66). Today's patients, of course, may bring printouts. While this may be helpful in focusing clinical discussion, and may constitute one of the few truly effective spurs toward continuing education, the information may also be misleading or incorrect. Sometimes the search for cure leads to an adverse outcome. In June 2000, the *Boston Globe* reported the tragic death of a child who had been treated by unorthodox means in a program that was discovered on the internet by a desperate parent after more conventional treatments had disappointed (Pertman, 2000).

The ready availability of information and the diversity of treatment approaches now being advertised have created a care system without walls. In response to this situation, the National Library of Medicine (NLM) has developed Medline Plus, a website for consumers that complements the one available for clinicians. This site provides carefully selected, evidence-based information on diseases and treatments. A branch of the National Institutes of Health (NIH), the NLM has hyperlinked its site to others that describe ongoing drug research, Federal Drug Administration (FDA) activities, and a wealth of information about currently available drugs. The patient may also be helped to find a health care practitioner and can obtain information about prospective treaters and institutions. A nonprofit organization, Health on the Net (HON), which is subsidized by the Swiss government, has taken the lead in screening health sites and establishing requirements for the reliability of information as the cost of providing its imprimatur. Despite such efforts, however, it can be assumed that our patients, driven by the imperative of illness, will continue to search the net widely and will outstrip our best efforts to stay informed. While this presents problems, it also offers an unprecedented opportunity for partnership.

Perhaps as a manifestation of the importance of face-to-face contact, technological forms of communication are now adding a visual component. Teleconferences are common in the business world, but less so among clinicians and even less so between physicians and patients. The limiting factor is the complexity and cost of equipment, a variable that is improving. Visual contact is possible in some telephone systems and may also take place using desktop computers. Digitalized images of talking heads have also been developed to simulate a personal contact; the application of such technology to health care cannot be far distant. While these early prototypes create digitalized re-creations of people talking, complete with facial animation and lifelike voices, later versions will also be interactive. Such devices may allow a patient to have electronic communication on a face-to-face basis with an office manager, secretary, or case manager, and it is not too far-fetched to envision a role in computer-assisted psychotherapy. With the advent of virtual reality and its introduction to mental health care, the possibilities expand even farther.

VIRTUAL EMPATHY

Virtual reality (VR) techniques have been developed and are being used in the treatment of patients with certain types of mental disorder, most notably phobias, where images are used to facilitate desensitization through immersing the patient gradually in a feared environment (Rothbaum et al., 1997; North et al., 1998). The limitations thus far are in the cumbersome equipment (head-mounted displays) and the crudeness of the technology (Bullinger et al., 1998). The possibility of networked VR, with the creation of a virtual space in which patients might interact with each other, with their families and friends and with their caregivers, has been raised by Ohsuga and Oyama (1998), an application that would offer advantages over chatrooms, the use of simulated talking heads, or teleconferencing. While such interaction is conceivable using current equipment, it is unlikely. The use of more specialized settings, such as the Cave automated virtual environment (CAVE), which does not rely on head-mounted gear but places the subject in an enclosed space and uses projective equipment to create its effects, is also impractical and too expensive for common use. Given the history of the computer technology evolution, however, advances that lead to broader usage are certainly not out of the question. Alessi and his colleagues at the University of Michigan have considered an even more ambitious prospect: the development of a virtual human. In considering the limitations of efforts to date to create virtual humans, Alessi has pointed to the absence of qualities that would encourage genuine attachment. These qualities of "relatedness" include evidence of attentiveness, and attunement to the emotional state of the other person and to his/her uniqueness and affective tone. Alessi calls such a profile "virtual relatedness fidelity" and suggests how this type of resource might be developed and used as an extender for a health care provider (Alessi & Huang, 1998).

We have taken a leap into the future, but one that is not hard to envision. Can human qualities be simulated? Undoubtedly so. Can technology create a substitute for an empathic listener? Probably not. Can technology contribute to the activities of an empathic psychotherapist, extending his/her availability and subserving functions that *reflect* empathic awareness rather than *simulate* it? I see no reason why not. An example would be the use of computerized resources to search for an appropriate self-help program for a patient suffering from a rare disorder. Another might be the development or location of a support group that uses linked VR or video conferencing to provide a forum for a patient who has become depressed while engaged in the care of a demented spouse or parent. Both cases would reflect the clinician's tailored and empathic response and expand the impact of his/her understanding of the patient's state of mind. Many other possibilities come to mind as well, all of which build on and expand empathic understanding beyond the consulting room door and the treatment setting, creating or enhancing the healing environment. Technology is here to stay. It need not corrupt.

PRESERVING AN ENDANGERED SPECIES

We have come a long way from *Einfuhlung*. As the new century, the first of a new millennium, begins, we are left with many of the same questions that were present a thousand years ago: about the fundamental nature of mankind, the causes of illness, the mystery of mind, the challenge of treating and healing the sick. Interpersonal skills are not prioritized in training or in practice in the current scientific era; for this reason, we have considered the empathic function as it contributes to the healing process as endangered. How will future generations of caregivers retain and hone this capacity?

To address this question, let us first consider the emerging context in which practitioners of this century will work. In chapter one, I predicted that the health care system of the twenty-first century would be characterized by the following ten features:

1. Prospective payment, which prioritizes the needs of populations rather than individual patients.

2. Patients who are treated for documentable states of illness that may be characterized in terms of impairments relative to baseline states.

3. Interventions that are evidence-based, focused, and directed toward recovery of function.

4. Collaborative patterns of care that involve multiple treaters and significant others.

5. Blurred boundaries between the formal health care system and alternative or complementary medicine.

6. Increasing use of technology in diagnostic appraisal, treatment, and assessment of outcome.

7. Selective use of psychosocial treatment methods, including psychotherapy, alone or in combination with biologically based interventions.

8. Psychotherapies that are configured to the specific goals of therapy and based on evidence of efficacy and effectiveness.

9. Improved integration of mental health and medical practice.

10. An atmosphere characterized by scrutiny of treatment, resulting in continued erosion of the insular environment in which psychotherapy has historically taken place.

Preparation of a clinician to serve within such a system will require changes in education. First, new skills must be learned. There must be comfort with technology but a recognition that technology complements personal caregiving and does not replace it. The old dualism must be replaced with a holistic approach to patient care that integrates body and mind, respects the healing potential in every human being, and seeks to free this capacity from the impasse of illness. Idiosyncratic practice patterns must either be validated as demonstrably preferable or honed to conform to the evidence of what works and what does not. The blurred boundaries between the formal and informal health care system, mainstream and complementary medicine, must be crossed with greater confidence in the value of each, as that value is confirmed by data and by credible evidence. Ideology must be subordinated to the overarching objective of treatment: recovery from illness in preparation for healing. Responsibility for the population served as well as for those individuals who emerge from that population to become patients must guide clinical decision-making, balancing advocacy with allocation, sympathy with justice.

Of all the systemic and personal barriers to empathy explored in earlier chapters, two stand out. First, the selection process as well as the training of contemporary health care practitioners have been shaped by dualistic thinking. Second, and as a product of such thinking, acculturation of new practitioners to the clinical environment has systematically dulled normal empathic capacities by favoring objective over subjective clinical data, the disease over the illness, and the illness over the person who has it. The answer to the first is in selection, to the second in modeling and retraining.

Although there have been efforts to teach empathy, this appears an ill-fated approach. The emphasis, rather, should be on identifying those points in the educational process when a natural capacity for empathy is blunted or undermined. There is some evidence that general medicine may be leading the way toward the necessary reforms in education. According to the *New York Times* (Langone, 2000), initiatives at such medical schools as Harvard, Yale, and the Universities of Texas, New Mexico, South Carolina, and Kansas seek to enhance doctor–patient communication and reinforce the students' natural tendencies toward compassionate care. The American Academy on Physician and Patient (AAPP), an organization of Canadian and American health care professionals, has, as its stated goal, "no less than to change the practice of medicine by helping doctors relate more effectively to each patient" (AAPP, 2000). The AAPP pursues this ambitious goal through establishing educational standards, disseminating literature and videotapes, and bringing together leaders in medical training who are concerned about such issues. Through such organizations as the Bayer Institute for Health Care Communication and the Fetzer Institute, position statements have been crafted, drawn from a growing literature on teaching models that emphasize the doctor–patient relationship (Greenfield *et al.*, 1985; Simpson *et al.*, 1991; Novack *et al.*, 1992; Keller & Carroll, 1994; Stewart *et al.*, 1995; Kurtz & Silverman, 1996; Silverman *et al.*, 1998). It is ironic that general medicine should take the lead, while psychiatry and the other mental health professions appear to be moving in the opposite direction, perhaps taking such matters for granted.

The doctor–patient sequence at Harvard Medical School illustrates one approach to preserving the humanistic core of medical practice in the next generation of physicians. Medical students are exposed to a three-year course on the doctor–patient relationship. Teaching takes place in small groups, offering the opportunity for consensual validation as students reflect on the personal transition involved. In the third year, when students participate for the first time as team members on the various hospital services, the transition is supported through experiential learning and consideration of the various ethical, interpersonal, and cultural problems universally encountered. Through a tutorial and clinical exercises that use simulated patients, as well as through bedside instruction, students are encouraged to engage with a patient in a personal and empathic manner. The topics covered in tutorial sessions pertain to the human aspects of practice: students refer to this as "the other stuff." These include such matters as: the delivery of bad news to a patient, the dilemmas associated with end-of-life care, special issues pertaining to the treatment of gay and lesbian patients, the duty to warn and protect, truth-telling and disclosure of information, and a variety of ethical challenges related to the constraints and financial limitations of contemporary practice. Students read for, plan, and lead the sessions, which are facilitated by health care professionals drawn from the various specialties. Although there is reading involved, the focus is on the interactive tutorial and the method of learning is experiential. An important aspect of teaching is the elicitation from the students themselves, of their personal responses to the important transition they are undergoing in moving from the preclinical to the clinical training years. Several times during the course students are asked to write a reflective paper that briefly presents any personal experience in the clinic or on the ward that has had a profound impact. After some hesitation, most students write openly about themselves: their reactions, their fears, their disappointments, and successes. The papers are read and discussed in the group.

Midway through the course, an exercise is conducted with a simulated patient, an amateur but trained actor (most of these actors are patients who have had serious illnesses and are concerned about improving the system). The brief interview involves sharing with the simulated patient that s/he has a serious illness that cannot be cured. Students are observed by a preceptor and are videotaped; feedback from the "patient" as well as the preceptor leads to discussion. The strengths and limitations of a student are addressed and carefully considered with him or her, and, when necessary, an opportunity is presented to repeat the exercise. Tutors in this program hear what drives a student, what accounts for the choice of medicine as a career, what facilitates and what blocks the human dimension.

At this early point in the development of a professional identity, the importance of balancing caring with precision, empathy with objectivity, involvement with appropriate boundaries, must be reinforced. A report describing this program (Branch et al., 1993) emphasized the struggle that students at this point in their career are likely to experience between empathic attunement to their patients and acculturation to the role of doctor, when the models they see often fall short of their vision. One student, for example, described his distress at finding staff attitudes toward a markedly obese woman neglectful of her emotional state, her shame, her pain, and his discomfort when jokes were made about her and he couldn't decide whether or not to laugh. Another described herself as the "listener" of the treatment team, a job for which others had too little time. She shared her difficulty in setting limits with patients so that she could get her work done. "I get too involved," she said. A third student presented a poignant account of his connection with a dying patient and his later difficulty attending the autopsy.

EMPATHY REDUX

We began by noting that the health care system appears to have lost its heart. Although it is fashionable to blame the sad state of affairs in our disorganized, costly, and largely inefficient system on managed care, there are many reasons to expect that health care in this country will continue to be managed. Mental health care, though much belabored, is a highly valued social and medical resource that is being made progressively more available to larger numbers of people. Advances in treatment efficacy hold great promise; the challenge is to follow the emerging science without abandoning the art.

We have traced the roots of empathy as a feature of the art of psychotherapy from its origins in aesthetics, through its use over the past hundred years in the various forms of psychotherapy, recognizing its role in creating and sustaining helping relationships and promoting the process of healing. Empathy lies at the very heart of psychotherapy, no matter what the theoretical orientation of the practitioner, and psychotherapy lies at the very heart of mental health care. Now, more than ever, it is imperative that we find a way to reconcile the empathic process with emerging models of health and illness. To lose this perspective would impoverish not only psychiatry but health care in general.

In this book, I have tried to present a way of thinking about empathy that bridges the biopsychosocial gap created by dualistic thinking, replacing *dualism* with *duality*. Our nature is, in fact, dual. We are biological creatures who are at the very same time spiritual. The experience of our spirituality is in our mental life, a blessing that relates to but is more than the brain that brings it about. Illness that affects the mind is particularly painful because it distances and alienates us from the context that sustains and reinforces our humanity. The treatment of such illness, therefore, must return us into that context; this is the job of the treater. To accomplish this job, the treater must herself be, more than anything else, human. As Buber has taught us (1957), the highest form of communication is the interhuman. Empathy is the heart of such communication.

During the course of this short book, we have considered empathy from a number of perspectives. We have examined the forces that undermine its use in practice, both those emanating from the context in which practice takes place and those that are more personal reflections of our limitations, also because we are human. We have also considered those factors, personal and contextual, that support our efforts to relate empathically and examined the manner in which empathic communication supports clinical objectives. The emerging science of brain provides new clues as to how empathy develops and what its neurological substrate appears to be, while the evolutionary perspective suggests its importance to our survival and success as a species. We have considered empathy to be a nonlinear process in which one person ventures past the boundary that separates him from another, and enters, for a brief time, the life space of that other. The act is volitional, but it draws on a ubiquitous capacity that is inborn and as biological in nature as it is psychological. The empathic cycle is both cognitive and affective, though either entry point may be used; most important, empathy is iterative, calling for validation that ultimately is determined in a clinical situation by one consideration alone: does it help? Clinical empathy is a refined use of an inborn capacity that can be honed, can be blunted, can be suppressed, can be facilitated. The process, as described and as illustrated through case reports, is a creative one that draws on the reservoir of life experience of the empathizer, his/her knowledge of the other, observations made and experienced both cognitively and somatically—listening, in the fullest sense of the word. Imagination, inference, and affective resonance are all part of the empathic experience. To use empathy is to make demands on the self and to place the self at the disposal of the other, consciously, strategically, and to a degree that is consistent with clinical need.

The use of an empathic means of knowing remains a fundamental component of the art of practice, but also its science. Because we share the human experience with our patients, we are able to find the person who tends to become lost in the illness and help that patient reemerge. Contemporary ideas about the impact of experience on gene transcription, neural networks, and implicit memory lead us to a new duality: human beings are shaped by forces often out of the sphere of conscious awareness. Most important to our task as treaters, this shaping process occurs not once, but continuously from womb to tomb. Our presence in the lives of our patients, albeit often episodic or brief, may be catalytic to this process, and corrective of previous influences. Our job is to get the patient back on his or her optimal developmental track. This is the healing function that is inseparable from treatment and, for many of our patients, it signifies the beginning of a new beginning. Although our goal is to initiate recovery from the painful state our patient brings to our door, a companion goal must be to begin a reeducative process by setting the stage for more lasting healing. In the service of such objectives, clinical empathy is the tool that blends our science with our art.

In the clinical encounter, we have observed that empathy is corrective for us as well as the patient, coming into play for the most part to fill in the blanks: to bridge a gap, understand an inconsistency, pursue and clarify an implicit motive. It is empathy that constitutes one of our major routes of access to procedural memory, the type of neural processes that underlie patterns of behavior and relating and the codes that determine them. Empathy, therefore, subserves multiple functions. In these times, when the care of populations draws us away from our individual patients, it is particularly important that we remember we are not treating disease, but people. This perspective is most apparent to us when we, as humans, establish connection with the human who is our patient. To practice psychotherapy in such a fashion is to ask a great deal of both oneself and the other: to extend toward each other, engage in the joint task, connect. The purpose of the clinician, in partnership with the patient and those others in the patient's environment who will accompany him or her on the journey from illness to health, is to treat: to mitigate the barriers to healing and open the pathway to healing. To do so successfully is the reward of the practitioner and the fulfillment of the professional role. This was true in antiquity, and it is no less the case today.

REFERENCES

Alessi, N. E., & Huang, M. P. (1998). The potential relevance of attachment theory in assessing relatedness with virtual humans. *Studies in Health Technologies and Informatics, 58*, 180–187.

Alexander, F., & French, T. M. (1974). *Psychoanalytic therapy: Principles and applications.* Lincoln: University of Nebraska. (Original work published 1946.)

American Academy on Physician and Patient (AAPP) (2000). *Application for Membership.*

American heritage dictionary of the English language (1969). Boston: Houghton Mifflin Company.

Banki, C. M., Bissette, G., Arato, M., O'Connor, L., & Nemeroff, C. B. (1987). CSF corticotrophin-releasing factor-like immunoreactivity in depression and schizophrenia. *American Journal of Psychiatry, 144*(7), 873–877.

Bertolucci, M., Perego, L., & De Simoni, M. G. (1996). Central opiate modulation of peripheral IL-6 in rats. *Neuroreport, 7*(6), 1181–1184.

Blake-Mortimer, J., Gore-Felton, C., Kimerling, R., Turner-Cobb, J. M., & Spiegel, D. (1999). Improving the quality and quantity of life among patients with cancer: A review of the effectiveness of group psychotherapy. *European Journal of Cancer, 35*(11), 1581–1586.

Branch, W., Pels, R. J., Lawrence, R. S., & Arky, R. (1993). Becoming a doctor: Critical-incident reports from third year medical students. *New England Journal of Medicine, 329*, 1130–1132.

Braverman, S. (1995). Intergenerational work as an adjunct to psychoanalysis and psychotherapy. *Journal of the American Academy of Psychoanalysis, 23*(3), 379–393.

Brosschot, J. F., Godaert, G. L., Benschop, R. J., Olff., M., Ballieux, R. E., & Heijnen, C. J. (1998). Experimental stress and immunological reactivity: A closer look at perceived uncontrollability. *Psychosomatic Medicine, 60*(3), 359–361.

Buber, M. (1957). Elements of the interhuman. *Psychiatry, 20*, 105–113.

Budman, S. H., & Gurman, A. S. (1988). *Theory and practice of brief therapy.* New York: Guilford Press.

Bullinger, A. H., Roessler, A., & Mueller-Spahn, F. (1998). From toy to tool: The development of immersive virtual reality environments for psychotherapy of specific phobias. *Studies in Health Technology and Informatics, 58*, 103–111.

Carr, D. J. (1991). The role of endogenous opioids and their receptors in the immune system. *Proceedings of the Society of Experimental Medicine, 198*(2), 710–720.

Castilla-Cortazar, I., Castilla, A., & Gurpegui, M. (1998). Opioid peptides and immunodysfunction in patients with major depression and anxiety disorders. *Journal of Physiology and Biochemistry*, *54*(4), 203–215.

Darko, D. F., Risch, S. C., Gillin, J. C., & Golshan, S. (1992). Association of beta-endorphin with specific clinical symptoms of depression. *American Journal of Psychiatry*, *149*(9), 1162–1167.

Frank, J. (1974). *Persuasion and healing.* New York: Shocken Books.

Greenfield, S., Kaplan, S., & Ware, J. E. (1985). Expanding patient involvement in care: Effects on patient outcome. *Annals of Internal Medicine*, *102*, 520–528.

Havens, L. (1989). *A safe place: Laying the groundwork of psychotherapy.* Cambridge: Harvard University Press.

Hennig, J. Laschefski, U., & Opper, C. (1994). Biopsychological changes after bungee jumping: Beta-endorphin immunoreactivity as a mediator of euphoria? *Neuropsychobiology*, *29*(1), 28–32.

Herbert, T. B., & Cohen, S. (1993). Stress and immunity in humans: A meta-analytic review. *Psychosomatic Medicine*, *55*(4), 364–379.

Hooley, J. M., Orley, J., and Teasdale, J. D. (1986). Levels of expressed emotion and relapse in depressed patients. *British Journal of Psychiatry*, *148*, 642–647.

Johnson, D. H., & Gelso, C. J. (1980). The effectiveness of time limits in counseling and psychotherapy: A critical review. *The Counseling Psychologist*, *9*, 70–83.

Johnson, S. M., & Williams-Keeler, L. (1998). Creating healing relationships for couples dealing with trauma: The use of emotionally focused marital therapy. *Journal of Marital and Family Therapy*, *24*(1), 25–40.

Keller, V., & Carroll, J. G. (1994). A new model for physician-patient communication. *Patient Education and Counseling*, *23*, 131–140.

Kennedy, S., Kiecolt-Glaser, J. K., & Glaser, R. (1988). Immunological consequences of acute and chronic stressors: Mediating role of interpersonal relationships. *British Journal of Medical Psychology*, *61*, 77–85.

Kiecolt-Glaser, J. K. (1999). 1998 Norman Cousins Memorial Lecture. Stress, personal relationships and immune function: Health implications. *Brain, Behavior and Immunity*, *13*(1), 61–72.

Kronfol, Z., and Remick, D. G. (2000). Cytokines and the brain: Implications for psychiatry. *American Journal of Psychiatry*, *157*(5), 683–694.

Kurtz, S. M., & Silverman, J. D. (1996). The Calgary–Cambridge observation guides: An aid to defining the curriculum and organising the teaching in communication training programmes. *Medical Education*, *30*, 83–89.

Langone, J. (2000, 22 August). Medical schools discover value in dispensing compassion. *New York Times*, p. D7.

Lewis, J. M. (1998). For better or for worse: Interpersonal relationships and individual outcome. *American Journal of Psychiatry*, *155*(5), 582–589.

Links, P. S., & Heslegrave, R. J. (2000). Prospective studies of outcome: Understanding mechanisms of change in patients with borderline personality disorder. *Psychiatric Clinics of North America*, *23*(1), 137–150.

Luborsky, L. (1977). Measuring a pervasive psychic structure in psychotherapy: The core conflictual relationship theme. In N. Freedman & S. S. Grand (Eds.), *Communicative structures and psychic structures.* New York: Plenum Press.

Miklowitz, D. J., Goldstein, M. J., Nuechterlein, K. H., Snyder, K. S., & Mintz, J. (1988). Family factors in the course of bipolar affective disorder. *Archives of General Psychiatry*, *45*, 225–231.

Moyers, B. (1993). *Healing and the mind.* New York: Doubleday.

Nadelson, C. C. (1993). Ethics, empathy and gender in health care. *American Journal of Psychiatry*, *150*(9), 1309–1313.

Nathanson, D. L. (1995). Crime and nourishment: Sometimes the tried and true becomes the tired and false. *Bulletin of the Tomkins Institute*, *2*, 25–30.

Neims, A. H. (1999). Why I would recommend complementary or alternative therapies: A physician's perspective. *Rheumatic Disease Clinics of North America*, *25*(4), 845–853.

Nemeroff, C. B., Widerlov, E., Bissette, G.,. Walleus, H., Karlsson, I., Eklund, K., Kilts, C. D., Loosen, P. T., & Vale, W. (1984). Elevated concentrations of CSF corticotrophin-releasing factor-like immunoreactivity in depressed patients. *Science*, *226*(4680), 1342–1344.

North, M. M., North, S. M., & Coble, J. R. (1998). Virtual reality therapy: An effective treatment for phobias. *Studies in Health Technology and Informatics*, *58*, 112–119.

Novack, D. H., Dube, C., & Goldstein, M. G. (1992). Teaching medical interviewing: A basic course on interviewing and the physician-patient relationship. *Archives of Internal Medicine*, *152*, 1814–1820.

O'Hara, M. (1997). Relational empathy: Beyond modernist egocentrism to postmodern holistic contextualism. In A. C. Bohart & L. S. Greenberg (Eds.), *Empathy reconsidered: New directions in psychotherapy* (pp. 295–319). Washington, DC: American Psychological Association.

Ohsuga, M., & Oyama, T. (1998). Possibility of virtual reality for mental care. *Studies in Health Technology and Informatics*, *58*, 82–90.

Paris, J., & Braverman, S. (1995). Successful and unsuccessful marriages in borderline patients. *Journal of the American Academy of Psychoanalysis*, *23*, 153–166.

Pertman, A. (2000, 5 June). Girl's death spotlights therapies of desperation. *Boston Globe*, pp. 1, 10.

Rosten, L. (1970). *The joys of yiddish*. New York: Pocket Books.

Rothbaum, B. O., Hodges, L., & Kooper, R. (1997). Virtual reality exposure therapy. *Journal of Psychotherapy Practice and Research*, *6*(3), 219–226.

Semrad, E. (1963–66). Personal communication.

Sforzo, G. A. (1989). Opioids and exercise. An update. *Sports Medicine*, *7*(2), 109–124.

Silverman, J., Kurtz, S., & Draper, J. (1998). *Skills for communicating with patients*. Abingdon: Radcliffe Medical Press.

Simpson, M., Buckman, R., Stewart, M., Maguire, C. P., Lipkin, M., Novack, D., & Till, J. (1991). Doctor–patient communication: The Toronto consensus statement. *British Medical Journal*, *303*, 1385–1387.

Spiegel, D. (1990). Can psychotherapy prolong cancer survival? *Psychosomatics*, *31*(4), 361–366.

Spiegel, D. (1994). Health caring. Psychosocial support for patients with cancer. *Cancer*, *74*, 1453–1457.

Spiegel, D. (1995). How do you feel about cancer now? Survival and social support. *Public Health Reports*, *110*(3), 298–300.

Spiegel, D., Bloom, J. R., Kraemer, H. C., & Gottheil, E. (1989). Effect of psychosocial treatment on survival of patients with metastatic breast cancer. *Lancet*, *2*(8668), 888–891.

Spiegel, D., Sephton, S. E., Terr, A. I., & Stites, D. P. (1998). Effects of psychosocial treatment in prolonging cancer survival may be mediated by neuroimmune pathways. *Annals of the New York Academy of Sciences*, *840*, 674–683.

Spiegel, D., Morrow, G. R., Classen, C., Raubertas, R., Stott, P. B., Mudaliar, N., Pierce, H. I., Flynn, P. J., Heard, L., & Riggs, G. (1999). Group psychotherapy for recently diagnosed breast cancer patients: A multicenter feasibility study. *Psycho-oncology*, *8*(6), 482–493.

Stewart, M, Belle-Brown, J., Weston, W. W., McWhinney, I. R., McWilliam, C. L., and Freeman, T. R. (1995). *Patient-centered medicine: Transforming the clinical method*. Thousand Oaks, California: Sage Publications.

Teich, N. (Ed.) (1992). *Rogerian perspectives: Collaborative rhetoric for oral and written communication*. Norwood, NJ: Ablex Publishing.

Tomkins, S. S. (1962). *Affect imagery consciousness*, Vol. 1. New York: Springer.

Tomkins, S. S. (1963). *Affect Imagery Consciousness*, Vol. 2. New York: Springer.

Unützer, J., Klap, R., Sturm, R., Young, A. S., Marmon, T., Shatkin, J., & Wells, K. B. (2000). Mental disorders and the use of alternative medicine: Results from a national survey. *American Journal of Psychiatry*, 157, 1851–1857.

van der Pompe, G., Antoni, M., Visser, A., & Garssen, B. (1996). Adjustment to breast cancer: The psychobiological effects of psychosocial interventions. *Patient Education and Counseling*, 28(2), 209–119.

Vonnegut, K. (1998). *Cat's cradle*. New York: Dell. (Original work published 1963.)

Weiss, J., Sampson, H., and the Mount Zion Psychotherapy Group (Eds.) (1986). *The psychoanalytic process: Theory, clinical observation, and empirical research*. New York: Guilford Press.

Zhong, F., Li, X. Y., & Yang, S. L. (1996). Augmentation of TNF-alpha production, NK cell activity and IL-12 p35 mRNA expression by methionine enkephalin. *Chung Kuo Yao Li Hsueh Pao*, 17(2), 182–185.

BIBLIOGRAPHY

Adolphs, R., Damasio, H., Tranel, D., & Damasio, A. R. (1996). Cortical systems for the recognition of emotion in facial expressions. *Journal of Neuroscience, 16*(23), 7678–7687.

Adolphs, R., Tranel, D., & Damasio, A. R. (1998). The human amygdala in social judgment. *Nature, 393*(6684), 470–474.

Alessi, N. E., & Huang, M. P. (1998). The potential relevance of attachment theory in assessing relatedness with virtual humans. *Studies in Health Technologies and Informatics, 58*, 180–187.

Alexander, F., & French, T. M. (1974). *Psychoanalytic therapy: Principles and applications.* Lincoln: University of Nebraska. (Original work published 1946.)

American Academy on Physician and Patient (AAPP) (2000). *Application for Membership.*

American heritage dictionary of the English language (1969). Boston: Houghton Mifflin Company.

American Psychiatric Association (1980). *Diagnostic and statistical manual of mental disorders* (3rd ed.). Washington, DC: Author.

American Psychiatric Association (1987). *Diagnostic and statistical manual of mental disorders* (3rd ed., rev.). Washington, DC: Author.

American Psychiatric Association (1994). *Diagnostic and statistical manual of mental disorders* (4th ed.). Washington, DC: Author.

American Psychiatric Association, Work Group on Psychiatric Evaluation of Adults (1995). Practice guidelines for psychiatric evaluation of adults. *American Journal of Psychiatry, 152*(11), 65–80.

Amini, F., Lewis, T., Lannon, R., Louie, A., Baumbacher, G., McGuinness, T., & Schiff, E. Z. (1996). Affect, attachment, memory: Contributions toward psychobiologic integration. *Psychiatry, 59*, 213–239.

Aring, C. D. (1958). Sympathy and empathy. *Journal of the American Medical Association, 167*(4), 448–452.

Balint, M. (1957). *The doctor, his patient and the illness.* New York: International Universities Press.

Balint, M., Ornstein, P., & Balint, E. (1957). *The doctor, his patient and the illness.* New York: International Universities Press.

Balint, M., Ornstein, P., & Balint, E. (1972). *Focal psychotherapy: An example of applied psychoanalysis.* London: Tavistock Publications.

Banki, C. M., Bissette, G., Arato, M., O'Connor, L., & Nemeroff, C. B. (1987). CSF corticotrophin-releasing factor-like immunoreactivity in depression and schizophrenia. *American Journal of Psychiatry, 144*(7), 873–877.

Barnard, A., & Tong, K. (2000, July 9). The doctor is out: more and more physicians, frustrated with managed care, are trying new professions and finding life less stressful. *The Boston Globe*, p. 17.

Barrett-Lennard, G. (1993). The phases and focus of empathy. *British Journal of Medical Psychology*, 66, 3–14.

Basch, M. F. (1983). Empathic understanding: A review of the concept and some theoretical considerations. *Journal of the American Psychoanalytic Association*, 31, 101–126.

Bechara, A., Damasio, H., Tranel, D., & Damasio, A. R. (1997). Deciding advantageously before knowing the advantageous strategy. *Science*, 275(5304), 1293–1295.

Bennett, M. J. (1983). Focal psychotherapy—terminable and interminable. *American Journal of Psychotherapy*, 37, 365–375.

Bennett, M. J. (1984). Brief psychotherapy and adult development. *Psychotherapy*, 21(2), 171–177.

Bennett, M. J. (1988). The greening of the HMO: Implications for prepaid psychiatry. *American Journal of Psychiatry*, 145, 1544–1549.

Bennett, M. J. (1989). The catalytic function in psychotherapy. *Psychiatry*, 52, 351–365.

Bennett, M. J. (1992). Managed mental health in health maintenance organizations. In S. Feldman (Ed.), *Managed mental health services* (pp. 61–82). Springfield, IL: Charles C. Thomas.

Bennett, M. J. (1993). View from the bridge: Reflections of a recovering staff model HMO psychiatrist. *Psychiatric Quarterly*, 64(1), 45–75.

Bennett, M. J. (1993). The importance in teaching the principles of managed care. *Behavioral Healthcare Tomorrow*, 2, 28–32.

Bennett, M. J. (1996). Is psychotherapy ever medically necessary? *Psychiatric Services*, 47(9), 966–970.

Bennett, M. J. (1997). Focal psychotherapy. In L. I. Sederer & A. J. Rothschild (Eds.), *Acute care psychiatry: Diagnosis and treatment* (pp. 355–373). Baltimore: Williams and Wilkins.

Bennett, M. J. (2000). Retraining the practicing psychiatrist. *Psychiatric Services*, 51(7), 932–934.

Bennett, M. J., & Foos, J. (1996). *Best practices for assessing and managing the suicidal patient*. St. Louis: Merit Behavioral Care Corporation.

Beres, D., & Arlow, J. A. (1974). Fantasy and identification in empathy. *Psychoanalytic Quarterly*, 43, 26–50.

Bertolucci, M., Perego, L., & De Simoni, M. G. (1996). Central opiate modulation of peripheral IL-6 in rats. *Neuroreport*, 7(6), 1181–1184.

Bjork, J., Brown, J., & Goodman, M. (2000). *Casebook for managing managed care*. Washington, DC: APA Press.

Blake-Mortimer, J., Gore-Felton, C., Kimerling, R., Turner-Cobb, J. M., & Spiegel, D. (1999). Improving the quality and quantity of life among patients with cancer: A review of the effectiveness of group psychotherapy. *European Journal of Cancer*, 35(11), 1581–1586.

Blumgart, H. L. (1964). Caring for the patient. *New England Journal of Medicine*, 270(9), 449–456.

Bohart, A. C., & Greenberg, L. S. (1997). Empathy and psychotherapy: An introductory overview. In A. C. Bohart & L. S. Greenberg (Eds.), *Empathy reconsidered: New directions in psychotherapy* (pp. 3–31). Washington, DC: American Psychological Association.

Bohart, A. C., & Rosenbaum, R. (1995). The dance of empathy: empathy, diversity, and technical eclecticism. *The Person-Centered Journal*, 2, 5–29.

Bohart, A. C., & Tallman, K. (1997). Empathy and the active client: An integrative, cognitive-experiential approach. In A. C. Bohart & L. S. Greenberg (Eds.), *Empathy reconsidered: new directions in psychotherapy* (pp. 393–415). Washington, DC: American Psychological Association.

Bolognini, S. (1997). Empathy and "empathism." *International Journal of Psycho-Analysis*, 78(Pt. 2), 279–293.

Book, H. E. (1991). Is empathy cost efficient? *American Journal of Psychiatry*, 45(1), 21–30.

Branch, W., Pels, R. J., Lawrence, R. S., & Arky, R. (1993). Becoming a doctor: Critical-incident reports from third year medical students. *New England Journal of Medicine*, 329, 1130–1132.

Braverman, S. (1995). Intergenerational work as an adjunct to psychoanalysis and psychotherapy. *Journal of the American Academy of Psychoanalysis*, 23(3), 379–393.

Breuer, J., & Freud, S. (1955). Studies on hysteria. In J. Strachey (Ed. and Trans.), *The standard edition of the complete psychological works of Sigmund Freud* (Vol. 2, pp. 30, 33–37). London: Hogarth Press. (Original work published 1895.)

Brosschot, J. F., Godaert, G. L., Benschop, R. J., Olff., M., Ballieux, R. E., & Heijnen, C. J. (1998). Experimental stress and immunological reactivity: A closer look at perceived uncontrollability. *Psychosomatic Medicine*, 60(3), 359–361.

Brothers, L. (1989). A biological perspective on empathy. *American Journal of Psychiatry*, 146(1), 10–19.

Buber, M. (1947). *Between man and man*, London: Routledge & Kegan Paul.

Buber, M. (1957). Elements of the interhuman. *Psychiatry*, 20, 105–113.

Budman, S. H., & Gurman, A. S. (1988). *Theory and practice of brief therapy*. New York: Guilford Press.

Buie, D. H. (1981). Empathy: its nature and limitations. *Journal of the American Psychoanalytic Association*, 29, 281–307.

Bullinger, A. H., Roessler, A., & Mueller-Spahn, F. (1998). From toy to tool: The development of immersive virtual reality environments for psychotherapy of specific phobias. *Studies in Health Technology and Informatics*, 58, 103–111.

Burns, D. D., & Nolen-Hoeksema, S. (1992). Therapeutic empathy and recovery from depression in cognitive-behavioral therapy: A structural equation model. *Journal of Consulting and Clinical Psychology*, 60(3), 441–449.

Bursztajn, H. J., & Brodsky, A. (1999). Captive patients, captive doctors: Clinical dilemmas and interventions in caring for patients in managed health care. *General Hospital Psychiatry*, 21, 239–248.

Campion, E. W. (1993). Why unconventional medicine? *New England Journal of Medicine*, 328, 282–283.

Camus, A. (1948). *The plague*. New York: Basic Books.

Carek, D. J. (1987). The efficacy of empathy in diagnosis and therapy. *The Pharos*, 50(1), 25–29.

Carr, D. J. (1991). The role of endogenous opioids and their receptors in the immune system. *Proceedings of the Society of Experimental Medicine*, 198(2), 710–720.

Castilla-Cortazar, I., Castilla, A., & Gurpegui, M. (1998). Opioid peptides and immunodysfunction in patients with major depression and anxiety disorders. *Journal of Physiology and Biochemistry*, 54(4), 203–215.

Castonguay, L. G., Goldfried, M. R., Wiser, S., Raue, P. J., & Hayes, A. M. (1996). Predicting the effect of cognitive therapy for depression: A study of unique and common factors. *Journal of Consulting and Clinical Psychology*, 64(3), 497–504.

Chessick, R. D. (1998). Empathy in psychotherapy and psychoanalysis. *Journal of the American Academy of Psychoanalysis*, 26(4), 487–502.

Collins, K. S., Schoen, C., & Sandman, D. R. (1997). *The Commonwealth Fund survey of physician experiences with managed care*. http://www.cmwf.org/programs/health_care/physrvg.asp.

Coyle, J. T. (2000). Mind glue: Implications of glial cell biology for psychiatry. *Archives of General Psychiatry*, 57, 90–93.

Cummings, N., & Sayama, M. (1995). *Focused psychotherapy: A casebook of brief, intermittent psychotherapy throughout the life cycle.* New York: Bruner/Mazel.

Dalton, R., & Forman, M. A. (1994). Mind, brain, and psychiatry. *Harvard Review of Psychiatry, 2,* 133–141.

Damasio, A. (1994). *Descartes' error.* New York: G. P. Putnam's Sons.

Damasio, A. (1999). *The feeling of what happens.* New York: Harcourt Brace.

Darko, D. F., Risch, S. C., Gillin, J. C., & Golshan, S. (1992). Association of beta-endorphin with specific clinical symptoms of depression. *American Journal of Psychiatry, 149*(9), 1162–1167.

Darwin, C. (1979). *The origin of species.* New York: Gramercy Books.

Darwin, C. (1989). *The expression of the emotions in man and animals.* In F. Darwin (Ed.), *The works of Charles Darwin* (Vol. 23). New York: New York University Press.

Detre, T., & McDonald, M. C. (1997). Managed care and the future of psychiatry. *Archives of General Psychiatry, 54,* 201–208.

Deutch, H. (1963). Occult processes occurring during psychoanalysis. In G. Devereux (Ed.) *Psychoanalysis and the occult* (pp. 131–146). New York: International Universities Press. (Original work published in 1926.)

Dostoievski, T. M. (1943). *Notes from underground.* In B. G. Guerney (Ed.), *A treasury of Russian literature* (pp. 442–537). New York: Vanguard Press.

Drug focus shortchanges psychodynamics, Tasman says. (2000, July 7). *Psychiatric News,* p. 18.

Dyckman, J. (1997). The impatient therapist: Managed care and countertransference. *American Journal of Psychotherapy, 51*(3), 329–342.

Dyer, R. (1999, October 2). Ozawa conducts transcendent Mahler Second. *The Boston Globe,* p. F4.

Easty, D. (1981). *On method acting.* New York: Ivy Books.

Edelman, G. (1992). *Bright air, brilliant fire.* New York: Basic Books.

Edman, I. (Ed.) (1928). *The philosophy of Plato.* New York: Simon and Schuster.

Eisenberg, D. M., Davis, R. B. Ettner, S. L., Appel, S., Wilkey, S., Van Rompay, M., & Kessler, R. C. (1998). Trends in alternative medicine use in the United States, 1990–1997. *Journal of the American Medical Association, 280*(18), 1569–1575.

Eisenberg, L. (1986). Mindlessness and brainlessness in psychiatry. *British Journal of Psychiatry, 148,* 497–508.

Eisenberg, N., & Strayer, J. (Eds.) (1987). *Empathy and development.* Cambridge: Cambridge University Press.

Elliott, F. A. (1986). Historical perspectives on neurobehavior. *Psychiatric Clinics of North America, 9*(2), 225–239.

Emanual E. J., & Dubler, L. L.B. (1995). Preserving the physician-patient relationship in the era of managed care. *Journal of the American Medical Association, 273*(4), 323–329.

Emanual, E. J., & Emanual, L. L. (1992). Four models of the physician–patient relationship. *Journal of the American Medical Association, 267*(16), 2221–2226.

Emde, R. N. (1995). Diagnosis, assessment and individual complexity. *Archives of General Psychiatry, 52,* 637–638.

Engel, G. L. (1977). The need for a new medical model: A challenge for biomedicine. *Science, 196,* 129–136.

Enthoven, A. C. (1989). Effective management of competition in the FEBHP (Federal Employees Health Benefits Program). *Health Affairs, 8*(3), 33–50.

Eslinger, P. J. (1998). Neurological and neuropsychological bases of empathy. *European Neurology, 39,* 193–199.

Ferenczi, S. (1955). *Final contributions to the problems and methods of psychoanalysis*. New York: Bruner/Mazel.

Fitzgerald, F. (1999). Curiosity. *Annals of Internal Medicine, 130*, 70–72.

Fleischman, P. R. (1989). *The healing spirit: Explorations in religion and psychotherapy* (pp. 5–20). New York: Paragon House.

Fliess, R. (1942). Metapsychology of the analyst. *Psychoanalytic Quarterly, 11*, 211–227.

Frank, J. (1974). *Persuasion and healing*. New York: Shocken Books; Baltimore: Johns Hopkins University Press.

Freud, S. (1958). Recommendations to physicians practicing psychoanalysis. In J. Strachey (Ed. and Trans.), *The standard edition of the complete psychological works of Sigmund Freud* (Vol. 12, pp. 111–112). London: Hogarth Press. (Original work published 1912.)

Freud, S. (1959). *Delusions and dreams in Jensen's Gravida*. In J. Strachey (Ed. and Trans.), *The standard edition of the complete psychological works of Sigmund Freud* (Vol. 9, p. 45). London: Hogarth Press. (Original work published 1907.)

Freud, S. (1959). *Group psychology and the analysis of the ego*. New York: W. W. Norton. (Original work published 1921.)

Freud, S. (1960). Jokes and their relation to the unconscious. In J. Strachey (Ed. and Trans.), *The standard edition of the complete psychological works of Sigmund Freud* (Vol. 8, p. 186). London: Hogarth Press. (Original work published 1905.)

Freud, S. (1966). Project for a scientific psychology. In J. Strachey (Ed. and Trans.), *The standard edition of the complete psychological works of Sigmund Freud* (Vol. 1, pp. 281–397). London: Hogarth Press. (Original work published 1895.)

Gauss, C. E. (1973–74). Empathy. In P. P. Wiener (Ed.) *Dictionary of the history of ideas: Studies of selected pivotal ideas* (Vol. 2, pp. 85–89). New York: Scribner.

Gierer, A. (1998). Networks of gene regulation, neural development and the evolution of general capabilities, such as human empathy. *Zeitschrift für Naturforschung, 53*(7–8), 716–722.

Glenmullen, J. (2000). *Prozac backlash: Overcoming the dangers of Prozac, Zoloft, Paxil, and other antidepressants with safe, effective alternatives*. New York: Simon & Schuster.

Gold, M. R. (1999). ISO quick fix, free lunch, and share of pie. *Journal of Health Politics, Policy and Law, 24*(5), 973–983.

Goldbeck-Wood, S., Dorozynski, A., Lie, L. G., Yamauchi, M., Zinn, C., Josefson, D., & Ingram, M. (1996). Complementary medicine is booming worldwide. *British Medical Journal, 313*, 131–133.

Goldberg, A. (Ed.) (1978). *The psychology of the self: A casebook*. New York: International Universities Press.

Grattan, L. M., & Eslinger, P. J. (1989). Letter to the editor. *American Journal of Psychiatry, 146*(11), 521–522.

Greenberg, D. S. (1998). Rapid rise for U.S. health-care costs, yet again. *Lancet, 351*(9116), 1639.

Greenberg, L. S., & Paivio, S. C. (1997). *Working with emotions in psychotherapy*. New York: Guilford.

Greenfield, S., Kaplan, S., & Ware, J. E. (1985). Expanding patient involvement in care: Effects on patient outcome. *Annals of Internal Medicine, 102*, 520–528.

Greenson, R. R. (1960). Empathy and its vicissitudes. *International Journal of Psycho-Analysis, 41*, 418–424.

Guntrip, H. (1975). My experience of analysis with Fairbairn and Winnicott. *International Review of Psychoanalysis, 2*, 145–156.

Gustafson, J. P. (1981). The complex secret of brief psychotherapy in the works of Malan and Balint. In S. H. Budman (Ed.), *Forms of brief therapy* (pp. 83–128). New York: Guilford Press.

Halpern, J. (1993). Empathy: Using resonance emotions in the service of curiosity. In H. M. Spiro, M. G. MCCrea, E. Peschel, & D. St. James (Eds.), *Empathy and the practice of medicine: Beyond pills and the scalpel* (pp. 160–173). New Haven: Yale University Press.

Havens, L. (1974). The existential use of the self. *American Journal of Psychiatry, 131,* 1–10.

Havens, L. (1978). Explorations in the uses of language in psychotherapy: simple empathic statements. *Psychiatry, 41,* 336–345.

Havens, L. (1979). Explorations in the uses of language in psychotherapy: Complex empathic statements. *Psychiatry, 42,* 40–48.

Havens, L. (1989). *A safe place: Laying the groundwork of psychotherapy.* Cambridge: Harvard University Press.

Havens, L. (1989). *A safe place: Laying the groundwork of psychotherapy.* Cambridge: Harvard University Press.

Hennig, J. Laschefski, U., & Opper, C. (1994). Biopsychological changes after bungee jumping: Beta-endorphin immunoreactivity as a mediator of euphoria? *Neuropsychobiology, 29*(1), 28–32.

Herbert, T. B., & Cohen, S. (1993). Stress and immunity in humans: A meta-analytic review. *Psychosomatic Medicine, 55*(4), 364–379.

Herman, J. L. (1992). *Trauma and recovery.* New York: Basic Books.

Holmes, J. (1956). The eleventh commandment. *Harper's, 213,* 53–54. (As quoted in K. Menninger (1963), *The vital balance* (p. 350), New York: Viking Press.)

Hooley, J. M., Orley, J., and Teasdale, J. D. (1986). Levels of expressed emotion and relapse in depressed patients. *British Journal of Psychiatry, 148,* 642–647.

Horowitz, M. J. (1997). Configurational analysis for case formulation. *Psychiatry, 60,* 111–119.

Horowitz, M. J., Eells, T., Singer, J., & Salovey, P. (1995). Role–relationship model configurations: A summation. *Archives of General Psychiatry, 52,* 654–656.

Horowitz, M. J., Eells, T., Singer, J., & Salovey, P. (1995). Role-relationship models for case formulation. *Archives of General Psychiatry, 52,* 625–632.

Howard, K. I., & Orlinski, P. E. (1986). Process and outcome. In S. L. Garfield & A. E. Bergin (Eds.), *Handbook of psychotherapy and behavioral change* (3rd ed.) (pp. 311–381). New York: Wiley.

Howard, K. I., Kopta, S. M., Krause, M. S., & Orlinski, P. E. (1986). The dose–effect relationship in psychotherapy. *American Psychologist, 41,* 159–164.

Jackson, S. W. (1992). The listening healer in the history of psychological healing. *American Journal of Psychiatry, 149*(12), 1623–1632.

Jackson, S. W. (1994). Catharsis and abreaction in the history of psychological healing. *Psychiatric Clinics of North America, 17,* 471–492.

Jaynes, J. (1977). *The origin of consciousness in the breakdown of the bicameral mind.* Boston: Houghton Mifflin.

Johnson, D. H., & Gelso, C. J. (1980). The effectiveness of time limits in counseling and psychotherapy: A critical review. *The Counseling Psychologist, 9,* 70–83.

Johnson, S. M., & Williams-Keeler, L. (1998). Creating healing relationships for couples dealing with trauma: The use of emotionally focused marital therapy. *Journal of Marital and Family Therapy, 24*(1), 25–40.

Jordan, J. V. (1997). Relational development through mutual empathy. In A. C. Bohart & L. S. Greenberg (Eds.), *Empathy reconsidered: New directions in psychotherapy* (pp. 343–351). Washington, DC: American Psychological Association.

Kandell, E. R. (1979). Psychotherapy and the single synapse. *New England Journal of Medicine, 301*(19), 1028–1037.

Kandell, E. R. (1983). From metapsychology to molecular biology: Explorations into the nature of anxiety. *American Journal of Psychiatry, 140*(10), 1277–1293.

Kandell, E. R. (1998). A new intellectual framework for psychiatry. *American Journal of Psychiatry, 155*(4), 457–469.

Kaplan, H. I., Sadock, B. J., & Grebb, J. A. (Eds.) (1994). *Synopsis of psychiatry* (7th ed.). Baltimore: Williams & Wilkins.

Karlsson, H., & Kamppinen, M. (1995). Biological psychiatry and reductionism: Empirical findings and philosophy. *British Journal of Psychiatry, 167,* 434–438.

Kaysen, S. (2000). *Girl, interrupted.* Thorndike, ME: Thorndike Press.

Kendler, K. (1995). Genetic epidemiology in psychiatry. *Archives of General Psychiatry, 52,* 895–899.

Keller, V., & Carroll, J. G. (1994). A new model for physician-patient communication. *Patient Education and Counseling, 23,* 131–140.

Kennedy, S., Kiecolt-Glaser, J. K., & Glaser, R. (1988). Immunological consequences of acute and chronic stressors: Mediating role of interpersonal relationships. *British Journal of Medical Psychology, 61,* 77–85.

Kessler, R. C., McGonagle, K. A., Zhao, S., Nelson, C. B., Hughes, M., Eshleman, S., Wittchen, H. A., and Kendler, K. S. (1994). Lifetime and 12-month prevalence of DSM-III-R psychiatric disorders in the United States: Results from the National Comorbidity Survey. *Archives of General Psychiatry, 51*(1), 8–19.

Kiecolt-Glaser, J. K. (1999). 1998 Norman Cousins Memorial Lecture. Stress, personal relationships and immune function: Health implications. *Brain, Behavior and Immunity, 13*(1), 61–72.

King, L. J. (1999). A brief history of psychiatry: Millennia past and present, Part 1. *Annals of Clinical Psychiatry, 11*(1), 3–12.

King, L. J. (1999). A brief history of psychiatry: Millennia past and present, Part 2. *Annals of Clinical Psychiatry, 11*(2), 47–54.

King, L. J. (1999). A brief history of psychiatry: Millennia past and present, Part 3. *Annals of Clinical Psychiatry, 11*(3), 99–107.

King, L. J. (1999). A brief history of psychiatry: Millennia past and present, Part 4. *Annals of Clinical Psychiatry, 11*(4), 175–185.

Kleinman, A. (1980). *Patients and healers in the context of culture.* Berkeley: University of California Press.

Kleinman, A. (1988). *The illness narratives.* New York: Basic Books

Kline, S., & Cameron, P. M. (1978). Formulation, I. *Canadian Psychiatric Association Journal, 23*(1), 39–42.

Kohut, H. (1959) Introspection, empathy and psychoanalysis: An examination of the relationship between mode of observation and theory. In P. H. Ornstein (Ed.) *The search for the self* (Vol. 1, pp. 205–231). New York: International Universities Press.

Kohut, H. (1971). *The analysis of the self.* New York: International Universities Press.

Kohut, H. (1977). *The restoration of the self.* New York: International Universities Press.

Kronfol, Z., and Remick, D. G. (2000). Cytokines and the brain: Implications for psychiatry. *American Journal of Psychiatry, 157*(5), 683–694.

Krupnick, J. L., Sotsky, S. M., Simmens, S., Moyer, J., Elkin, I., Watkins, J., & Pilkonis, P. A. (1996). The role of the therapeutic alliance in psychotherapy and pharmacotherapy outcome: Findings in the National Institute of Mental Health Treatment of Depression Collaborative Research Program. *Journal of Consulting and Clinical Psychology, 64*(3), 532–539.

Kris, E. (1952). *Psychoanalytic explorations in art.* New York: Shocken Books.

Kurtz, S. M., & Silverman, J. D. (1996). The Calgary–Cambridge observation guides: An aid to defining the curriculum and organising the teaching in communication training programmes. *Medical Education, 30,* 83–89.

Langone, J. (2000, 22 August). Medical schools discover value in dispensing compassion. *New York Times,* p. D7.

LeDoux, J. E. (1993). Emotional memory systems in the brain. *Behavioural Brain Research, 58,* 69–79.

Levin, R. (1997). Speaking Mozart's lingo. In B. D. Sherman (Ed.), *Inside early music* (pp. 315–338). New York: Oxford Press.

Lewis, A. (1953). Letter from Britain. *American Journal of Psychiatry, 110,* 401–405.

Lewis, J. M. (1998). For better or for worse: Interpersonal relationships and individual outcome. *American Journal of Psychiatry, 155*(5), 582–589.

Lewis, T., Amini, F., & Lannon, R. (2000). *A general theory of love.* New York: Random House.

Liberman, R. P. (1988). *Psychiatric rehabilitation of chronic mental patients.* Washington, DC: APA Press.

Lindner, R. (1982). The Jet Propelled Couch. In *The fifty minute hour* (pp. 163–216). New York: The Dell Publishing Company.

Linehan, M. M. (1993). *Cognitive–behavioral therapy of borderline personality disorder.* New York: Guilford Press.

Linehan, M. M. (1997). Validation and psychotherapy. In A. C. Bohart & L. S. Greenberg (Eds.), *Empathy reconsidered: New directions in psychotherapy* (pp. 353–392). Washington, DC: American Psychological Association.

Links, P. S., & Heslegrave, R. J. (2000). Prospective studies of outcome: Understanding mechanisms of change in patients with borderline personality disorder. *Psychiatric Clinics of North America, 23*(1), 137–150.

Lipowski, Z. J. (1989). Psychiatry: Mindless or brainless, both or neither. *Canadian Journal of Psychiatry, 34,* 249–254.

Luborsky, L. (1977). Measuring a pervasive psychic structure in psychotherapy: The core conflictual relationship theme. In N. Freedman & S. S. Grand (Eds.), *Communicative structures and psychic structures.* New York: Plenum Press.

Luborsky, L., & Crits-Christoph, P. (1989). A relationship pattern measure: The core conflictual relationship theme. *Psychiatry, 52,* 250–259.

Mahrer, A. (1997). Empathy as therapist–client alignment. In A. C. Bohart & L. S. Greenberg (Eds.), *Empathy reconsidered: New directions in psychotherapy* (pp. 187–213). Washington, DC: American Psychological Association.

Mann, J. (1973). *Time-limited psychotherapy.* Cambridge: Harvard University Press.

Mann, J. (1981). The core of time-limited psychotherapy: Time and the central issue. In S. H. Budman (Ed.), *Forms of brief therapy* (pp. 25–43). New York: Guilford Press.

Marcia, J. (1987). Empathy and psychotherapy within a developmental context. In N. Eisenberg & J. Strayer (Eds.), *Empathy and its development* (pp. 81–102). Cambridge: Cambridge University Press.

Margulies, A. (1989). *The empathic imagination.* New York: W. W. Norton.

Margulies, A., & Havens, L. (1981). The initial encounter: What to do first. *American Journal of Psychiatry, 138*(4), 421–428.

McDougall, G. M., & Reade, B. (1993). Teaching biopsychosocial integration and formulation. *Canadian Journal of Psychiatry, 38,* 359–362.

Meissner, W. W. (2000). On analytic listening. *Psychoanalytic Quarterly, 69*(2), 317–367.

Menninger, W. W. (1996). Practitioner, heal thyself: Coping with stress in clinical practice. *An occasional paper from the Menninger Clinic*. Topeka: The Menninger Foundation.

Mental health: Does therapy help? (1995, November). *Consumer Reports*, pp. 734–739.

Meyer, A. (1917). Progress in teaching psychiatry. *Journal of the American Medical Association, 69*(11), 861–862.

Meyer, R. E. (1998). *Between mind, brain, and managed care: The now and future world of academic psychiatry*. Washington, DC: American Psychiatric Association Press.

Michels, R. (2000). *Thinking while listening*. Lecture no. 13, delivered at the Annual Meeting of the American Psychiatric Association, 16 May.

Miklowitz, D. J., Goldstein, M. J., Nuechterlein, K. H., Snyder, K. S., & Mintz, J. (1988). Family factors in the course of bipolar affective disorder. *Archives of General Psychiatry, 45*, 225–231.

Miller, I. J. (1989). The therapeutic empathic communication (TEC) process. *American Journal of Psychotherapy, 43*(4), 531–545.

Mohl, P. (1987). Should psychotherapy be considered a biological treatment? *Psychosomatics, 28*(6), 320–326.

More, E. S. (1994). Empathy enters the profession of medicine. In E. S. More & M. A. Milligan (Eds.), *The empathic practitioner: Empathy, gender and medicine* (pp. 19–39). New Brunswick, NJ: Rutgers University Press.

More, E. S., & Strayer, J. (Eds.) (1994). *The empathic practitioner: Empathy, gender and medicine*. New Brunswick, NJ: Rutgers University Press.

Moyers, B. (1993). *Healing the mind*. New York: Doubleday.

Nadelson, C. C. (1993). Ethics, empathy, and gender in health care. *American Journal of Psychiatry, 150*(9), 1309–1313.

Nahm, M. C. (Ed.) (1947). *Selections from early Greek philosophy*. New York: Appleton-Century-Crofts.

Nathanson, D. L. (1995). Crime and nourishment: Sometimes the tried and true becomes the tired and false. *Bulletin of the Tomkins Institute, 2*, 25–30.

Neims, A. H. (1999). Why I would recommend complementary or alternative therapies: A physician's perspective. *Rheumatic Disease Clinics of North America, 25*(4), 845–853.

Nemeroff, C. B., Widerlov, E., Bissette, G.,. Walleus, H., Karlsson, I., Eklund, K., Kilts, C. D., Loosen, P. T., & Vale, W. (1984). Elevated concentrations of CSF corticotrophin-releasing factor-like immunoreactivity in depressed patients. *Science, 226*(4680), 1342–1344.

Nietzsche, F. (1995). *Human, all too human: A book for free spirits*. Stanford: Stanford University Press. (Original work published 1878.)

Norretranders, T. (1998). *The user illusion*. New York: Penguin Putnam.

Novack, D. H., Dube, C., & Goldstein, M. G. (1992). Teaching medical interviewing: A basic course on interviewing and the physician-patient relationship. *Archives of Internal Medicine, 152*, 1814–1820.

North, M. M., North, S. M., & Coble, J. R. (1998). Virtual reality therapy: An effective treatment for phobias. *Studies in Health Technology and Informatics, 58*, 112–119.

O'Hara, M. (1997). Relational empathy: Beyond modernist egocentrism to postmodern holistic contextualism. In A. C. Bohart & L. S. Greenberg (Eds.), *Empathy reconsidered: New directions in psychotherapy* (pp. 295–321). Washington, DC: American Psychological Association.

Ohsuga, M., & Oyama, T. (1998). Possibility of virtual reality for mental care. *Studies in Health Technology and Informatics, 58*, 82–90.

Olden, C. (1953). On adult empathy with children. In B. Charles (Ed.), *The psychoanalytic study of the child* (Vol. 8, p. 115). New York: International Universities Press.

Olinick, S. (1984). A critique of empathy and sympathy. In J. Lichtenberg, M. Bornstein, & D. Silver (Eds.), *Empathy I* (pp. 137–167). Hillsdale, NJ: The Analytic Press.

Papez, J. W. (1937). A proposed mechanism of emotion. *Archives of Neurology and Psychiatry, 38*(4), 725–743.

Paris, J., & Braverman, S. (1995). Successful and unsuccessful marriages in borderline patients. *Journal of the American Academy of Psychoanalysis, 23*, 153–166.

Pasnau, R. O. (1987). The remedicalization of psychiatry. *Hospital and Community Psychiatry, 38*(2), 145–151.

Patients' rights, M.D. unions inch forward in Congress. (2000, July 21). *Psychiatric News*, pp. 1 & 26.

Peabody, F. (1984). The care of the patient. *Journal of the American Medical Association, 252*(6), 813–818. (Original work published 1927.)

Perry, J. C. (1989). Scientific progress in psychodynamic formulation. *Psychiatry, 52*, 245–249.

Perry, J. C., Luborsky, L. Silberschatz, G., & Popp, C. (1989). An examination of three methods of psychodynamic formulation based on the same videotaped interview. *Psychiatry, 52*, 302–323.

Pertman, A. (2000, 5 June). Girl's death spotlights therapies of desperation. *Boston Globe*, pp. 1, 10.

Pfleiderer, O. (1886). *The philosophy of religion on the basis of its history* (Vol. 1, p. 68). London: Williams and Norgate.

Post, R. M. (1992). Transduction of psychosocial stress into the neurobiology of affective disorder. *American Journal of Psychiatry, 149*(8), 999–1010.

Post, R. M. (1997). Molecular biology of behavior: Targets for therapeutics. *Archives of General Psychiatry, 54*, 607–608.

Post, R. M., Rubinow, D. R., & Ballenger, J. C. (1986). Conditioning and sensitization in the longitudinal course of affective illness. *British Journal of Psychiatry, 149*, 191–201.

Regier, D. A., Narrow, W. E., Rae, D. S., Manderscheid, R. W., Locke, B. Z., and Goodwin, F. K. (1993). The de facto U.S. mental and addictive disorders service system: Epidemiologic catchment area prospective 1-year prevalence rates of disorders and services. *Archives of General Psychiatry, 50*(2), 85–94.

Reich, W. (1982). Psychiatry's second coming. *Psychiatry, 45*, 189–196.

Reik, T. (1983). *Listening with the third ear: The inner experience of a psychoanalyst*. New York: Farrar, Straus & Giroux. (Original work published 1948.)

Reiser, M. F. (1984). *Mind, brain, body*. New York: Basic Books.

Reiser, M. F. (1999). Memory, empathy and interactive dimensions of psychoanalytic process. *Journal of the American Psychoanalytic Association, 47*(2), 485–501.

Reiss, D. (1995). Personality theory: Clinical practice, social development, and the biology of individual differences. *Archives of General Psychiatry, 52*, 633–635.

Reiss, D., Neiderhiser, J. M., Hetherington, E. M., & Plomin, R. (2000). *The relationship code*. Cambridge: Harvard University Press.

Remen, R. (1996). *Kitchen table wisdom*. New York: Riverhead Books.

Restak, R. M. (1984). Possible neurophysiological correlates of empathy. In J. Lichtenberg, M. Bornstein, & D. Silver (Eds.) *Empathy I* (p. 13). Hillsdale, NJ: Analytic Press.

Risk Management Foundation of Harvard Medical Institutions (1996). *Guidelines for identification, assessment and treatment planning for suicidality*. Cambridge: Author.

Roback, H. B., Barton, D., Castelnuovo-Tedesco, P., Gay, V., Havens., L., & Nash, J. (1999). A symposium on psychotherapy in the age of managed care. *American Journal of Psychiatry, 53*(1), 1–16.

Rogers, C. R. (1951). *Client-centered therapy: Its current practice implications and theory*. Boston: Houghton Mifflin.

Rogers, C. R. (1959). A theory of therapy, personality, and interpersonal relationships as developed in the client-centered framework. In S. Koch (Ed.), *Psychology: A study of a science. Foundations of the person and the social context*, Vol. 3 (pp. 210–211). New York: McGraw-Hill.

Rogers, C. R. (1961). *On becoming a person*. Boston: Houghton Mifflin.

Rogers, C. R. (1980). *A way of being*. Boston: Houghton Mifflin.

Rogers, C. R. (1980). Empathy: an unappreciated way of being. In *A way of being* (pp. 150–161). Boston: Houghton Mifflin.

Ross, W. D. (Ed.) (1938). *Aristotle selections*. New York: Charles Scribner's Sons.

Rosten, L. (1970). *The joys of Yiddish*. New York: Pocket Books.

Rothbaum, B. O., Hodges, L., & Kooper, R. (1997). Virtual reality exposure therapy. *Journal of Psychotherapy Practice and Research*, 6(3), 219–226.

Russell, B. (1945). *A history of western philosophy*. New York: Simon and Schuster.

Rutter, M. (1986). Meyerian psychobiology, personality development, and the role of life experiences. *American Journal of Psychiatry*, 143(9), 1077–1087.

Sacks, O. (1984). *A leg to stand on*. New York: Summit Books.

Santos, A. B. (1997). ACT now! Assertive community treatment. *Administration and Policy in Mental Health*, 25(2), 101–104.

Sarton, M. (1974). *Collected poems*. New York: W. W. Norton.

Savage, G. T., Campbell, K. S., Patman, T., & Nunnelley. L.L. (2000). Beyond managed costs. *Health Care Management Review*, 25(1), 93–108.

Saxe, J. G. (1936). The blind men and the elephant. In H. Felleman (Ed.), *The best loved poems of the American people* (pp. 521–522). New York: Doubleday.

Schafer, R. (1959). Generative empathy in the treatment situation. *Psychoanalytic Quarterly*, 28, 342–373.

Schroeder, T. (1925). The psycho-analytic method of observation. *International Journal of Psycho-Analysis*, 6, 155–170.

Schwaber, E. (1979). On the "self" within the matrix of analytic theory: Some clinical reflections and reconsiderations. *International Journal of Psycho-Analysis*, 60, 467–479.

Schwartz, A. (1987). Drives, affects, behavior, and learning: Approaches to a psychobiology of emotion and to an integration of psychoanalytic and neurobiologic thought. *Journal of the American Psychoanalytic Association*, 35(2), 467–506.

Seligman, M. E. P. (1996). Science as an ally of practice. *American Psychologist*, 51(10), 1072–1079.

Semrad, E. (1963–66). Personal communication.

Seruya, B. B. (1997). *Empathic brief psychotherapy*. Northvale, NJ: Jason Aronson.

Sforzo, G. A. (1989). Opioids and exercise. An update. *Sports Medicine*, 7(2), 109–124.

Sifneos, P. E. (1981). Short-term anxiety-provoking psychotherapy: Its history, technique, outcome, and instruction. In S. H. Budman (Ed.), *Forms of brief therapy* (pp. 45–81). New York: Guilford Press.

Silverman, J., Kurtz, S., & Draper, J. (1998). *Skills for communicating with patients*. Abingdon: Radcliffe Medical Press.

Simon, B. (1978). *Mind and madness in ancient Greece: The classical roots of modern psychiatry*. Ithaca: Cornell University Press.

Simpson, M., Buckman, R., Stewart, M., Maguire, C. P., Lipkin, M., Novack, D., & Till, J. (1991). Doctor–patient communication: The Toronto consensus statement. *British Medical Journal*, 303, 1385–1387.

Singer, M. T. (1974). Presidential Address. Engagement–involvement: A central phenomenon in psychophysiological research. *Journal of the American Psychosomatic Association, 36*(1), 1–17.

Shakespeare, W. (1909). *The tempest* (Act V, Scene 1). In *The works of William Shakespeare* (Vol. 18, p. 95). New York: Bigelow, Smith and Company.

Shapiro, T. (1974). The development and distortion of empathy. *Psychoanalytic Quarterly, 43,* 4–25.

Sharma, R. M. (1993). *Understanding the concept of empathy and its foundations in psychoanalysis.* Lewiston/Queenston/Lampeter: The Edwin Mellen Press.

Shem, S. (1978). *The House of God* (pp. 12, 13). New York: Michael Marek.

Shlien, J. (1997). Empathy in psychotherapy: A vital mechanism? Yes. Therapist's conceit? All too often. By itself enough? No. In A. C. Bohart & L. S. Greenberg (Eds.). *Empathy reconsidered: New directions in psychotherapy* (pp. 63–80). Washington, DC: American Psychological Association.

Sorian, R., & Feder, J. (1999). Why we need a patients' bill of rights. *Journal of Health Politics, Policy and Law, 24*(5), 1137–1144.

Sperry, R. W. (1988). Psychology's mentalist paradigm and the religion/science tension. *American Psychologist, 43*(8), 607–613.

Spiegel, D. (1990). Can psychotherapy prolong cancer survival? *Psychosomatics, 31*(4), 361–366.

Spiegel, D. (1994). Health caring. Psychosocial support for patients with cancer. *Cancer, 74,* 1453–1457.

Spiegel, D. (1995). How do you feel about cancer now? Survival and social support. *Public Health Reports, 110*(3), 298–300.

Spiegel, D., Bloom, J. R., Kraemer, H. C., & Gottheil, E. (1989). Effect of psychosocial treatment on survival of patients with metastatic breast cancer. *Lancet, 2*(8668), 888–891.

Spiegel, D., Sephton, S. E., Terr, A. I., & Stites, D. P. (1998). Effects of psychosocial treatment in prolonging cancer survival may be mediated by neuroimmune pathways. *Annals of the New York Academy of Sciences, 840,* 674–683.

Spiegel, D., Morrow, G. R., Classen, C., Raubertas, R., Stott, P. B., Mudaliar, N., Pierce, H. I., Flynn, P. J., Heard, L., & Riggs, G. (1999). Group psychotherapy for recently diagnosed breast cancer patients: A multicenter feasibility study. *Psycho-oncology, 8*(6), 482–493.

Spiro, H. M., McCrea, M. G., Peschel, E., & St. James, D. (Eds.) (1993). *Empathy and the practice of medicine: Beyond pills and the scalpel.* New Haven: Yale University Press.

Stanislavski, C. (1936). *An actor prepares.* New York: Theatre Arts Books.

Starr, P. (1982). *The social transformation of american medicine.* New York: Basic Books.

Stein, E. (1964). *On the problem of empathy.* The Hague: Martinus Nijhof.

Stern, D. (1985). *The interpersonal world of the infant.* New York: Basic Books.

Stewart, M, Belle-Brown, J., Weston, W. W., McWhinney, I. R., McWilliam, C. L., and Freeman, T. R. (1995). *Patient-centered medicine: Transforming the clinical method.* Thousand Oaks, California: Sage Publications.

Stolorow, R. D. (2000). From isolated minds to experiential worlds: An intersubjective space odyssey. *American Journal of Psychotherapy, 54*(2), 149–151.

Stone, D. (1999). Managed care and the second great transformation. *Journal of Health Politics, Policy and Law, 24*(5), 1213–1218.

Stone, M. H. (1997). *Healing and the mind.* New York: W. W. Norton.

Sullivan, H.S. (1931). Socio-psychiatric research: Its implications for the schizophrenia problem and for mental hygiene. *American Journal of Psychiatry, 10,* 977–992.

Sullivan, H. S. (1940). *Conceptions of modern psychiatry.* New York: W. W. Norton.

Sullivan, H. S. (1964). *The fusion of psychiatry and social science.* New York: W. W. Norton.

Szasz, T. (1985). Psychiatry: Rhetoric and reality. *Lancet, ii,* 711–712.

Tansey, M. J., & Burke, W. F. (1989). *Understanding countertransference: From projective identification to empathy*. Hillsdale, NJ: Analytic Press.

Teich, N. (1992). *Rogerian perspectives: Collaborative rhetoric for oral and written communication*. Norwood, NJ: Ablex Publishing.

Test, M. A., & Stein, L. I. (1976). Practical guidelines for the community treatment of markedly impaired patients. *Community Mental Health Journal, 12*(1), 72–82.

Thomas, L. (1983). *Late night thoughts on listening to Mahler's Ninth Symphony*. New York: Bantam Books.

Thompson, M. (1954). *Not as a stranger* (p. 391). New York: Charles Scribner & Sons.

Titchener, E. B. (1926). *Experimental psychology of the thought processes*. New York: Macmillan.

Toews, J. A. (1993). Case formulation in psychiatry: Revitalizing an ailing art. *Canadian Journal of Psychiatry, 38*, p. 344.

Tomkins, S. S. (1962). *Affect imagery consciousness*, Vol. 1. New York: Springer.

Tomkins, S. S. (1963). *Affect Imagery Consciousness*, Vol. 2. New York: Springer.

Tuch, R. H. (1997). Beyond empathy: Confronting certain complexities in self psychology theory. *Psychoanalytic Quarterly, 66*(2), 259–282.

Unützer, J., Klap, R., Sturm, R., Young, A. S., Marmon, T., Shatkin, J., & Wells, K. B. (2000). Mental disorders and the use of alternative medicine: Results from a national survey. *American Journal of Psychiatry, 157*, 1851–1857.

van der Pompe, G., Antoni, M., Visser, A., & Garssen, B. (1996). Adjustment to breast cancer: The psychobiological effects of psychosocial interventions. *Patient Education and Counseling, 28*(2), 209–119.

Viederman, M. (1986). Personality change through life experience, I: A model. *Psychiatry, 49*, 204–217.

Vonnegut, K. (1998). *Cat's cradle*. New York: Dell. (Original work published 1963.)

Wallerstein, R. S. (1991). The future of psychotherapy. *Bulletin of the Menninger Clinic, 55*, 421–443.

Warner, M. S. (1997). Does empathy cure? A theoretical consideration of empathy, processing and personal narrative. In A. C. Bohart & L. S. Greenberg (Eds.), *Empathy reconsidered: new directions in psychotherapy* (pp. 125–140). Washington, DC: American Psychological Association.

Webster's New Universal Unabridged Dictionary, Deluxe Second Edition (1979). (pp. 594, 1848). New York: Simon and Schuster.

Weerasekera, B. A. (1993). Formulation: A multiperspective model. *Canadian Journal of Psychiatry, 38*, 351–358.

Weiss, J., Sampson, H., and the Mount Zion Psychotherapy Group (Eds.) (1986). *The psychoanalytic process: Theory, clinical observation, and empirical research*. New York: Guilford Press.

Wellek, R. (1970). *Discriminations*. New Haven: Yale University Press.

Wind, E. (1963). *Art and anarchy*. London: Faber & Faber.

Winnicott, D. W. (1965). *The maturational process and the facilitating environment: Studies in the theory of emotional development*. New York: International Universities Press.

Winnicott, D. W. (1968). Playing: Its theoretical status in the clinical situation. *International Journal of Psycho-Analysis, 49*, 591–599.

Wispe, L. (1987). History of the concept of empathy. In N. Eisenberg & J. Strayer (Eds.), *Empathy and development* (pp. 17–36). Cambridge: Cambridge University Press.

Wolfe, T. (1957). *Look homeward, angel*. New York: Charles Scribner's Sons. (Original work published 1929).

Wortis, J. (1988). The history of psychiatry. *Biological Psychiatry, 23*, 107–108.

Young, G. B., & Pigott. S. S. (1999). Neurobiologic basis of consciousness. *Archives of Neurology*, *56*, 153–157.

Yudofsky, S. C. (1987). Neuropsychiatry: An idea whose time has come—again. *Hospital and Community Psychiatry*, *38*(7), 701.

Zealberg, J. J. (1999). The depersonalization of health care. *Psychiatric Services*, *50*(3), 327–328.

Zhong, F., Li, X. Y., & Yang, S. L. (1996). Augmentation of TNF-alpha production, NK cell activity and IL-12 p35 mRNA expression by methionine enkephalin. *Chung Kuo Yao Li Hsueh Pao*, *17*(2), 182–185.

Zohar, D. (1990). *The quantum self*. London: Bloomsbury Publications.

INDEX

S

T